HOW TO BE AVANT-GARDE

Also
by
Morgan
Falconer

*Painting
Beyond
Pollock*

HOW TO BE AVANT-GARDE

Modern Artists and the Quest to End Art

MORGAN FALCONER

W. W. NORTON & COMPANY
Independent Publishers Since 1923

Copyright © 2025 by Morgan Falconer

All rights reserved
Printed in the United States of America
First Edition

For information about permission to reproduce selections from this book, write to Permissions, W. W. Norton & Company, Inc., 500 Fifth Avenue, New York, NY 10110

For information about special discounts for bulk purchases, please contact W. W. Norton Special Sales at specialsales@wwnorton.com or 800-233-4830

Manufacturing by Lake Book Manufacturing
Book design by Lovedog Studio
Production manager: Anna Oler

ISBN 978-1-324-05142-8

W. W. Norton & Company, Inc.
500 Fifth Avenue, New York, NY 10110
www.wwnorton.com

W. W. Norton & Company Ltd.
15 Carlisle Street, London W1D 3BS

1 2 3 4 5 6 7 8 9 0

Art
has
poisoned
our
life.
—
Theo
van
Doesburg

CONTENTS

Introduction: On the Coast		1
1.	Leaving Montmartre	15
2.	Can You Make Works Which Are Not Works of Art?	41
3.	The Wandering Prophets	65
4.	The Pope	93
5.	The Monument without a Beard	117
6.	Saint-Peter of the Straight Line	143
7.	The School, the Cathedral, and the Whitewashed Die	171
8.	Situations	197
Epilogue: The Future of an Illusion		223
Acknowledgments		233
Notes		235
Illustration Credits		251
Index		253

HOW TO BE AVANT-GARDE

INTRODUCTION

On the Coast

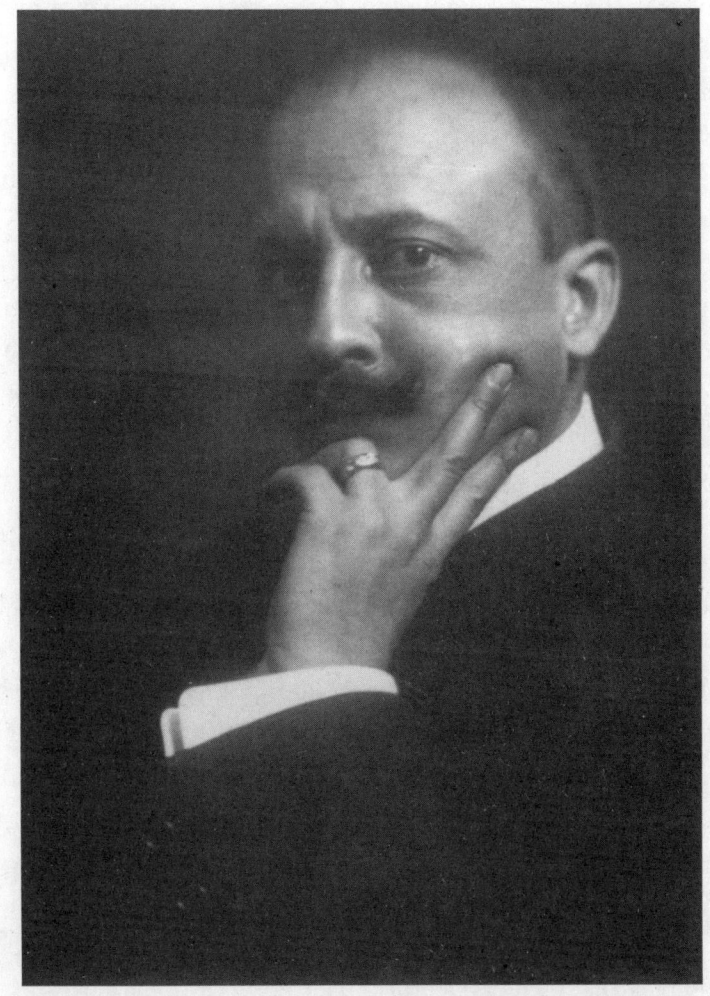

Filippo Tommaso Marinetti, 1913.

WHEN FILIPPO TOMMASO MARINETTI WAS A child, his mother would take him on walks in the late evening around the harbor of Alexandria. They would stroll around the tight, horseshoe arc of the old port, they would breathe the cool air drifting in from the Mediterranean, and they would observe the stars domed overhead. Far away, she would say, is Italy. And she would point into the night sky to find the Star of Venus, and she would call it the Stella d'Italia, the star that the young nation of Italy had claimed as its own. Tom, as his family called him, was born in Egypt, but he was going to be raised in the sure and certain knowledge that he was Italian.[1]

His mother, Amalia, was the daughter of a literature professor from Milan. His father, Enrico, was a lawyer from Piedmont. They had arrived in Alexandria in 1873, at a time when thousands of Europeans were doing the same. Alexandria was a small town of maybe six thousand souls at the end of the eighteenth century; a century later, it was a bustling city of nearly a quarter million, and nearly a fifth of those were foreign-born. This growth was fueled in part by thriving business throughout the Middle East but also by the policies of Egypt's rulers, viceroys of the Ottoman Empire, who were enthusiasts for European industry and keen to attract its expertise.[2] Enrico was one of those fortune hunters, and he quickly succeeded. He established offices across Egypt and became an adviser to one of the country's wealthiest landowners, Ali Pacha Chérif. He was, as his son would later put it, "the legal steelyard of the Egyptian ports."[3]

Alexandria had once been a great capital of the classical world, a renowned center of learning. Under the Ptolemaic dynasty, at the beginning of the third century BC, a follower of Aristotle was commissioned to build a site modeled on the Athenian Mouseion, which had held the philosopher's library.[4] The result was an extraordinary complex that included lecture halls, observatories, a park and a zoo, and most famously, a library that grew to become the jewel of the classical world, until it was burned, no less than twice. When Arab cavalrymen rode into Alexandria in the seventh century, it is said that they had to shield their eyes from the glare of the city's shining marble. But all that was far in the past by the time Napoleon visited it in the nineteenth century, and little was left of its history but a few monuments. It was, as the writer Michael Haag put it, "an immense and silent cemetery."[5]

Marinetti would soon become one of the twentieth century's loudest champions of modernity, one of its most violently aggressive and hyperbolic, so one wonders what his young mind thought of this ancient city. In his recollections of the period he often exoticizes and poeticizes the place. He writes, in his typically rapid stream of objects and images, of "mud-caked buffaloes emerging from the Mahmudieh Canal . . . squawking hens bristle-haired dogs and long ribboned tails that dusk studs with stars." He remembers "the old abandoned forts where pimps thieves whores ragpickers fight among themselves." Sometimes, it's contrasts of old and new, speed and grandeur, that strike him, as when he recalls "my first bicycle shiny spinning spokes chasing after plumed carriages of beautiful women and proud Arabian horses."[6]

Marinetti's earliest days were dominated by the presence of women, mostly a Sudanese nurse and his mother. Amalia would read to him from Dante, Leopardi, Rousseau, and Baudelaire, and it's said that his father hired women to read erotica to him.[7] At the age of eight, he was enrolled at the city's Collège Saint-François Xavier, and there he followed the humanist education of a French lycée, studying philosophy, rhetoric, math, and music. The ritual of Catholicism caught his imagination. The boys, dressed in red and white lace, carried gilded censers, the smell of the smoke drifting upward as showers of rose petals cascaded down. For a time, he wanted to be a priest, but then he fell in love with an Egyptian girl and put those ambitions aside.[8]

There seems to have been much in Marinetti's early life to supply easy pleasure and languor, but there were also shocks and conflicts. At age five, his father taught him to swim by picking him up and throwing him into the water. From that day on, he would always think of water as a powerful force. At school, the Jesuits liked to group the boys by nationality and set them to fight in the college gardens. Marinetti would defend the honor of Italy by hurling leather balls at the other boys and deflecting their returning fire with an iron shield. Fighting was encouraged but,

Marinetti believed, thought was not: he later claimed that he was expelled from school for reading Zola's novels. In fact, his father had decided to return to Italy; he proposed to leave the boy in Egypt, but Marinetti objected and instead his parents sent him to Paris to finish his baccalaureate. While he was there, his beloved elder brother, Leone, died in Italy of rheumatic fever at the age of twenty-one.[9]

The poetry Marinetti wrote in those years borrows its tone from the previous generation of Symbolist poets. "The Conquest of the Stars" is typical of this phase, and it begins with an "Oracle-Song of the Waves," in which the poet imagines the waters rising up ("Don your heavy / golden armor, encrusted with emeralds / devoured by moss and rust!") and readying to attack the stars. The imagery is natural, Romantic, freighted with symbols, sumptuously descriptive, and, it's fair to say, studded with the poeticisms of an earlier time ("O ancient waves, O Veterans of the Sovereign Sea," he begins). But changes were coming to Marinetti's outlook, and they began in 1898 when he moved to Milan, a city his parents no doubt knew well and rhapsodized about while homesick in Egypt. It was not the place he expected to find. Prior to Italy's unification in 1861, it had been a largely agricultural and artisanal place.[11] In one memoir, Marinetti evoked the nineteenth-century city in terms that seem hardly urban at all, claiming it had "rural and genteel graces."[12] But change had quickly come over Milan at the end of the century. It was now ringed with factories and bustling with newcomers. Old working-class neighborhoods had been razed, and grand, new modern buildings put up in their place. New gas lines were sunk underground and electric arc lamps illuminated the Duomo's piazza. When the sun rose over Milan, thousands poured onto the city's trams and trains. And so it was that, one night with friends at his father's apartment, Marinetti was led to an epiphany:

> For hours we had trampled our atavistic ennui into rich oriental rugs, arguing up to the last confines of

logic and blackening many reams of paper with our frenzied scribbling.

An immense pride was buoying us up, because we felt ourselves alone at that hour, alone, awake, and on our feet, like proud beacons or forward sentries against an army of hostile stars glaring down at us from their celestial encampments. Alone with stokers feeding the hellish fires of great ships, alone with the black specters who grope in the red-hot bellies of locomotives launched down their crazy courses, alone with drunkards reeling like wounded birds along the city walls.

Suddenly we jumped, hearing the mighty noise of the huge double-decker trams that rumbled by outside, ablaze with colored lights, like villages on holiday struck and uprooted by the flooding Po and dragged over falls and through gorges to the sea.

Then the silence deepened. But, as we listened to the old canal muttering its feeble prayers and the creaking bones of sickly palaces above their damp green beards, under the windows we suddenly heard the famished roar of automobiles.

"Let's go!" I said. "Friends, away! Let's go."[13]

The stars still twinkle from above, and the waters of rivers and seas still catch his glance, but now it is cars and trams and their beautiful noise that seize his imagination. Marinetti had awoken to the modern world. He would never be the same.

THE MIAMI BEACH CONVENTION CENTER sits a few blocks from the water, and has done so since the 1950s. Then, it was a long, unadorned slab. Today, following a recent makeover, it is faced with a succession of curving fins and resembles a sleeping animal with its ribs lengthened and resting in the sun. It has welcomed generations of individuals who want to come together to meet, talk and work—but not too seriously. Ideally, in Miami, you arrive and cast off your jacket in sheer gladness to feel heat and breathe tropical air, and by 4:00 p.m. you're holding a frozen daiquiri and can barely remember your place of employment.

I had made the trip for Art Basel Miami Beach, the hugely successful offshoot of the Swiss art fair that rides into town for a few days every December. Dealers fly in with cases of their more mood-elevating paintings, and financiers, tech bros, and a fairy-dust sprinkling of movie stars follow them in search of brand-name cultural expression, all put together in an air of fizzy exuberance and congratulation. The business of art used to take place during exhibitions; today, it takes place in malls we call fairs.

The art in these fairs isn't bad—often it's extraordinarily good. There is old and odd work by celebrated names; startling new work by lesser-known names from far across the globe; and there are ambitious displays of some overlooked genius that we'd be thankful to see in the greatest museums. But then there's also a huge lot of expensive this and that. I arrived around noon, and by late afternoon I'd seen a great deal—at least, much had passed before my eyes. I'd seen landscapes of Los Angeles and outline drawings of cats. I'd seen a tall painting with fields of cloudy pastels that felt new in some unimportant way. There were yellow glass flowers and photographs of African politicians giving speeches; there were emotive, vulnerable portrayals of rappers, and paintings collaged with advertisements for melons from a German grocery store. I'd seen a watercolor of a boy standing out of the sun under some trees; I'd stood for a while looking at some charcoal drawings of rowing boats that were lying out to dry; photographs of fallen trees in England in the 1940s; and a painting with a long, bounding green figure, stretched out like a wet, distended gummy bear and stepping into a Day-Glo foreground. And there was a painting in which a hand stretched down from above, through broad, spattered strokes of paint, and grabbed a shoe. So, so much, and yet it didn't add up to anything that made any sense. Now I was standing at the beginning of another long, long corridor of art feeling dazed, and distinctly not myself.

I'm a person who likes art. I have the credentials to prove that I like it: as a critic I spent years writing about it, and as a teacher I've spent yet more years discussing its history. Something was wrong. I couldn't blame the heat: the convention center had been cooled to the temperature of a walk-in fridge. Was I going to be sick? Or did I just need to sit down? I emptied the entire contents of my wallet to purchase a coffee and fell into a chair. It was late in the day, but the light was suspended in a continuous, uniform glare, lending the impression that the day might never end, which I felt was quite likely if I was going to be forced to see all this art. I could decide that I had "seen" the art in the convention center, but then there were other fairs, more mini convention centers, and there were also probably some small galleries I should see, lest anyone ask if I saw *that* when I was in Miami. Finally, I decided I had indeed seen enough and made for the beach. I sat down at a picnic table and tried to rouse my soul with another espresso and an intensely refrigerated pastrami sandwich. Before me, figures lay prostrate on towels next to cans of Bud. I realized that I didn't want any more art. Not today; I was tired. But not tomorrow either. I wondered, in fact, whether I'd ever want to see any more art again.

We're supposed to be ever thankful for art. The more art the better, we're told, and in recent times we've been offered more and more of it. Museums have grown to become tourist attractions for a global audience, commercial galleries have proliferated, and art fairs have sprung up across the world. In 2022, the global art market generated $67.8 billion, and that doesn't begin to count the money that flows through the gleaming museums.[14] All this growth should surely bring art ever closer to our ordinary lives, and yet all the wealth that nurtures it seems only to increase its aura of power and mystique, and hence its distance from us. To say no to all this still seems like an ungrateful and philistine act. You don't say no to art.

And yet, Marinetti had once had the courage to do so. He had his famous moment of awakening in his father's apartment, and he had recalled the events, setting the scene for us, how all his friends were gathered around one night "under hanging mosque lamps with domes of filigreed brass," and how together they came to a realization about the modern world. And then he tells us what they're going to do about it:

"We will destroy the museums, libraries, academies of every kind."[15]

He calls the museums "cemeteries," "public dormitories," "abattoirs."

Venice, too, he dismissed as a reeking and feeble pile of old bricks, its gondolas being "rocking chairs for cretins."[16] He and his friends will bulldoze the palaces, fill in the canals, let in trains and cars, and install artillery for defense.

"Admiring an old picture is the same as pouring our sensibility into a funerary urn."

"Set fire to the library shelves! Turn aside the canals to flood the museums!"

Of course, Marinetti's complaint was about the art of the past, and he was fully open to the prospect of an art of the future. The problem these days is the art of the present, an obsession with what's contemporary and what's coming next. I wondered for a moment whether we might need an anti-futurist movement: "We will destroy art fairs, galleries, institutes of contemporary art of every kind! Art fairs are cemeteries, public dormitories, abattoirs!" Might I lead this movement? It would give me purpose. But I wasn't certain about the end of all galleries. That sounded like the end of art itself. I was willing to grant that, even if my distress continued and I no longer wanted any more art in my life, ever, it was likely that others would want some—and who was I to take it away from them?

But what if I did? What if there was no art? If art just, well, ended? I tried to think what that would be like, but my mind went blank. I looked up and saw a small plane fly by trailing a banner for a DJ set that night.

It occurred to me, sitting there at the picnic table, that Marinetti wasn't alone in railing against art. There were others who had also wanted an end to it, and one might reasonably suppose that they liked art too—or did at some point in their lives. André Breton, the leader of the Surrealists, frequently called for the end of literature. Emmy Hennings and her partner, Hugo Ball, the founders of the Dada movement, talked about the end of art while they desolately wandered the streets of Zurich in the depths of the First World War. The Russian poet Vladimir Mayakovsky felt that war actually killed it: "Art is dead," he wrote in December 1914, "because it found itself in the backwater of life; it was soft and could not defend itself."[17] A few years later, however, Theo van Doesburg, the leader of the De Stijl movement, found that it was still alive and still needed to die: "Art has poisoned our life," he complained.[18] Even his mild-mannered friend and associate, Piet Mondrian, wanted done with it. In fact, Mondrian was convinced that we wouldn't miss it when it was gone. "One day," he reflected, "the time will come when we shall be able to do without all the arts, as we know them now; beauty will have ripened into palpable reality. Humanity will not lose much by missing art."[19]

It's fair to say that these individuals were not all calling for exactly the same thing, nor were they driven to do so by the same feelings. But we can still find some commonalities if we take up Mondrian's weird idea that "humanity will not lose much by missing art." As he says, it's premised on the dream that, one day, "beauty will have ripened into palpable reality." What Mondrian hoped for was that the beauty now confined to art, to little painted pictures, could be made to somehow burst out of its confines and suffuse our everyday lives. Art would enter life.

We're accustomed to a lot of slack talk about art and life, of being told that someone is living artfully, or that some art really captures life, so when I say that there was a group of modern artists who wanted to merge art and life, it can sound like I'm merely saying they wanted to spice things up. But these individuals had bigger plans. One of Marinetti's favorite entertainments was the *serate*, rowdy evenings of poetry and politics that were staged before packed audiences at theaters. Marinetti likened them to a "well-primed grenade."[20] Following suit, Hennings and Ball established a political cabaret that embraced high and low art, music, and abstract language. Their particular spirit of dark satire and irrational attitude would spread like a virus to groups in Berlin, Hanover, Paris, Cologne, and New York. A few years later in Paris, André Breton began to replace art with séances, word games, and aimless strolls through the city. In the Netherlands, van Doesburg led a search for "de stijl," the single style that would transcend fine art and become the basis for all design. In Russia, when Vladimir Tatlin set about designing a monument to celebrate the Communist Third International, he envisaged not a figure in bronze but a vaulting tower in glass and steel in which entire sections would rotate. His friend Mayakovsky described it as "the first monument without a beard." These artists didn't necessarily believe that they had solved the problem of art; they knew they were pioneers generating no more than prototypes for an artless world.

And who were these pioneers? They were the avant-garde. There were plenty of great moderns who explored limits: Pollock dripped paint and achieved an extreme abstraction, and Rothko conveyed emotion with nothing more than panels of color, but both obeyed the basic conventions that artists paint pictures and those pictures are hung on walls. We might not know what the artists are saying, but we know what they're doing: they're making art. But the likes of Marinetti, Hennings, Mondrian, and Van Doesburg, they were different: they were avant-garde. We generally take that phrase to denote something that might be advanced, ahead of its time. That's a useful understanding of it, though today we tend to use the term very loosely to acclaim all kinds of phenomena, everything from fashion to music, even food—I've heard a bowl of noodles being described as avant-garde. (Maybe they were forward-thinking noodles, difficult noodles.)

But it's worth remembering the literal translation of the French, which means "before the front." And that's where Marinetti always wanted to be. He spent his youth wavering between a romance with Alexandria's antiquity and the seduction of a capitalist modernity that he could only imagine from afar; when he was finally committed to the modern, his devotion was complete and his hatred of the antique was vicious and absolute.

For Marinetti, anger was a fuel, it was an energy: he once described it as "the caffeine of Europe."[21] And all his violent talk wasn't merely a performance: Marinetti was an avant-gardist who made that military metaphor seem very appropriate. He *loved* war. His first taste of it came when he worked as a correspondent reporting conflict in Libya and the Balkans. He departed for the adventure saying that he hoped "to shoot some Turks," and returned claiming to have killed three.[22] He started a fight with a journalist who revealed the dreadful treatment that the Italian army meted out to Arab rebels. And he composed poems evoking the clamor of the battlefield. Then he volunteered to fight in the First World War (he would be arrested along with Mussolini during pro-war demonstrations in Rome); then he volunteered to fight in the Abyssinian War; then he volunteered for the Second World War and served on the Eastern Front at the age of sixty-five. Somehow, a little while later, he died of natural causes. Art, war, and modern life: they lit a fire in Marinetti. He didn't want to be a lonely poet, scorned by the world, he wanted to be a leader, and it drove him to proselytize everywhere from London to St. Petersburg, and to rally writers and artists around him as if he were forming a political party—which eventually he did.

The term "avant-garde" first came into common use in Paris at the turn of the twentieth century and pointed to artists who were behaving in distinctly new ways. It's true that sometimes they painted pictures, just as countless generations of artists had done before them, but often they created objects that defied all the prior categories of art. They bound together in cultish cells, they explored obscure knowledge, and they scorned the public. In the coming pages I'm going to be looking at the roots of this kind of avant-garde behavior that started in the years around 1910, but my real focus is on what happened next, an extraordinary change of attitude and approach that was initiated by the First World War, but that endured for many decades afterward. All of a sudden, artists who had been behaving like devotees of some new religion of art decided that they needed to kill their god. Art needed to end, and in various places across Europe and beyond, groups got together to work out how that might be done.

Why did the avant-garde pursue this quest? Some were driven by a desire to challenge the patron class, to be offensive or productively confusing, to *épater la bourgeoisie*. Many disliked the refined, elevated sphere in which art lived. They wondered why it couldn't descend from its Delphic heights and speak to the people. Some were frustrated by the confines of little squares of canvas, or little sculpted figurines, and how, whenever you wanted to view them, you had to go to special quiet rooms. Why couldn't art be a seamless, enveloping, immersive environment in which everyone will live and work? And then some were fired by a fierce belief that changes in art could bring changes in life, and that a new society was just over the horizon if they succeeded. They were suspicious that art had become an impediment to change in life itself, that art had become society's pressure valve, so when the people's anger mounted at the state of things, at the fallen circumstances of their lives and times, they paid artists to do the lamenting for them and never got around to actually making changes.

Today, unfortunately, it is in museums that we encounter so much that the avant-garde left behind (and in tribute to them, I'm hesitant to call it art). Wasn't Marinetti going to destroy all the museums with his "well-primed grenade"? Maybe it failed to detonate. But the fact that we must go to an art museum to learn about these attempts to end art means that we tend to forget just how strange, radical, and promising these ideas were when they were first born. Yesterday's inventions have become today's commonplace tools. We need to recall what an extraordinary thing it could be for art to enter life. And maybe we need to consider trying it out once again. While I was trudging around the art fair in Miami, I could see one good, if banal reason to end art: I might never have to go to an art fair again. So where do I start? Could I restage one of Marinetti's *serate* in the halls of Art Basel Miami Beach and create such explosive energy that it would just shut the place down? Sounds good, but would it work as it had for Marinetti? And what might I destroy in the process? If I could snap my fingers and be rid of art, the fairs would vanish, and there would be no more chilly and intimidating galleries in the big cities; maybe that would be progress. But would there be no more long and pleasurable moments of looking at an object, of taking in its shape and form and patterning and resonance? Or might I find those pleasures elsewhere? I told a friend recently that my latest pair of sneakers was a masterpiece, so in the absence of art was I going to have to contemplate sneakers? Or had my sneakers become art, and I was going to have to return them? I'd like to explore all these ideas, all these schemes to end art, and test out whether it's possible, today, to take up the tools of the twentieth-century avant-garde and, well, do the job right this time.

During the tumultuous early years of the twentieth century, Western artists experienced crises of all kinds—political, economic, social—and they responded by provoking a crisis in art, one that many hoped would bring an end to it. It was the rich possibility of this idea that prompted them to talk and travel and work as never before. Marinetti's wanderlust only set a pattern for the whole period, in which artists created a network of interlocking lives and conversations, uniting disparate figures from Moscow to Munich, Paris to New York. If you wander the halls of Miami

Basel, you'll find people from all those places and more. We live in such an interconnected world that, if a good idea catches light in Djibouti, it could be changing lives in Toronto soon after. Yet if we look at the art in those booths in Miami, hanging quietly and expensively on the walls, ready to be parceled up and sent to decorate a living room, you might wonder what happened to all those good ideas that the avant-garde put forward. Couldn't we revive them once more? What's to stop us?

ONE
Leaving Montmartre

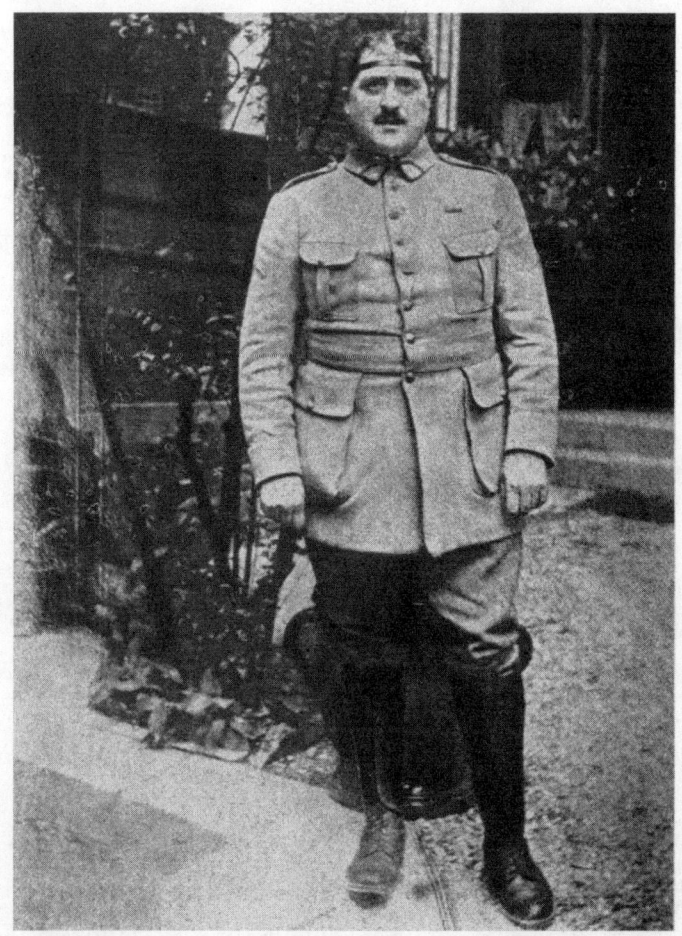

Guillaume Apollinaire

SOMETIME LATE IN 1909, GUILLAUME APOLLINAIRE left Montmartre. It was the first place he moved to after he left home, and he had remained there for over two years. He had had great exploits. But his friend, the poet André Salmon, had recently gotten married and had left the hillside. Around the same time, Picasso did the same, leaving behind the thin, damp walls of his studio in the Bateau Lavoir for the sturdy respectability of a bourgeois apartment on the boulevard de Clichy. Apollinaire was a poet and critic, and he didn't have the funds for Picasso's level of comfort, so he took rooms behind a gasworks in Auteuil. They were in an old house set back from the road at the end of a little garden with a privet hedge.[1] He lived on the second floor, above a saddlemaker's shop. It stank of leather, but Apollinaire was undeterred. From there he could walk a few streets to where his lover, Marie Laurencin, lived with her mother.

In the coming months he would regularly venture back up the hill to see old friends among the many artists and writers who remained. The area had been bypassed by the great rationalization of Paris carried out by Baron Haussmann in the 1860s. Instead of broad boulevards, the hillside was a tangle of tree-lined streets and alleyways. For centuries, windmills dotted the area, milling wheat brought in from the plains north of the city, and the hillside still retained qualities of rural life. Draft horses brought the grain up the hill; no buses made the journey. Grass grew between the paving stones. Colorful festivals and processions still survived, vestiges of folk traditions. But Montmartre was still unmistakably a part of the city's social life. Laborers lived at the northern end. Prostitutes worked their trade among the crowds that passed through the more commercialized bars and cafés at the bottom of the hill. And woven among them were the *classes dangereuses*, what the art historian T. J. Clark describes as "tramps, street-porters, organ-grinders, rag-pickers, knife-grinders, tinkers, errand-boys, and all those who lived by the thousand little occupations of the streets of Paris."[2] They were the street types that the writer Théophile Gautier referred to as the "hideous toads who hop in the mires of Paris."[3] And among them lived artists and writers. The painters liked the quality of light—sharper than could be found in studios on the Left Bank—and for everyone the living was cheap.

Montmartre was the dwelling place of Bohemians, that ill-defined and motley group that thrived at the margins of Parisian society in the nineteenth century, as it did in many European cities then. Bohemian is a term that today we use imprecisely, just as we do avant-garde. Sometimes we might use the two interchangeably, and it's true that some Bohemians possessed qualities of avant-gardism—and vice versa. Apollinaire was one of those. Many of the key avant-garde figures passed through this Bohemian world in its last days. Yet Bohemian and avant-garde are not the same, and it's important to distinguish one from the other. In fact, we might say that one was born out of the other, and that Bohemianism was to the nineteenth century as avant-gardism was to the twentieth.

For the French novelist and poet Henry Murger, who did so much to shape its myth, Bohemia was a place "bordered on the North by hope, work and gaiety, on the South by necessity and courage; on the West and East by slander and the hospital."[4] Murger gave Bohemia its earliest defining sketches in the 1840s when he published stories in a small Paris newspaper. They became a roaring success after they formed the basis of a play, *Scenes of Bohemian Life*, in 1849. By the time Giacomo Puccini penned the opera *La Bohème* at the end of the century, Bohemia was fondly recognized by all.[5] It was a hazy section of nineteenth-century European society that lay on the margins of the bourgeoisie, at a time when that class had only just come into being and was still finding a shape. It was a place where those who couldn't yet afford bourgeois society lay in wait of success, a place to loiter and scorn polite society before you had the money to join it yourself. It was also a place where those implacably opposed to that society found allies, and where those without any class, any stable profession, any stable identity, scratched out an existence.

Henry Murger knew of what he wrote, for he was very much a Bohemian—a typical one, if we can say that such misfits formed a type. He was born in 1822, the son of a tailor who also served as a concierge. As the scholar Jerrold Seigel tells us, those occupations were frequently combined in the nineteenth century because the sedentary work of tailoring could be combined with the job of overseeing a building.[6] It meant that the family straddled social classes: they were working class by virtue of the father's trade but surrounded by the successful bourgeoisie who occupied the building. Henry himself never fitted in: for much of his life he struggled with purpura, which causes rashes of purple spots formed by leaking blood vessels; he also suffered from facial tics and watery eyes, and he was frequently confined to the hospital. In poor clothes he could look like a scarecrow; in finer outfits he could still look no better than a tailors dummy. His mother hoped he would be a lawyer, but he fell in with a group of artists. He wrote some poetry, then gave that up for prose, playwrighting. He would fuel himself through all-night bouts of writing on enormous quantities of coffee. His social life brought him to the fringes of radical politics, and his stumbling romances to the edge of criminality (his greatest love was a married woman whose husband mixed a career as a teacher with forging, fencing goods, robbing banks, and spying for the police). He was only in his late twenties when he found success, but a little over a decade later he died in poverty. This was Bohemian life.

Seigel quotes a stage character of the 1840s explaining, "By Bohemians, I understand that class of individuals whose existence is a problem, social condition a myth, fortune an enigma, who have no stable residence, no recognized retreat, who are located nowhere and whom one encounters everywhere!"[7] Bohemia promised youth, art, hope, experience, danger, and license. As Seigel argues, social life in eighteenth-century France was corporate; it was lived among guilds, estates, orders, and councils.[8] The revolution destroyed that, and in its place emerged a class who celebrated individualism and made a virtue of cultivating the self. But the boundaries of that individualism were never easily determined, and one of Bohemia's important roles was to offer a space where newly liberated energies could be let loose. Here, outside the strictures of bourgeois society, the effort of fashioning that gloriously free self became its own art. *Life* became art. That's not the same as the later avant-garde ambition to bring the products of art *into* life: for the Bohemians, life itself, living it fully, experiencing extremes, cultivating the self, was the art form. This didn't mean, of course, that art was redundant; on the contrary, the Bohemian life was felt to supply the essential experiences an artist required if they were to speak truly of life in the modern world. The magical, muddled case of Guillaume Apollinaire is testimony to that. Yet it's fitting that, in 1909, Apollinaire should have left Montmartre, the home of the Paris Bohemians, for he was a transitional figure, one stamped by both the Bohemian life and the avant-garde spirit.

Born in Rome in 1880, raised in Monaco, and educated in Nice and Cannes, he was at first Guillaume Albert Wladimir Alexandre Apollinaire de Kostrowitzky—though school friends liked to mangle his surname into Cointreau-Whiskey, which should point to his habits even at a young age.[9] He was the illegitimate son of a handsome Italian officer and a dark-haired and beautiful woman who descended from Polish nobility, and whose family had taken political refuge at the papal court.[10] Anxious to keep their liaison a secret, his mother registered Guillaume's birth under a false name, baptized him under his real name, and only later legally registered his birth.[11] The couple had another child but soon enough their relationship came to an end, and the story of their children's births was concealed for decades. Apollinaire liked to claim that he had been fathered by a Vatican dignitary of no lesser rank than a cardinal. He attended Catholic schools and experienced religious intensities while praying all night in the school chapel. But soon enough he put God aside to devise a school newspaper with an anarcho-syndicalist line.

His mother prepared him for living well and living on his wits. When he was nineteen, she took him on a gambling jaunt in Belgium, in the company of a banker and speculator whom she had grown attached to. While she and her lover made for the tables, Apollinaire and his brother were left to fend for themselves in a boardinghouse in the Ardennes. But when the couple lost their money at the tables, they told the boys to flee without paying the bill. They did, stuffing all they could into a trunk and a valise and dashing through the night.

When the family finally settled in Paris, in 1899, it was under straitened circumstances, and for a time Apollinaire lived with his mother in a rented villa in the suburbs, along with her young lover and a macaque monkey.[12] She would beat Apollinaire when he displeased her, just as she did her lover. Nevertheless, he could not have been happier. He wandered the city with glee, rummaging in the booksellers' kiosks on the Seine. "I knew no one in Paris," he recalled, "and every passer-by interested me."[13]

PICASSO ARRIVED IN PARIS for the very first time, probably just before his nineteenth birthday, in October 1900, stepping off the train at the newly opened Gare d'Orsay.[14] He was in the company of his childhood friend Casagemas; the two of them were identically dressed in black corduroy suits. First they headed for Montparnasse, where a friend said they could find a cheap studio. But immediately afterward, when they visited another acquaintance in the lofty reaches of Montmartre, he convinced them that it was where they needed to be, where the Catalan artists lived, and where *la vie de bohème* was a reality. So they doubled back to Montparnasse, tore up the agreement of earlier in the day, and hauled their luggage back up the hill. Marcel Duchamp's brother, Jacques Villon, passed them as they arrived and laughed to see what he thought were two impecunious Spaniards running out on the rent. Picasso never forgot the slight.

Picasso's early days on the hill seemed to have been everything the lusty young Spaniard imagined Bohemian life to be. He and Casagemas worked until light failed, they talked of sending pictures to exhibitions across Europe, they met writers, they drank into the small hours, and they took up with women from the neighborhood. At times it was blissful—a "dirty arcadia," Casagemas called it.[15] To live with this license, to mix with thinkers, to pick up and cast off lovers, and to brush up against agitators and criminals: this was *la vie de bohème*.[16]

When Picasso looked back on his life, he felt that the times spent in Montmartre were his best. In particular, he fondly recalled the Bateau Lavoir, a ramshackle complex of studios and living quarters on the rue Ravignan, where he moved in 1904. Although named after the floating laundries that commonly sat by the edges of French rivers, the Bateau was no boat at all but a piano factory turned locksmith's workshop that had finally been converted to house artists' studios. The walls were thin, there was no gas or electricity, there was one filthy toilet and a single tap. But the warren of studios had long been popular with artists, and over the years everyone from Amedeo Modigliani to Juan Gris and Henri Matisse would pass through.

Recollections of the first meeting between Picasso and Apollinaire are inevitably theatrical—all the recollections of Bohemian Montmartre are tinted by myth. They were said to have been introduced by Jean Mollet, one of Apollinaire's acolytes who served as his housekeeper and procurer—of new friends as much as new lovers. They met in an English bar on the rue Amsterdam in October 1904, where Apollinaire was in the company of a short, fat, red-haired Englishman and two Black women wearing gaudy costumes and huge plumed hats. Picasso arrived to find Apollinaire opining on the differences between German and English beers; Apollinaire gave the newcomer a knowing wink, and from that moment on, the two were fast friends.

Picasso's lover, Fernande Olivier, penned this vivid recollection of Apollinaire:

> He was pleasant-looking, distinguished, with sharp features, small eyes rather close together, a long, thin Roman nose, and eyebrows like commas. A little mouth,

> which he often seemed to make deliberately smaller when he spoke, as though to give more bite to what he was saying. He was a mixture of distinction and a certain vulgarity, the latter coming out in his loud, childish laugh. His hands and his unctuous gestures made you think of a priest.... What struck you above all was his evident good nature. He was calm and gentle, serious, affectionate, inspiring confidence the moment he spoke—and he spoke a great deal.[17]

Apollinaire just did a little of this, a little of that, passions leading where they may. On a typical Tuesday, he would drop into an office in Saint-Germain-des-Prés to edit some pornography, he would take a leisurely lunch, and then he would mix with the leading writers and artists at the Café de Flore.[18] Otherwise, he could be found wandering the city, telling anyone who would listen about its landmarks, and composing his poetry in his head as he strolled. He was known to break off from these walks and disappear for days; he smoked opium, and there were rumors of orgies. Apollinaire was industrious at life and somehow also at work, though rarely at the same time, and if there was anything routine in his life it was the frequency with which the turbulence of his various love affairs would derail him.

His brushes with criminality are also typical of the Bohemian life. At one point, out of indulgence, Apollinaire employed as his secretary a Belgian petty criminal named Géry Pieret, a man who Picasso's biographer, John Richardson, describes as a "boxer, card sharper, drug pusher, jockey, pimp, blackmailer and convicted felon."[19] Pieret had spent four years in the American West and returned to Paris to wreak havoc, boasting of having got "disgustingly" rich, a situation that the French racetrack quickly took care of. It seems that at some point Picasso wondered out loud about owning an Iberian sculpture that was displayed in the Louvre, so Pieret stole it for him, and stole another to install in Apollinaire's apartment.[20] When the escapade came to light, Pieret fled to Marseilles; meanwhile, someone informed on Apollinaire, who was arrested, and he implicated Picasso. Both being foreign nationals, Apollinaire and Picasso were terrified of what the consequences could be. When Picasso was brought before the judge, the artist looked at his friend standing there in handcuffs and denied knowing him. Picasso then somehow avoided charges while his friend was detained for several days and given only a provisional release. Apollinaire's final indignity came when he was paraded in front of the press before he was released. He was incense. He would have his revenge on Picasso.

Such a disordered life, and one with such diffuse activities, is what makes Apollinaire characteristically Bohemian. Disorder was a Bohemian ideal to be held up against the ordered world of the bourgeois. As Seigel has put it, it was a life of "perpetual dispersion."[21] The editorial program of one of Apollinaire's early literary reviews, *Les Lettres Moderne*, promised its readers not to publish too regularly because to do so would be "disloyal to the Bohemianism we are calling for."[22] Bohemia offered a radicalized version of the freedom that the nineteenth century middle class had claimed when they threw off their aristocratic overlords. But the Bohemians claimed freedom through absolute self-reliance and tasted it through intense experience. It was a banquet, and these were—to borrow the title of Roger Shattuck's classic account of the period—the banquet years.[23]

A real banquet does sum up the spirit of Bohemia in its last years, and it was organized in part by Apollinaire. It took place at the Bateau Lavoir in November 1908, and it was intended to celebrate—or perhaps humiliate?—Henri Rousseau, the customs agent and self-taught painter of crisp, scintillating jungle scenes and folk dreamscapes. It wasn't a glamorous dinner or a sober homage, it was—in the Montmartre slang of the period—a "rigolo," a comic amusement.[24] It was a *fumisterie*, something the writer Émile Goudeau described as "a kind of disdain for everything, an inner spite against creatures and things, that translated itself on the outside by innumerable acts of aggression, farces, and practical jokes."[25] The banquet was staged in Picasso's studio on the rue Ravignan, and everyone of note was invited: poet André Salmon; critic Maurice Raynal; Gertrude Stein and her brother Leo; Georges Braque and his wife, Marcelle Lapré; the illustrator and printmaker Ramon Pichot; and the sculptor Auguste Agero.

The night began with drinks at a café a short walk from the studio, and it unraveled from there. Apollinaire was sent off to retrieve the old man Rousseau, and left to her own devices, his lover, Marie Laurencin, drank with gusto. By the time Gertrude Stein arrived, Laurencin was swaying back and forth. Picasso had lately purchased Rousseau's *Portrait of a Woman* (1895), and it hung in pride of place in the studio, draped in flags and wreathes and flanked by statues. Stein described Rousseau as "a little small colorless Frenchman with a little beard"; in Rousseau's own estimations, he was a Great; the yawning chasm between the two assessments was at the root of the hilarity, and the homage to him was certainly partly in jest as much as it was prompted out of genuine fondness for the man and his work.

The crowd eventually strolled over to the Bateau Lavoir where Fernande Olivier served *riz à la Valencienne*, a dish she had lately learned on a trip to Spain. Everyone had sat down to eat by the time Apollinaire arrived with the guest of honor. But it didn't sober the proceedings. Marie Laurencin, after earlier being helped to stand by Gertrude and Leo Stein and taken out to be brusquely sobered up by Apollinaire, had sat down in some state of renewed calm before recommencing what Stein described as "wild movements and outcries." At one point a local character who came in with a donkey was helped to a drink and left. A group of Italian street singers heard the hullaballoo and tried to invade, only to be expelled by Fernande. Apollinaire gave a eulogy, Raynal gave a toast, and then André Salmon stood on the table and gave forth before throwing back another drink and starting a fight. He had to be dragged into an adjoining studio and locked in. Marie Laurencin, sobered by the meal, sang some Norman songs, Agero's wife sang some from Limousin, and then Pichot performed a Spanish religious dance that ended with him lying on the floor in the position of the crucified Christ. The whole affair heaved on until 3:00 a.m., when Salmon was released from his confines, uttered a wild yell, and tore off down the hill.

APOLLINAIRE'S MOST FAMOUS POEM is "Zone," which he began writing sometime in 1909.[26] It begins with a mood of weariness that might make you wonder if he had written it while hungover from the kind of night I've just described:

> In the end you are weary of this ancient world
> Shepherdess Eiffel Tower this morning the flock of bridges
>   is bleating
> You've had enough of living in ancient Greece and Rome
> Here even the cars seem old[27]

The poem is circadian, meaning that it spans twenty-four hours in the life of Paris, and the poet is addressing himself. The lines quoted here are separate stanzas, their brevity only serving to slow down the city's movement and underline the mood of exhaustion. The morning brings the crowds onto the streets as they rush to work, "Executives workers beautiful typists," but Apollinaire has no appointments and merely wanders the streets while his mind does its own wandering. He notes the modern scenes, "the hangars at the airport," "the inscriptions on walls / the Billboards." And he throws this modernity into greater relief with incongruous images and references to rural life, religious ritual, and the locales from his youth, places that in his recollection now seem exotic:

> Here you are in Marseilles surrounded by water-melons
> Here in Coblenz at the Hotel du Géant
> Here in Rome sitting under a Japanese medlar tree

The poem ends with Apollinaire returning to his apartment in Auteuil, and to his collection of tribal art, to "Sleep among your fetishes from Guinea and the South Seas." By this time he has passed through bars and restaurants, stood at the "the counter of a cheap bar / You drink cheap coffee with the derelicts," and a new day is dawning with a strange and awful, bloody image of a decapitated sunrise, one that Apollinaire's recent translator, Martin Sorrell, renders as "Sun sundered head."[28]

In French, a "zone" can denote an area in the general sense, as it does in English, but it can also denote an area of urban dereliction, often on the margins of the city. A wasteland. And indeed, just as "Zone" is often said to have inaugurated modern poetry in French, it also prefigures T. S. Eliot's poem *The Waste Land*, which was published in 1922 and which is said to have inaugurated modern poetry in English.[29] We could also describe it as modernist, in the sense that it expresses the experience of the modern city and does that in a manner that necessitates some significant transformation of the traditional conventions of poetry.[30] That explains why "Zone" describes the city in disconnected thoughts and images, entirely without punctuation. Apollinaire's experiences and emotions mingle and collide, his mind moves from place to place, from one memory to another, all while the city intrudes on those thoughts. Modern and ancient also mix: the Eiffel Tower is likened to a shepherdess, and the cars rumbling over bridges are likened to sheep. For Apollinaire, the motifs of classical pastoral poetry must be updated by reference to the modern city. And Martin Sorrell points out, while the poem is fragmented in its images, the length of its stanzas, and much else, it is held together by a traditional French verse form, *rimes suivies*, which shape the lines into couplets of full rhyme and near rhyme.[31] To take an example from two lines

I quoted earlier, "Here in Coblenz at the Hotel of the Giant / Here in Rome seated beneath a loquat tree," the original French contains a rhyme: "Te voici à Coblence à l'hotel du *Géant* / Te voici à Rome assis sous un néfier du *Japon*."

Now Apollinaire's life and work offer examples of a variety of important cultural phenomena in this period. He was a Bohemian in his lifestyle and in many of his attitudes, a modernist in his poetry, and also a proponent of the emerging avant-garde. To explain the latter term, we must begin with the writing of the early nineteenth-century French social theorist Henri de Saint-Simon, who employed the first use of the term "avant-garde" in an artistic context. Saint-Simon was among a wide range of French thinkers who reflected on the nation's direction in the wake of the revolution. The country had deposed and executed Louis XVI, but in 1814 it restored the House of Bourbon to the throne under the late king's brother, Louis XVIII. Saint-Simon came to feel that France needed a modern form of government, but his solution was not a conventional form of constitutional democracy. He believed France should be led by an elite triumvirate of scientists, industrialists, and artists. The artists, "the men of imagination," as Saint-Simon put it, would be the nation's "avant-garde," who might rethink the way the nation was governed.[32] Utopian thinking would be their remit: they were to "take the Golden Age from the past and offer it as a gift to future generations."[33] Of course, the French never implemented these bold propositions, but the notion that artists might play a leadership role at the forefront of society proved influential, and in the late nineteenth century we start to see artists taking on some of those ideas.

The French government did much to support artists in the mid-nineteenth century, and an expanding—and increasingly varied—middle class fueled a growing market for their work. But as Paris became ever more renowned as a center for creativity, the institutions struggled to keep pace with demand. The Salon was the greatest event in the calendar of the visual arts in Paris, and although it grew and grew, accommodating more and more artists in an increasingly unwieldly format, it still could not accommodate all who sought to be noticed. That forced those on the margins to find new ways to set themselves apart, and so artists began to collaborate, meeting in cafés, exhibiting together, and publishing limited-circulation magazines that spread their ideas. They began to think of themselves as leaders.

In doing so, artists also sought new ways to set themselves apart in the eyes of the public, and one of the first to approach this in a distinctively avant-garde manner was Félix Fénéon.[34] He would be many things—an artist, critic, publisher, collector, and gallerist—and in the mid-1880s he coined the term "Neo-Impressionism" to carve an identity for painters associated with Georges Seurat, Paul Signac, and Camille Pissarro and his son Lucien. At that time, France's art scene was starting to generate a series of waves of young talent, and Fénéon's coining represented a novel and striking means of packaging the group. It signaled their newness while also suggesting their link to—and bold supersession of—Impressionism.

Outrage was in the DNA of the avant-gardes from the very beginning, and it is again explained in part by changes in the way the artists exhibited their art and organized themselves in late nineteenth-century France. The dominance of the academy system meant that there was a broad uniformity in the styles and ideas of the leading artists in France, and therefore a shared understanding of artists' concerns among the public. The collapse of that system meant the collapse of that understanding, and as artists increasingly innovated, and did so at increasing pace in the last years of the century, that understanding was replaced by incomprehension and hostility. The public became the enemy of advanced art.

It's notable that Fénéon was an anarchist, for in the coming decades that creed, and its calls for freedom, resonated with many avant-gardists who sought to test the boundaries of art. Anarchism wasn't uncommon among circles of artists in the late nineteenth century: for all the famous glitter of the Belle Epoque, it was a time of stark income inequality. Artists living in Montmartre were close to the industrial suburbs of Paris, where that inequality was on full view, and many harbored a distrust of the government following the brutal suppression of the Paris Commune in 1871. Anarchism offered an ideology that was antiauthoritarian, anticlerical, anticapitalist, anti-colonial, and spoke to artists' yearning for artistic freedom and radical individualism. Fénéon was totally committed, contributing anonymous articles to anarchist journals in the 1890s. But he was also supportive of the anarchist notion of the "propaganda of the deed," the use of violence to further the movement's aims. In early April 1894, a bomb exploded in the Restaurant Foyot, and a few weeks later Fénéon was arrested along with twenty-nine others during a series of police raids. He was found to have in his possession eleven detonators and a vial of mercury. He and most of the others were eventually acquitted. Some have claimed that Fénéon planted the device, but the evidence is thin; more likely he knew those who did and gave them his support.[35]

As a supporter of anarchism, Fénéon was a man of his time, but as an avant-gardist, packaging and promoting the new, he was ahead of it. As David Cottington argues, it wasn't until the decade before the First World War that the idea of an avant-garde really began to take hold in Paris. It did so in part due to shifts outside of the field of art.[36] The years around the turn of the century produced a realignment in French politics, with a coalition forming that brought together liberal intellectuals and artists with sections of the working class. That group, the *Bloc des gauches*, began to enjoy a stronger role in government, and it led to the launch of a series of new initiatives designed to promote art to a broad public, to encourage workers to enjoy art and appreciate French cultural heritage. Some significant artists played a part: Albert Gleizes, who would soon have a key role in Cubism, founded a school for adult education.

But the optimism behind that progressive wave collapsed under the strains of a series of political crises around 1905. Some sections of the politically organized working class began to be dissatisfied with what parliamentary government was delivering, and they launched protests. Coupled with that, the German kaiser made a contentious visit to Morocco, which was then a French protectorate, leading to an outcry among French nationalists. The consequence was the breakdown of the coalition that had brought artists new power, and in the wake of its collapse the artists began to shift their positions. As Cottington puts it, they swapped social militancy for the aesthetic kind, and political solidarity for aesthetic elitism. Artists became avant-garde.

This thesis is enormously helpful in explaining the context around a seminal painting like Picasso's *Les Demoiselles d'Avignon* (1907). It notionally depicts five prostitutes posing in a brothel on Avignon Street in Barcelona. The women stare at us, boldly and confrontationally, in a manner very rare in images of the female nude at that time. The picture was once seen as inaugurating Cubism, since it is one of the first in which Picasso introduces a radical new kind of fragmentation and angular faceting to the figures and the shallow backdrop. Now it is seen more as a key work in the artist's transition to the style, but whatever its place in his development, it is an astonishing work. Braque felt it was "as if someone had drunk kerosene to spit fire." Picasso seems to have been aware of how shocking it was because he appears to have hidden it, showing it to remarkably few people and only letting it go for brief exhibitions during the First World War.[37] *Les Demoiselles* threatened the avant-garde shock of the new. But Picasso wasn't trying to reach the wider public, as Cottington argues; that moment had passed, and French artists were now only talking among themselves, devoted to the goal of leadership in art alone.

While we're on the topic of definitions and distinctions, it is worth pointing out that avant-gardism is a distinctly Western phenomenon. It's a response to the marginal position of modern art in Western society. We might say that in societies in which art does not occupy this peripheral role, it isn't necessary. It's for that reason that this book confines its scope to Europe, Russia, and North America. In fact, Picasso's *Les Demoiselles* offers an instructive example of where modern, Western art is situated in relation to its own society and that of the non-Western world. Scholars have long noted the similarity between the head of the woman in the top right of the picture and masks from the Etoumbi region of the Congo.[38] People in the northern Congo often used masks in rituals associated with boys' initiations and circumcisions. Picasso probably knew nothing of this, but he was attracted to the masks because they allowed him to bring change to the Western tradition of painting the figure (he was a modernist), and to do so in a manner that appeared to contemporary viewers to be shocking and extreme (he was an avant-gardist). For the people of the Etoumbi region, the masks were a part of life (albeit a special, ritual part of life), whereas for Picasso, the masks were an inspiration for art—and one whose extremism would ensure that it was first seen only by those most devoted to the religion of art.

Art that was as extreme and as unconventional as this required critics to explain it to the public, and Apollinaire was at the heart of the effort in the years before the war. He praised Fauvism, he coined the term "Orphism" to describe Robert Delaunay's art, and he was the first to use the term "Surrealism."[39] Wave after wave of new art arrived and Apollinaire gave his views and invented new labels to describe it. By 1912, the invention of "isms" had become a kind of journalistic sport, and Apollinaire could comically set forth his views on what he described as "the transcendent school of excentroconcentroconcepticorationaloorphism."[40]

Apollinaire wrote one of the first books on Cubism, the 1913 volume *The Cubist Painters*, and in it he described the style as "pure painting," meaning that it wasn't concerned with the world, it was concerned with art. That's quite characteristic of the avant-gardes before the war: political shifts had cut them adrift from the broad public they sought, and their response was to turn inward and concern themselves with art itself. Now, that might be a little surprising given what I said in the introduction: I drew attention to the way they called for the end of art. They didn't want to work on art's traditions and conventions and bring changes to them. They wanted to rip them up and transform the very place that art had in the world. So, why did avant-garde artists go from separating art from life, making it special and different, to striving to dissolve it entirely in the flow of life? First, the habits of the French avant-garde started to go stale: as Apollinaire's joke about "isms" suggests, everyone came to know the moves. Second, the war arrived and changed everything, changed the personalities and changed their priorities.

/

I'LL COME TO THE IMPACT of that cataclysmic event later, but for now it's worth noting that the seeds of change were already present in the prewar years. New ways of working, new ways of conducting yourself as an artist, an agitator, an avant-gardist, were being presented. Marinetti was a prominent example: he had no interest in secluding himself in a studio and courting a small public of devotees. After the revelations that came to him that night in his father's apartment in Milan, the revelations of the modern world, nothing would satisfy him but a mass audience. And so he set about attracting a public in the same way as the politicians of his day—he wrote a manifesto. It was in that winter of 1908 that Marinetti drafted the eleven theses that formed the centerpiece of the Futurist Manifesto. He intended to publish them immediately, but on December 28 an enormous earthquake shook Messina, in the northeast of Sicily. The death toll reached two hundred thousand, Italy declared a state of emergency, and Marinetti stalled. Instead, he printed the theses as a leaflet in French and Italian and sent it to intellectuals and journalists. It wasn't until the beginning of 1909 that he dreamt up and wrote that romantic narrative of his modern epiphany and of the movement's "founding," the text that now always appears along with the theses. The story about Marinetti gathering his friends in his father's apartment, of the hanging mosque lamps, the oriental rugs, and them "blackening many reams of paper with our frenzied scribbling"—most likely none of it occurred, yet it sets an inspiring, lyrical tone. Satisfied, Marinetti published the entirety on the front page of the French daily newspaper *Le Figaro* on February 20, 1909. He later claimed to have received ten thousand letters in response, most of them angry.

The tone of Marinetti's rhetoric, and his loud public address, no doubt clashed with the mood of Bohemian Paris, but that Paris was dying. What was being born was a new, avant-garde city. The old Bohemian world, with its uproarious life, its poverty, its petty criminality, was fading away, to be replaced by a more ordered life, and notably one dominated more by the professional middle classes. In this world, you didn't struggle in a garret and hope to get noticed; you made public assaults, you courted the press, you launched your brand. Sound familiar?

Nothing would encapsulate the tone of the new avant-garde like the Futurist Manifesto. The world had had manifestos before, some even with lyrical beauty. Maybe you aren't familiar with the specifics of policy laid out in 1848, in Marx and Engels's anonymously published *The Communist Manifesto*, but you likely are familiar with the poetry of the essay's opening salvo, "A specter is haunting Europe—the specter of Communism." The genius of Marinetti's manifesto was to dump the policy and elevate the poetry. The Futurist Manifesto isn't without prescriptions, but they aren't things we can grasp with much specificity. "We intend to sing the love of danger, the habit of energy and fearlessness," reads the first of the theses. Vague or otherwise, declaiming intentions became their mode. Between 1909, when Marinetti published the first manifesto, and 1915, when Italy entered the First World War and the movement disintegrated, the group issued more than fifty such statements covering everything, including painting, sculpture, architecture, music, noises, lust, and cooking (Italians' love of pasta was absurd and was going to be abolished and replaced with a diet based on scientific principles). Marinetti didn't write all of them, but he shaped and advised on many.

It didn't matter what the topic, the Futurists seemed to have no end of causes and opinions, and their opinions can sound extreme. That's a characteristic they share with a lot of the avant-gardes who would be forever calling for the ultimate this or that. It can be difficult to empathize with them, though blocking empathy is part of their aim; they wish to disorientate us, to refuse to be the usual, reasonable, rational individual of the public world. The resemblance that some avant-gardes took to political factions also encouraged a love of rhetoric. But sociologists have also argued that group dynamics encourage extremism, so while some of this might be rhetorical, some is also very real.[41]

The future would be important to Marinetti, but the political present would be a passionate cause as well. That had been true from his earliest days, when his interest was kindled by his parents' patriotism and his own remoteness from Italy, and it only increased as he grew older. He had returned to Italy in a climate in which many Italian intellectuals were expressing disillusionment over the cultural fruit of the Risorgimento. That nineteenth-century movement had unified the peninsula of city-states into a modern nation, but some still complained of a lack of national consciousness.[42] Marinetti looked to the working class to spur this regeneration, among whom the Futurists would, in time, excite a surprising following. His animus was also fueled by a personal feeling that, although he had inherited a considerable sum from his father, funds that would be crucial to his activities as an impresario, he was excluded from the upper echelons of Milanese society.[43] His disgust at the state of the nation was only amplified by military humiliations and territorial grievances. Italy's forces had almost been annihilated in the first Italo-Ethiopian War in the 1890s, and resentment lingered over the fact that the Austro-Hungarian Empire maintained control of the Italian-speaking areas around Trento and Trieste.

Guglielmo Oberdan, an Italian nationalist, had set out in 1882 to assassinate the Austrian emperor, was captured by the Austrians, and executed. He subsequently became a martyr for the Italian nationalists. In 1908, Marinetti went to Trieste to carry a wreath at the funeral of Oberdan's mother and was arrested for a speech against Austria.[44] Positions like this would be central to the Futurists' message, though they could surface in comical ways. Marinetti's 1912 novel, *The Pope's Aeroplane*, describes a bizarre, imagined war between Italy and Austria-Hungary. It concludes with a scene in which the pope, kidnapped from the Vatican and flown toward Trieste, at some point finds himself dangling from a plane above the Adriatic Sea "like a piece of stinking black manure," while Austrian soldiers point cannons at him. The Italians exploit this distraction to march on Vienna, while the pilot lets the pontiff drop into the sea.

These political passions were closely allied to Marinetti's fascination with war. It was "the sole hygiene of the world," he would claim.[45] We can look back to his earliest days in Alexandria, and to his fights with the other schoolboys, to see where that ground was prepared, but it was reinforced soon after by a deeper belief in the efficacy of violence. He was powerfully persuaded by the arguments of George Sorel, the influential anarchist writer who saw violence not only as necessary to bring about revolution, but something that was vital and creative. So, when Italy invaded Tripoli in October 1911, Marinetti happily went along as a correspondent. He recalled the two months he spent there as "the most beautiful of my life."[46] In 1912, he served as a kind of poet-correspondent for a French newspaper, covering the First Balkan War (though his Futurist associates complained of his absence, Umberto Boccioni moaning that while "war is beautiful, to see it is better, but ours and my future concern me more."[47]) Then, in 1913, he visited the Bulgarian trenches at Adrianople, and he would celebrate that experience in the poetry published in the volume *Zang Tumb Tumb*. When he couldn't observe conflict, he was ready to start it himself. In the wake of Italy's invasion of Libya, the English journalist Francis McCullagh accused Italy of piracy. He was at home one day in an isolated house on the Surrey Downs (with, reportedly, no one other than "a maid servant") when there was a knock at the door, and he found an angry Marinetti and Boccioni, who had driven from London. Marinetti wanted a duel. When McCullagh tried to dismiss him, Marinetti threatened to kill McCullagh on the spot.[48]

It's clear that Marinetti emerged as the leader of the Futurists because he had the forceful charisma to make himself so, but it's worth acknowledging that the artists he gathered around him had good reason to let him. Marinetti provided services, he promoted and organized, and that left the artists free to pursue their own work. One of his important early initiatives was an exhibition staged at the Galerie Bernheim-Jeune in Paris. Who should have invited him to organize it but Félix Fénéon—it was inevitable that their paths would cross. Over the next two years, "The Exhibition of Futurist Painters" toured Europe, setting down in London, Berlin, Brussels, and ten other destinations, where it was generally launched with press conferences and discussions.

The exhibition consisted of the work of four of the leading Futurist painters: Umberto Boccioni, Luigi Russolo, Carlo Carrà, and Gino Severini. But that doesn't represent all those who would later be recognized as Futurists. The group had no formal membership structure, artists simply chose to appear under the movement's banner or they declined to do so. They might appear as Futurists one day and distance themselves from the group on another. Marinetti might denounce them himself, or they might simply fall away from the group and their involvement be forgotten. The Surrealists and the Situationists had more rigid membership lists, mainly because they were led by domineering personalities who ran things that way, but most avant-gardes had elastic boundaries. Marinetti's struggle was to maintain cohesion among factions in different cities, and despite his ceaseless travel he began to lose his grip on them around 1913, and tensions developed between the groups in Florence and Milan.[49]

While in a practical sense Marinetti was simply a promoter, a glorified press officer for the Futurists, the promotion had an outsize importance for the group, and certainly for Marinetti himself. One of his favorite modes of presentation was the *serate*, a series of performances held at theaters, most of which sold out. The first was held in Trieste in January 1910 and was promoted aggressively beforehand, with leafleting and street antics on the day (promotion for the promotion). They certainly were not conventional nights at the playhouse: Marinetti described them as his way of "introducing the fist into the artistic battle," of "enabling the brutal entry of life into art."[50] One typical event, held at a theater in Rome in 1913, was said to have led to such chaos in the streets beforehand that the police had to intervene, and in the end four thousand people were admitted—more than the famed tenor Enrico Caruso ever attracted at the same theater. The night was to consist of a Futurist symphony, performances of Futurist poetry, Boccioni presenting his manifestos on painting and sculpture, and Marinetti giving a speech, "Advice to the Romans." How much of this was actually seen and heard by the audience, however, is open to question, since the evening seems to have quickly descended into chaos, and that was part of its anticipated pleasure. A journalist reported that, for over two hours, there was a "continuous battle of whistling, howling, rioting, fisticuffs, thrashings, assaulting the Futurists with potatoes, chestnuts, tomatoes, apples and other objects." And this wasn't a rough crowd: the audience consisted of a cross-section of Italian society, including Roman aristocracy, the city's intellectuals, and students. When the orchestra struck the first notes of the Futurist symphony, a shower of fruit and vegetables were said to have rained down on them, and a scion of an ancient noble family threw lumps of coal, of which he had brought an entire sack to the theater. (Marinetti responded from the wings: "You syphilitic lout! Son of a priest!")[51] Some of this sounds too incredible to be true, yet clearly the attraction of the events was the chaos and outrage they generated. They were not the kinds of conventional scandals that resulted from a bad response to a new artwork: their aim and purpose was outrage. Marinetti lived to cause offense, and when he wasn't doing that from the stage, he was doing it on the page. No less than three obscenity trials resulted from the publication of his 1910 novel, *Mafarka the Futurist*, possibly because one of the protagonists has an eleven-foot-long penis that he wraps around himself while sleeping.

If you're familiar with the noise and violence of Futurist rhetoric, it can be disconcerting to encounter the art that was first made under the movement's banner. Painters like Boccioni and Carrà at first worked in a Divisionist style inherited from late nineteenth-century French art. In this mode, artists divided color into tiny dots to produce what they hoped would be a richer saturation and vitality of hue. But it also tended to produce paint surfaces that are softly, delicately textured, and that can be incongruous when they are brought to bear on typical Futurist subject matter. Boccioni's *The City Rises* (1910) depicts surging horses and straining workers, but the dynamism of the scene is undercut by the way the clouds of dots produce such feathery forms. It wasn't until the Futurists became aware of Cubism that they fashioned a style more appropriate to their own movement's aims; how that came about is an amusing and telling example of the atmosphere of competition that cloaked the Paris art world.[52] Gino Severini was the only Futurist living in Paris in the movement's early years, so he was the only one aware of new developments like Cubism. When Marinetti started planning the show at Bernheim-Jeune, Severini persuaded him to delay it until the Italians could be sent on a research trip to Paris to discover the new styles and update their approach—lest the Paris debut of Futurism look incongruously old-fashioned. Marinetti agreed and organized a two-week jaunt to the French capital for Boccioni, Carrà, and possibly Russolo. Severini took them to the studios of Picasso and Braque, and brought them to see pictures by another Cubist group at the Salon d'Automne. When the Italians returned to Milan, their style quickly shifted in a Cubist direction, their forms becoming more angular and their palette more muted; they began to claim that their work depicted movement in new and dramatic ways. Boccioni even painted new versions of earlier subjects in an updated style. With this advance achieved, the Futurists' exhibition at Bernheim-Jeune went ahead in February 1912. But this success didn't allay the Italians' fears about rivals in Paris: barely four months later, Boccioni was ordering Severini to conduct some kind of espionage and report back on Picasso's and Braque's latest work. Of course, for the Futurists, this was a war, the Cubists were the enemy, and reconnaissance was a necessary part of the fight. Victory would go to those who were the true avant-garde.

The Futurists were anxious to place themselves in the forefront of modern style, and doing so required them to beat the Parisians at their own game. But they would always be adventurous in their desire for novelty. While Picasso held on to the traditional genres of the still life and the portrait as foundations on which to stage his Cubist innovations, the Futurists cast conventions aside. One typical example is Boccioni's *Dynamism of a Speeding Horse and Houses* (1915). It was assembled from bits of wood, cardboard, copper, and iron, but he did much with these simple materials, crafting an extraordinary composition of surprising forms and volumes, a vividly imagined three-dimensional scene. To suggest, in 1915, that such a mixed assemblage of material might be art, might join the sculptural tradition of Michelangelo, Donatello, and Rodin, was to upset and insult a great many people, it was to curse in a church, spit on a memorial. Arguably, the Futurists did much of this, producing innovative forms of art that broke with tradition in dramatic ways. The scholar and critic Marjorie Perloff credits them with inventing almost the entire inventory of avant-garde forms, forms that would be taken up again and again by subsequent avant-gardes.[53] She points to collage, ready-made sculpture, sound poetry, performance, nonlinear typography, chance-generated text, experimental architecture, assemblage, abstract photography, and, of course, the manifesto.[54]

All this took energy to direct, and Marinetti had that in ample supply. While Apollinaire wandered Paris, lunched, and otherwise diverted himself, Marinetti drove himself forward with the determination of a freight train. He is said to have "practically commuted" between Paris and Milan.[55] The Futurist writer Giovanni Papini recalled that "[Marinetti's] arrival in the peaceful Florence of those days was like a meteorite landing in an old palace garden."[56] He would fire off telegrams, take calls, jump in cars for appointments across the city—flashes of modernity entirely alien to sleepy Florence. On one occasion, while sitting in a bath, he was introduced to a guest and held the conversation while shouting over the rushing water.[57]

TWO

Can You Make Works Which Are Not Works of Art?

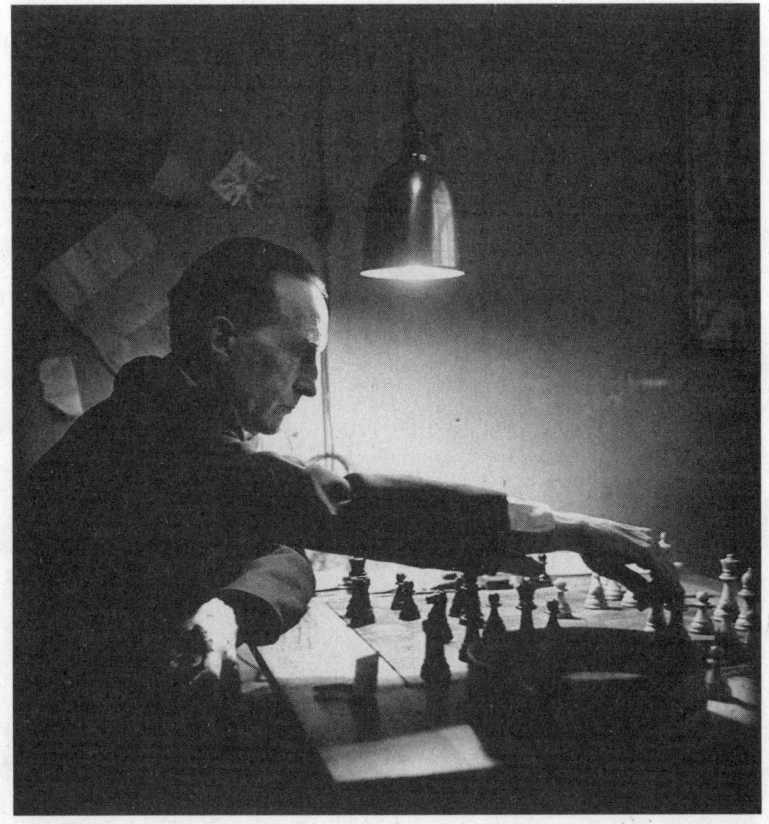

Marcel Duchamp

*I*TOOK UP PAINTING RECENTLY. I WAS STAYING IN A small town in North Carolina with time to kill, and I went to Walmart and bought a small selection of oil paints and some cheap, prefabricated canvases. I sat by a river and made a copy of one of Mondrian's slate gray, geometric pictures of the sea. It was a pleasure. I liked the result and hung it next to a flyswatter in the kitchen. When I got back to New York, I carried on painting at a small desk in the corner of my apartment. My family began to refer to it as "the studio." There were scattered tubes of paint, solvents, dirty brushes; there was some grumbling about this in the household, but I persisted. I tried out different paints and experimented with different layerings and solvents. I stretched my own canvases, bought a box of pastels. And the more curious I became about the material fabric of art, the more I found myself looking at art in new ways. I was peering at the surfaces of pictures, at tiny passages of paint, at the texture of thickly worked oil. I was looking closely. I felt that the pictures had something new to teach me, and I had something to learn.

I was a novice at all this and had never attended an art class, so feeling unprepared to make my own grand statements, I continued to copy other artists' work. One painter I was particularly drawn to was Henri Matisse. I was hopeful that I could approximate the simple drawing, the flat, brilliant color, and the loose handling of paint in his Fauvist portraits, as they appeared to have a brash simplicity. In my efforts, the figures looked skewed and the colors lifeless and off pitch, but it made me see his pictures more clearly. As clumsy and lurid as my Matisses were, they shone out joy in my apartment, and so I moved on to attempt his larger and far stranger 1904 picture, *Luxe, Calme et Volupté* (*Luxury, Calm and Voluptuousness*), which depicts women bathing by the sea. Matisse painted it while staying with Paul Signac in St. Tropez, so it's warmed by the dry heat of France's southern coast. Patches of ground the women lie on are baked to a fierce red; the sky opens up in an opalescent sweep of hues, yellows and purples and blues; and the cooling water beckons below. It's painted in the Pointillist style in which Signac himself worked, and I thought the disconnected dabs of paint that color it might require even less management than in other Fauvist works. I realized again, however, that Matisse's steady hand was steering all that apparently loose and easy paint, and whatever simple passages there were, such as the dabbed color on the water, came up against the perfectly judged shapes of the nudes. So I was disappointed in my efforts, but lessons were learned, and as I worked I was drawn further into the scene. I smelled the fragrant heat as I massed the reds together to describe the earth; I felt the cooling water as I spaced out the blues; and as I outlined the legs and arms of the reclining women, I felt the sensuality wash over me.

Luxe, Calme et Volupté might not describe the shape of some new society of the future, but arguably it was in keeping with Henri de Saint-Simon's call for the artists of his "avant-garde" to do utopian thinking and to "take the Golden Age from the past and offer it as a gift to future generations." I wouldn't say I felt closer to the promised land when I'd completed my work on the canvas, but I felt my body and soul were a little bit closer together. My hand was bringing shapes and forms out of nowhere, my eye was making observations, my mind was off in the south of France. I wondered why anyone would want to give up on making art, and yet, a little more than a decade after Matisse painted it, more and more artists were committed to doing just that.

Marinetti would probably have complained that Matisse's sensual world was an irrelevant fantasy. In his time, electric lights threaded the streets of Milan and trains wove the cities together, massed workers bent over turbines in the factories. Why were artists still sitting alone in studios, worrying over their archaic handicrafts and refining their delicate feelings? Modern politicians were rallying a mass public through the newspapers, so why were artists trying to court a handful of perfumed connoisseurs? And Marinetti might also have felt some disappointment at the purposes Matisse imagined his work being put to. "It's an armchair for the tired businessman," the Frenchman famously said. Here he was bringing arcadian visions to life, drenched in water and light, and its only purpose was to calm a rich man's nerves?

What Matisse is acknowledging here is a gap between the freedom and aspirations of the studio and the reality of art's life in the world. His ambitions might be utopian, but he doesn't live in a utopia, and he has to accept that. It's a reality that every artist experiences if they're lucky enough to be able to sell their work. Some accept it with equanimity, as did Matisse, while others protest it. Some might wish to address the public on politics and society and regret their work disappearing into private homes. And some might feel that magic is lost, work is lost, the process of creation itself is lost when the norms of art require an artist to communicate by making a certain type of object in one room and putting it for exhibition and sale in another. And some might feel that if the inspiration for the art is a vision of freedom and utopia as enlivening as *Luxe, Calme et Volupté*, then the sincerity of the whole effort is thrown into question if it's on sale for such-and-such a price, plus tax and shipping.

I suspect that Marcel Duchamp had some disconnected thoughts like this; maybe not these thoughts exactly, but ones that are similar. He never issued any long statement about the Paris and New York art worlds that he inhabited in the years around the First World War, when he was making his most consequential work. But critics suspect that what prompted that work was a frustrated rejection of those worlds. He couldn't see an alternative to them, but he wouldn't play along, and so he decided on a strategy to expose all the nonsense and pretense of those worlds. It was one typical of the man's brevity and wit. He proposed to exhibit a urinal, an object he bought at a hardware store and titled *Fountain*. In so doing, he started an argument about what could be accepted as art. And just momentarily, Duchamp seemed to promise the possibility of bringing art to a halt.

/

DUCHAMP PROBABLY WASN'T PROPELLED into a career as an artist by a fierce belief in his own talent. He probably became an artist simply because it was what people like him did—at least, it was what his family did.[1] His grandfather, Emile Nicolle, had been a successful landscape engraver. His father, Eugène, pursued a more conventional and predictable career as a notary, a profession that furnished the family's bourgeois comforts, but the next generation failed to follow his lead. Marcel's eldest brother, Gaston, initially pleased their father by training to be a lawyer, and then mightily displeased him by throwing it over to become an artist and finding a place in Montmartre. The second eldest, Raymond, did something similar, training in medicine and then abandoning it for art. The eldest daughter, Suzanne, was already attending art school in Rouen at the age of sixteen. Only the younger daughters, Yvonne and Magdeleine, failed to pursue a career in art. Finally, the youngest of all, Marcel, declared for art, and in the fall of 1904, at the age of seventeen, he left the family home in the small Normandy town of Blainville and moved in with Gaston in Montmartre.

The brothers' apartment was part of a row of six-story buildings across from which was an open field of scrubland with winding footpaths, kitchen gardens, sheds, and pens for animals. Gaston had already been living on the fabled hill for several years, long enough to have laughed at Picasso that day when the Spaniard changed his mind on his lodgings. Montmartre was a lark, but it was distracting. Gaston, being both a diligent and hospitable sort, found his friends were constantly harassing him. "They came over to smoke their pipes," he complained, "brought along their women, and stopped me working. I had to make up at night for the time they wasted during the day."[2]

Eventually, Gaston decided that enough was enough, and in 1906 he moved out to the suburban village of Puteaux, on the western edge of the city. The following year, Raymond joined him, along with the Czech artist František Kupka, and the three moved into a series of small houses with artists' studios and a shared back garden.[3] Soon afterward, Marcel moved to Neuilly, a short walk across the bridge from his brothers (in fact, he had little choice after he was evicted for holding a Christmas party that went on for two days). And on Sundays, everyone would gather in the two brothers' garden, where the branches of a grand old chestnut tree reached down to the ground. Friends would be invited to lounge, eat, and talk, and the Duchamp brothers' two Siamese cats and fat old collie would roam about entertaining.[4] When the weather was fine, they'd play chess, *boules*, or archery. Marcel also devised a steeplechase game, laying down pieces of canvas to create a model of the racetrack at Auteuil, and players would roll dice to advance a wooden horse that Marcel had made. It was all very satisfyingly distant from the noise on the hill.

SO DUCHAMP WAS STARTING LIFE as an artist, and he was close to his beloved brothers: it must have felt good. It's said that as a young man Duchamp was handsome, with hooded gray eyes and thin lips, pale skin, and hair brushed back over a high forehead. The Surrealist's leader, André Breton, idolized him, and said he had "a face of admirable beauty." Yet his own career in art was encountering obstacles.[5] He took a few art classes at a private academy, and he would occasionally make quick drawings in a pocket sketchbook, capturing his family, or Parisian street types, but in the spring of 1905, when he took the exam to enter the École des Beaux Arts, he failed. More problems followed when a new conscription law made it mandatory for all young Frenchmen to enlist for two years. The only way to lessen this term was if you were a lawyer or doctor, or engaged in a handful of other professions deemed essential, in which case you could get away with a single year's service. Duchamp discovered that among those deemed essential were "art workers," meaning printers or engravers or other skilled technicians in the applied arts. So he promptly made for Rouen, where his parents had recently moved, and found a position as an apprentice at a print shop. There he spent five months mastering the trade, learning etching, engraving, and typesetting. For his final examination, he found one of his grandfather's original copper plates titled *The Hundred Towers of Rouen*, from which he pulled a series of exquisite prints. Having finally gained a qualification as an artist, Duchamp reported for military service. A year later he came back to Paris.

If we're to understand the increasingly strange direction Marcel Duchamp's career took, it's instructive to look back at those early years. For having failed the entrance exam for the École des Beaux Arts, Duchamp never obtained a qualification as a "fine artist." He obtained one as an "art worker," and upon returning to Paris, he found work drawing humorous illustrations for newspapers. Work like this was lower down the rungs of art's hierarchy, but it could pay well, and satirical illustration had some prestige in this period.

Another likely reason why Duchamp was not inclined to take the profession of fine artist too seriously was the company he was keeping. Francis Picabia, whom Duchamp met in the fall of 1911, was the much-indulged son of a rich Cuban widower, whose French wife, Picabia's mother, had died young, leaving him to be raised as a splendid playboy alongside his father, grandfather, uncle and servants.[6] The house was described as "les quatre sans femmes" ("the four without women"), though Picabia's friends, aware of his penchant for women, would later jest that it should have been called "les quatre cents femmes" ("the four hundred women"). His uncle was a collector of art and rare books, and his father enjoyed the none-too-taxing position of chancellor of the Cuban embassy in Paris, while his son was said to want for nothing. Tales of his exploits were whispered in cafés. It was said that, as a child, he had used a toy scale to weigh darkness and light and decided that darkness was heavier (he was destined to be a pessimist). He quit school at the age of eighteen to run off to Switzerland with the lover of a prominent French journalist. He claimed to have met Nietzsche and had supported himself by painting landscapes on smooth, flat stones retrieved from a lake. When Apollinaire finally split with Marie, he found himself at loose ends and fell in with Picabia, and they spent many nights talking, drinking, and smoking opium. In various states of intoxication, they would roar around Paris in what William Camfield, Picabia's biographer, excitedly describes as "his magnificent automobiles." (Mark Polizzotti, André Breton's biographer, claims that there were no less than 127 of them, over the years.)[7] These splendid carriages would forever be Picabia's temptation and he used them to explore the world.

Duchamp undoubtedly found his friend's lifestyle a wonderful distraction, and it was perhaps one that was all the more welcome in preventing him from dwelling on his friend's accomplishments—and indeed those of his brothers. Picabia was six years older than Duchamp, and by the time they met, in 1911, he had tried Impressionism, dabbled in the different modes of Seurat and Van Gogh, borrowed from Toulouse-Lautrec and Fauvism, and was on the cusp of a shift into Cubism. Gaston and Raymond also were significantly older than Marcel, Raymond by eleven years, Gaston by twelve, and their progressing work had lifted them into the company of increasingly prominent figures. Gaston now styled himself as Jacques Villon. It's thought that Gaston took his new name in tribute to François Villon, the medieval French writer renowned as much for his criminality as his poetry. Gaston had had a long spell working for satirical magazines, and he likely thought it advisable to have a pseudonym so as to spare his father embarrassment. Raymond then adopted Duchamp-Villon in solidarity.

Today, we tend to remember Picasso and Braque as the founders of Cubism, and the Futurists' anxiety about their innovations would suggest that they led the field unchallenged. Yet Cubism was pursued by a much broader group of artists in the years before the war. Picasso and Braque worked in Montmartre and held relatively low-profile shows at Kahnweiler's gallery. By contrast, the period around 1911–12 saw another group of Cubists emerge around Montparnasse, and they were much more intent on publicity. They organized prominent displays of their work at the Salon des Indépendants and the Salon d'Automne, and consequently they are known today as the Salon Cubists. The group initially consisted of Robert Delaunay, Jean Metzinger, Albert Gleizes, Henri Le Fauconnier, and Fernand Léger. They first began to congregate at each other's studios, and in the fall of 1911 they began to be drawn to the Sunday afternoon meetings hosted by the Duchamps in Puteaux.

What Picasso and Braque were striving for in their own brand of Cubism has produced more commentary than I could helpfully summarize here, but to put it most broadly and succinctly, their aim was to take apart the conventions of Western painting. They were interested in how objects are described in pictures, how three-dimensional objects are rendered on a two-dimensional surface, and what codes and conventions artists use to achieve it. The circle around the Salon Cubists tended to have more wide-ranging and esoteric interests, and their styles were more varied.[8] Two paintings by František Kupka, *Amorpha, Warm Chromatic* and *Amorpha, Fugue in Two Colors* offer some sense of this.[9] It's thought that their origins lie in a drawing Kupka made around five years earlier of a young girl holding a ball. Through a steady series of revisions of the drawing, he arrived at these abstractions of intersecting curves and circles. He knew they were ambitious statements, and he gave them a size to match: *Amorpha, Fugue in Two Colors* is seven-foot square, far larger than most Cubist pictures by Picasso and Braque. And to ensure the greatest audience for his achievement, he exhibited them in October 1912 at the Salon d'Automne, a successful young salon that enjoyed a prestige location in the Grand Palais. They were among the very first abstract pictures to be exhibited in Paris, and they drew considerable attention. Film company Gaumont shot newsreel footage of them and showed it in movie theaters across Europe and the United States. The critic Gustave Kahn proclaimed that they played "games which are not within everyone's reach."

Kupka's interests were expansive. He had attended lectures on physics and biology at the Sorbonne, and he blended ideas drawn from those with esoteric references. It was a mixture that was typical of the Puteaux crowd. They looked at art through a peculiarly scientific lens and believed that modern art might serve as a kind of technical drawing for the latest advances. In comparison to most artists of their time, they were unusually well-read in scientific fields, and several of them had made their way through weighty texts on the latest physics and geometry. One enthusiasm was non-Euclidean geometry, which sprang in part from the writing of the late nineteenth-century French scientist Henri Poincaré, who argued that the modern principles of geometry were only conventions, not absolute truths. It's said that few among the Salon Cubists genuinely understood these ideas; it didn't help that much of their information came from Maurice Princet, an actuary and an unreliable amateur mathematician who was one of Picasso's hangers-on. But they were enthusiasts nonetheless, many being fascinated by the possibility of a fourth dimension, a widely popular topic in the period and something that was said to point to some higher, cosmic, transcendental truth.

So it was in this milieu that Duchamp learned about the mores of the prewar avant-garde, how it competed, how it networked. At first, he couldn't settle on a style. Like Picabia before him, he tried this, he tried that, moving between Post-Impressionism, Fauvism, and touches of Cézanne. Trying on different styles was part of the learning process in modern art, part of what Duchamp called his "swimming lessons." Then, around 1911, his painting finally took on a new authenticity, a style of its own that was more distinct and adventurous, and also a whole lot stranger. He borrowed from Cubism and took steps toward abstraction, and he began to arrange figures in strange, ritualistic groups. *Sonata* (1912) depicts his three sisters each playing a musical instrument, their mother looking on from above them. It may be based on childhood memories, but the posing of the figures is oddly rigid and hierarchical. The Duchamp scholar Arturo Schwarz suggests that the picture also contains a portent of Suzanne's coming marriage, since she sits at the bottom of the picture, her faced turned away from her family.[10]

These developments were probably all very promising, especially from the perspective of the Salon Cubists (and the judgment of peers was constant), but then he shifted once more. In 1912, he painted a picture titled *Nude Descending a Staircase*. It shows a geometric, apparently mechanical figure coming down a spiral staircase. He was pleased, so he painted another version, the one we now know as *Nude Descending a Staircase No. 2*. In this picture, the backdrop is less distinct and instead all the focus is on a robotic body whose juddering movements are followed, as if in a slow-motion sequence, down the stairs. Again, he was pleased, but when Gleizes and Metzinger saw it they were aghast. Apollinaire had recently praised the Salon Cubists for a "noble and restrained" art, and this wasn't that. Moreover, it probably felt too close to the new Futurist style that had emerged in the wake of the group's visit to Paris. Finding a style in the Paris art world of 1912 wasn't just about crafting a shape for your feelings, it was about positioning. It was about being in advance of the enemy, anticipating their moves, shutting them down. It was about being avant-garde. And in this competitive game, Duchamp's work strayed too near to the opposition.

It was decided that the artist's brothers should put him straight, and the day before the exhibition's opening, Raymond and Gaston turned up at Marcel's studio in Neuilly, dressed in black, to relay the bad news. Marcel recalled being told that the picture was "a little off beam." Couldn't he at least change the title? He refused. "It was a turning point in my life," Duchamp later reflected. "I saw that I would never be much interested in groups after that."[11] It would also mark the end of Duchamp's life as a committed painter.

CRITICS HAVE OFTEN CONFESSED to being puzzled about Duchamp's motivations at different stages of his life, and there are a few spells that are a complete mystery. The first of those came when he took himself to Munich in June 1912. He stayed a few months, made some notes and drawings, and painted a couple of pictures; otherwise, no one knows what he did there, or what preoccupied him. Yet it was likely consequential, because shortly after his return, he started to do things differently. He took the front wheel of a bicycle, still in its fork, and fixed it to the top of a kitchen stool. As with so many of Duchamp's works, there isn't a very substantial explanation for that object to which—like every other work of art—we now give a title, *Bicycle Wheel*, and the artist was happy not to provide one. He merely said that he liked to spin it around as the mood took him. "[It] just came about as a pleasure," he recalled, "something to have in my room the way you have a fire, or a pencil sharpener, except that there was no usefulness. It was a pleasant gadget, pleasant for the movement it gave."[12]

But it was strange and interesting enough to prompt him to try something else, and that's why in 1914 he went to a large housewares store in Paris and bought a bottle-drying rack. French shops in that period occasionally sold wine directly from the barrel, and families brought along their empties to be refilled. Duchamp didn't intend to use the bottle rack for drying bottles, though he doesn't seem to have been very clear on what he was going to do with it. He scribbled in his notes a question: "Can one make works which are not works of art?" Before he had come to any definitive conclusions about this question, the First World War broke out. Gaston and Raymond were promptly called up; Marcel, having satisfied the requirements of military service a few years earlier, was temporarily exempt. When in January 1915 his orders finally came, a medical exam found that he had a rheumatic heart murmur, and he was excused from service. But that didn't excuse him from the accusations of those who did have to fight, and deciding he was better out of the country, he left for New York.

Duchamp had never set foot in New York, yet he already had a reputation there. After the Salon Cubists had rejected *Nude Descending a Staircase No. 2*, he had sent it across the Atlantic to appear in the

Armory Show, a huge, broad—and enormously successful—survey of some thirteen hundred examples of European and American art that opened at the 69th Regiment Armory in New York in March 1913. It is credited with turning America's attention to new trends, and while it included many examples of late nineteenth-century art, and more American work than French, it was examples of the most recent French art that caught the press's attention. Among the most controversial pieces were Matisse's *Blue Nude* (1912), which was accused of "leering effrontery," and Constantin Brancusi's *Mademoiselle Pogany I* (1912), which was compared to "a hard-boiled egg balanced on a cube of sugar."[13] Picabia, alone among the French artists in having the funds to attend, contributed a Cubist picture, *Dances at the Spring (II)* (1912), and was happy to offer himself for interviews to mildly scandalized reporters. Duchamp's picture also amused the press: one cartoonist likened it to a scene of commuters rushing to catch a subway train and titled his sketch "The Rude Descending a Staircase."

When Duchamp's boat drew into New York in June 1915, the heat was intense. He recalled being "dumbfounded—I thought there must have been a fire somewhere."[14] When the winter arrived, more climatic surprises were in store when snow blanketed the city and people came outdoors to clear the sidewalks. Duchamp had never seen a snow shovel before; enchanted, he bought one with a galvanized iron blade and wooden handle. Again, he didn't intend to use it, but this time he concluded that objects like these could be artworks of a special kind. Borrowing a term Americans used in the period to describe ready-to-wear clothes, he decided to call them "Readymades." It seemed that for these objects to be artworks, they could simply be chosen by the artist, as he had done with the bottle rack in Paris, though he realized that they also needed to be named. On the side of the Readymade snow shovel, he painted the words, "In Advance of the Broken Arm," which then became the work's title. Only now did Duchamp realize what he had been striving to create with the earlier objects, the bicycle wheel and the bottle rack, which he had left behind in Paris. He quickly wrote his sister, Suzanne, who had recently cleared out his studio on the rue Saint-Hippolyte, and asked her to inscribe his name on the bottle rack. Alas, it was too late: Suzanne had discarded both of them, presumably thinking they were junk, which they were until Duchamp decided they were not.

The Readymade was born. Now he had to get people to pay attention. Apparently, he exhibited two more Readymades at the Bourgeois Galleries in New York in April 1916, but we don't know which ones they were, and positioned outside the main exhibition in the gallery's vestibule where visitors hung their hats, they were barely noticed.[15] He needed a different approach and he finally arrived at one when he became involved with Society of Independent Artists.[16] Its mission was to promote modern art. The United States had been slow to respond to the new styles, but the Armory Show revealed that there was an audience for them, and many were eager to repeat its success. The New York society was modeled on the Parisian Société des Artistes Indépendants, to which the Salon Cubists had contributed, and the centerpiece of its calendar was a large annual show to which anyone could submit work. There would be no jury to judge entrants, none of the kind of gatekeepers that guarded traditional academies. It would simply have an initiation fee of one dollar, and a fee of five dollars would entitle the member to exhibit two works. Duchamp endorsed the liberal principles of the endeavor and signed on as one of twenty founding members, and in typically avant-garde fashion, he banded together with Roché and the artist and ceramicist Beatrice Wood to also found a magazine, *The Blind Man*, to provide a forum for the exhibition.

It's said that the plan was hatched over lunch. Duchamp sat down with the painter Joseph Stella and the art collector Walter Arensberg, and afterward the three of them visited the J. L. Mott Iron Works, at 118 Fifth Avenue, and selected a "Bedfordshire" porcelain urinal. Duchamp wrote "R. MUTT 1917" on the side, and two days before the exhibition's opening, he delivered it to the society, along with a membership fee from the fictional Mr. Mutt and a false address in Philadelphia. What happened next was inevitable, and Duchamp knew it.

There was said to have been a standoff between George Bellows, a painter who sat on the society's board, and Arensberg. Bellows called the work "indecent" and refused to exhibit it, while Arensberg reminded him that the whole purpose of the show was to be open to all artists and all art. Moreover, Arensberg argued, the work had a "lovely form." Bellows wasn't impressed and retorted that if they were to let anything go on show, someone could send in "horse manure glued to a canvas [and] we would have to accept it." "I'm afraid we would," Arensberg happily replied. Alas, Bellows had his way, and his fellow painter William Glackens, the president of the society's board, pronounced final judgment, stating that the object was "by no definition, a work of art." Rejecting the work was difficult under the society's rules, but a way was found by dismissing it on a technicality, claiming that its documentation had been improperly completed.[17]

At this point, Duchamp had probably achieved no more than he had in the previous exhibition of the Readymades. If they had been overlooked because there was nothing to draw attention to them, paradoxically, *Fountain* risked being completely unknown because it *couldn't* be overlooked. So Duchamp decided to publicize the society's refusal in *The Blind Man.* The row erupted only a few days before the opening, making it too late for the first issue, but the second (which was to be its last) appeared to coincide with the show's closing, and it carried an unsigned editorial titled "The Richard Mutt Case." It's thought that it was penned by Beatrice Wood but more or less dictated by Duchamp and succinctly put his case. It was not immoral, nor did it matter that Mr. Mutt had not made the work himself. "He CHOSE it," the article argued. "He took an ordinary article of life, placed it so that its useful significance disappeared under the new title and point of view—created a new thought for that object." Significantly, the article was accompanied by a photograph taken by Alfred Stieglitz, who was then not only a prominent photographer but also one of the few leading gallerists exhibiting modern art in the United States. Duchamp didn't know Stieglitz well, but in seeking him out and persuading him to photograph the object, he effectively had the work baptized as art.

ALTHOUGH DUCHAMP'S MOTIVATION for creating the first two Readymades isn't entirely clear, it is easy to see what he hoped to achieve with *Fountain*. His intention was to test the principles of the Society of Independent Artists. Still smarting from the rejection he experienced in Paris, when his friends blocked him from exhibiting alongside them, he wanted to find out if American society was genuinely open to all and to everything. He probably wasn't surprised by the second rejection: the avant-gardism that had taken shape in Paris before the war put a great emphasis on artistic freedom, but it was clear that that freedom existed within certain limits. It was also clear that freedom could work hand in hand with the shape of the modern, commercial art world that was then taking shape in the city: well-calibrated scandals were good marketing. Duchamp knew this, and he could have been accused of staging his own lucrative scandal, if only he had followed through with a big show and a clutch of sales. But that wasn't his style. The original *Fountain* actually disappeared. No one knows for sure what happened to it. Some say that William Glackens broke it, others that it was sold to Arensberg, who then lost it (the versions we see today, in museums across the world, are all replicas that the artist authorized at various times).

The scandal having blown over, one might have expected Duchamp to reveal himself as the force behind *Fountain*, yet he didn't. Remarkably, he kept the identity of R. Mutt a secret from all but a few friends throughout the affair, and for a long while afterward. He immediately resigned from the society, but officially did so in sympathy with Mr. Mutt, not because he had been the cause of the row. He even lied in a letter to Suzanne, claiming that the sculpture was the work of "one of my female friends under a masculine pseudonym."[18] Indeed, for almost thirty years afterward, until Duchamp settled in New York again in the 1940s, the work remained more or less unknown, never exhibited, and never reproduced. And partly as a consequence, Duchamp remained largely unknown to wider audiences until the late 1950s.[19]

In fact, in the years following *Fountain*, Duchamp was doing something very unusual for an artist in the wake of a great *succès de scandale*. Nothing. His inactivity was such that some were concerned. The painter Georgia O'Keeffe and her husband-to-be, Stieglitz, paid a visit to his studio in New York in 1922 and were alarmed. "The room looked as though it had never been swept," O'Keefe recalled, "not even when he first moved in. There was a single bed with a chess pattern on the wall above it to the left. Nearby was a makeshift chair. There was a big nail in the side of it that you had to be very careful of when you got up or you'd tear your clothes or yourself . . . and the dust everywhere was so thick that it was hard to believe."[20] Duchamp had stopped working.

If he was disinclined to make work before the war, after it he was fully committed to doing nothing, and Duchamp's nothing and his silence about so much have been the cause of an outlandish amount of debate ever since. Between 1918 and 1933, he dabbled at the fringes of art but did no more than that. Spending time in Buenos Aires during the first months of peace, he organized an exhibition of Cubism, but as he wrote to Arensberg, "I will exhibit nothing, according to my principles." He would make what he wanted to make and make no more. He produced one single Readymade during several months spent in Paris in 1921; he told people that he intended to return to New York and get a job in the movies. From the late 1920s through the mid-1930s, his chief preoccupation was playing chess. He was selected for the French national chess team, and in 1932 he published a serious study of end games. Some years later, offered a job running a gallery, he refused on the grounds that "there can be no more question of my life as an artist's life: I gave that up ten years ago."

"I've never worked for a living," he once said. He felt it was stupid to do so, but he didn't explain why. That's not strictly true, of course, because Duchamp was not independently wealthy and had to work to pay his bills. When younger, he could subsist on a modest allowance paid to him by his father, but when he moved to the United States he started teaching French. At one point he worked as a librarian in J. P. Morgan's private library; at another he was a personal secretary to a French army captain on a military mission to New York.[21] He dabbled in art dealing for a time, but it didn't lead to much.

Ultimately, his surest and best source of income was from the wealthy American collectors whose company he kept in later years, and they ultimately saved Duchamp's reputation from himself. For if his peculiar inactivity and secrecy meant that, for much of his life, he was little known outside avant-garde circles, this began to change in the mid-1950s, when Walter Arensberg donated his collection of the artist's work—and much else—to the Philadelphia Museum of Art. The fact that this elite support existed for Duchamp tells us something important about how the avant-garde found pockets of toleration and encouragement within the cultures and societies they rejected. Duchamp was tolerated—even cherished—as an exception, an original whose ideas might eventually feed back into art and society and change it, as indeed they did, finally, in the 1960s, when Duchamp entered his last years. Only then did he become widely renowned and acclaimed as a kind of prophet.

As the scholar Christopher Green points out, Duchamp's relationship with patrons was unusual, for while Matisse, Picasso, and other modern masters cultivated collectors who bought their work, Duchamp "collected the collectors themselves," not to buy his work, because there wasn't enough of it to sell, but to fund his eccentric projects.²² A classic of this type was his 1935 effort to devise what he described as an optical "playtoy," a disc of cardboard printed with a spiral design that could be spun around on an ordinary record turntable and would create the illusion of three-dimensional shapes, such as a wineglass, an eggcup, and a swimming fish. He called them *Rotoreliefs*, and he decided to market them to the ordinary consumer. Henri-Pierre Roché made an investment in the project, allowing Duchamp to manufacture five hundred. Then Duchamp took a stall at an annual inventor's fair in Paris. Roché came by on the opening day to see what his money was doing and was charmed. "All the discs were turning around him at the same time," he recalled, "some horizontally, others vertically, a regular carnival."²³ Nevertheless, it was clear that they weren't going to set the world alight. "I must say that his stand went strikingly unnoticed," Roché lamented. "None of the visitors, hot on the trail of the useful, could be diverted long enough to stop there. A glance was sufficient to see that between the garbage-compressing machine and the incinerators on the left, and the instant vegetable chopper on the right, this gadget of his simply wasn't useful. When I went up to him, Duchamp smiled and said, 'Error, one hundred per cent. At least, that's clear.'"²⁴

Artists' biographers rarely waste time wondering why anyone becomes an artist, but Duchamp's biographers—in addition to the time spent trying to discern why he did what he did—have spent a whole lot of time wondering why he stopped. They aren't the first to find Duchamp inscrutable. Beatrice Wood, who was infatuated with him, complained of a certain cold-blooded "deadness" in him (she said that while he was always "extremely cordial," he exhibited "elegance in its fatal form").²⁵ André Breton idolized him but couldn't work him out at all, saying that the man had "a polished surface that conceals everything going on behind it."²⁶ The principal reason why Duchamp stopped making conventional art was that freedom was all-important to him. When he looked back at his early days as an artist, the years of his "swimming lessons," he said, "I *had* no aim. I just wanted to be left alone to do what I liked."[27] He was a *respirateur*, he liked to say, a breather. Calling himself an "artist" seemed to imply too much. He would sometimes say he ran out of ideas, but the one-upmanship of the prewar avant-gardes also irritated him; if that was art's game, he wouldn't play. As early as 1915, he was complaining of the "little Cubists, monkeys following the motion of the leader without comprehension of their significance. Their favorite word is discipline." Freedom was what he wanted. "Not to be engaged in any groove is very important for me," he said. "I want to be free, and I want to be free for myself, foremost."[28]

This craving, and Duchamp's opposition to the conventional art world or studio and sale, was probably born out of a sense that he didn't belong to it. Maybe this was due to the nature of his relations with his brothers, who for much of his youth had seemed so far ahead of him; or maybe it was due to the distance he gained from the professional art world as a result of failing to win a qualification as a "fine artist," and instead becoming an "art worker." Or maybe it was something wider, a sense he and so many others had in the years around the First World War that Europe's elite, and the high culture they supported, had lost all credibility. That's something we see throughout the avant-garde in this period, a rejection of the culture of a class. Sometimes its motivation and direction is clear, as when the Constructivists lent their support to the Bolshevik revolution. But there are other instances in which the case is more complicated. Marinetti's father left him a relatively wealthy man, but one without the status to win entry into the elite circles of Milan, and that certainly grated on him, as did what he perceived as the parlous state of the country led by these people.

Whatever the limitations of "the Richard Mutt case," it does seem to have revealed to Duchamp a way in which he *could* live and work in the freedom of his own terms. With *Fountain*, he made a conceptual intervention in the art world, and that would largely be his modus operandi for the rest of his days. Although Duchamp claimed that he was no longer an artist, in truth he was living a double life. He was making art, just not much of it, and making that art in secret. One major project was *The Bride Stripped Bare by Her Bachelors, Even*, a work that Duchamp described as "an object painted on transparent glass," and which today we tend to refer to as *The Large Glass*. It was mostly conceived, though not made, prior to his departure for New York in 1915, and he eventually left it in the Arensbergs's apartment, declaring it "definitively unfinished" in 1923. He produced a series of minor works throughout his life, but nearly all of them are, like the *Rotoreliefs*, eccentric things existing at the borderline between art object and ordinary object. One of the weirdest was his 1924 issue of a series of bonds. They were priced at five hundred francs each, and the revenue was used to try out his own gambling system at roulette tables at Monte Carlo (hence they are referred to as the *Monte Carlo Bonds*) and to invest in mining. The idea was to make a 20 percent return for investors. It's not clear if that happened, and there were never enough investors to issue the full set of planned bonds. But they remain attractive photocollages, with Duchamp's head, completely lathered in soap, appearing in the circle of a roulette wheel. Critics suspect that the soap was intended to furnish a pun, with Duchamp being the *homme savon/savant* (soap man/intellectual man).[29]

DUCHAMP WAS ONLY ONE of several artists who, in the 1910s, started to regard the norms of the art world as exhausted and corrupted. In the early years of the century the avant-garde had made great achievements by advancing the innovations of a previous generation. Yet it was becoming clear to the likes of Duchamp that the moderns' noble struggle against the traditionalists of academic art had degenerated into a game of position taking among the moderns. That new game was also fully supported by a reconfigured system of exhibition and sale, with small, nimble operators like

Kahnweiler and Stieglitz replacing the old, lumbering exhibition juggernauts like the Salon.

What we're going to see in the coming chapters is a series of different attempts to challenge this situation, or simply circumvent it, and in most of those cases the artists began with an idealistic program of reform in mind, new proposals for how art should exist in the world. But for Duchamp, there weren't any perceivable alternatives to the Paris art world of the prewar years. The only available option for those who rejected it was a kind of conscientious objection, which was the stance he took. He said no. Perhaps that's why this first avant-garde attempt to end art is, in some respects, so disappointing. Duchamp was a prankster without a program, and consequently his great attack on art, his work that was not a work of art, promptly became one, and he abetted the process. All the *Fountain* could do was reveal the creative *un*freedom that existed within this new and supposedly liberated art world, and it had to *become* artwork in order to do so.

In certain respects, the art world today is the same as the one Duchamp inhabited a hundred years ago. For sure, much has changed, but the way artists make a living largely has not. They are still represented by relatively small commercial galleries that exhibit their work and make long-term investments in their careers. The likes of Kahnweiler and Stieglitz have simply been replaced by the likes of Gagosian and Pace. It is difficult to imagine that Duchamp would have been much happier in this climate than he once was. He would just have had different sorts of freedoms and restrictions. What is certain is that today, it will take something more than a urinal—or something different, at least—to jam the gears of the commercial art world.

That was conclusively proven at Art Basel in Miami Beach in 2019 when Maurizio Cattelan, the Italian artist and provocateur, exhibited nothing more than a single banana, duct-taped to the wall.[30] It was titled *Comedian*; it was issued in an edition of three with two artists' proofs; and it was priced at around $120,000. It caused no scandal, no outrage, only excitement as visitors thronged to take selfies with the banana and prove themselves free-spirited enough to be open to anything. We could take that as evidence that audiences are more tolerant since Duchamp's day, though what it really proves is merely that Duchamp's original provocation has been digested and institutionalized by the art world. It has lost its teeth. It may be true that the fairgoers in Miami are a tolerant bunch, though one can bet that if a local Republican politician were to come down to the fair, cut some ribbon, and give a brief speech on the problems of our time, there would be a riot.

In one respect, though, Cattelan's *Comedian* did resuscitate the *frisson* of Duchamp's original stunt, and that was in its heedlessness and triviality. Duchamp's *Fountain* outraged an audience that had higher standards of public *politesse* than in our own time (newspaper reports spoke of it euphemistically as a "bathroom fixture"), but it surely also angered them because it suggested that art didn't warrant any seriousness of purpose, any elevating response, that art itself was worth no more than a urinal. It's possible to find critics today who, while they might admire aspects of *Fountain*'s provocation, do feel that the criticism still sticks. And art today remains a worthwhile public exchange that relies on norms and conventions in order to function. Sadly, Cattelan's *Comedian* managed to remind us of that important point while failing to make any others of value. It pointed to a sorry fact about the contemporary art world that is too often thrown into relief by art fairs: that for all the excitement about art, there isn't much broad public confidence in its intrinsic value. Avant-garde artists at the beginning of the last century were contesting certain entrenched beliefs about the value of bourgeois culture, and the fight was contentious because enough people felt that high culture mattered. But Cattelan's *Comedian* merely pushes at an open door and panders to a gleeful defeatism.

THREE

The Wandering Prophets

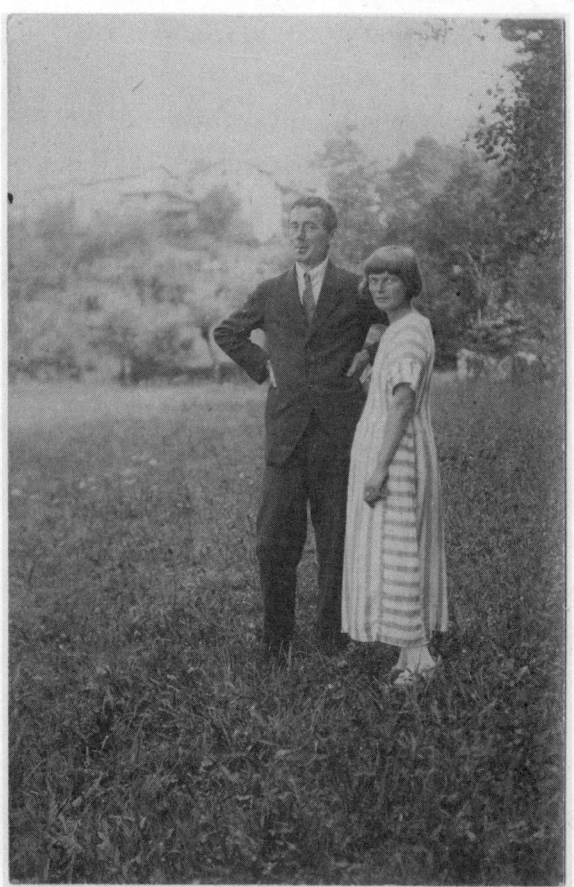

Hugo Ball and Emmy Hennings

WASSILY KANDINSKY HAD A VIVID MEMORY OF being a three-year-old boy and watching a coachman strip spirals of bark from thin branches. The man "cutting away both layers of bark from the first spiral," Kandinsky recalled, "and from the second only the top layer." To the boy, they were like horses, with the outer bark a "brownish yellow ... which I disliked, and would gladly have seen replaced," and the second layer a "juicy green ... which I loved most particularly and which, even in a withered state, still had something magical about it." The stripped wood was "ivory-white ... which smelled damp, tempting one to lick it, but soon withered miserably and dried, so that my pleasure in this white was spoiled from the outset."[1]

He realized that he felt things powerfully, felt them differently than others, perhaps. He felt *everything*. "My soul was in a state of constant vibration by other, purely human disturbances," he complained, "to the extent that I never had an hour's peace."[2] He said that "everything 'dead' trembled. Everything showed me its face, its innermost being, its secret soul." A beautiful landscape might speak to him, but so, too, might the things most people overlooked, and to Kandinsky they would spring into almost human life, like that "patient white trouser-button looking up at you from a puddle on the street."[3] To Kandinsky, even inert objects sprang into life with personality, with expression. And colors suggested sounds, suggested moods. Kandinsky had synesthetic perception.

Another impression of what this felt like comes forth in a letter he once wrote to Lily Klee, wife of the painter Paul, thanking her for some polenta. "The eye perceives that wonderful yellow," Kandinsky explains, "then the nose savors an aroma that definitely includes the yellow within itself." He said it had a "deep softness," along with something that recalled "the middle range of the flute."[4] On another occasion, he explained his reaction to paint as it oozed from tubes: "One squeeze of the fingers, and out came these strange beings ... which one calls colors—exultant, solemn, brooding, dreamy, self-absorbed, deeply serious, with roguish exuberance, with a sign of release, with a deep sound of mourning, with defiant power and resistance, with submissive suppleness and devotion, with obstinate self-control, with sensitive, precarious balance."[5]

Kandinsky was born in Moscow in 1870, his father a prosperous tea merchant. He would go on to study economics and law, and he would mature with the manners of his class. Peggy Guggenheim said he reminded her of a Wall Street broker; Igor Graber, the Russian painter and art historian, thought he looked like a Russian lawyer; others have described him as having an aristocratic demeanor, or that of a diplomat.[6] It kept people at a distance, and he seemed to want that. Nicholas Fox Weber, who wrote a vivid account of his life, conjures a striking image of the artists always clouded with smoke from his cigarettes; it was just another method of concealment.[7] Kandinsky would say that he had a "smooth surface" under which beat "an ardent heart."[8] And this passion, and passion for art, coupled with his sensitivity, meant that he would inevitably depart from a conventional path: when he was almost thirty, married, and with the offer of a university teaching post, he came to Munich to be a painter. Shortly afterward, his wife left him and returned to Russia.

Kandinsky arrived in Munich in 1896 and enrolled in an art school. He wasn't alone. The city was a beacon for artists and writers in the period, second only to Paris in its lively modernist culture. It had been that way for decades: Ludwig I, the king of Bavaria, had first encouraged the city's growth as a cultural center in the mid-nineteenth century. He melted down cannons for monuments, turned military parades into carnival processions, and built museums. His marriage to Therese von Sachsen Hilburghausen, in 1810, was the occasion for the creation of Oktoberfest. This tradition continued under his son, Maximilian II. Universities were established, more museums were constructed, poets were nurtured. And again under Maximilian own son, Ludwig II—until the man was declared insane and later found dead in Lake Starnberg. The city shone with grand buildings, palaces to art and culture, and artists came from throughout Europe and beyond, particularly students, who were drawn by some of the finest academic training outside Paris. The city grew rapidly: in 1875, its population was thought to be nearly two hundred thousand; by 1910, it was three times that. In the 1890s, the novelist Thomas Mann, and the artists Paul Klee and Lovis Corinth, all called Munich home. "Munich was luminous," recalled Mann.[9] Kandinsky would come to adore the city, spending eighteen years there. He once remarked that Schwabing, the city's Bohemian district, wasn't so much a place as "a spiritual island."[10] It made him feel "reborn."

Kandinsky found Munich profoundly affecting, but it was not just the beauty and exuberant liberty of the city that impressed them, it was also the shock of the new, something that was being experienced across Germany. When Mark Twain visited Berlin in 1892, he was stunned, remarking that Chicago looked "venerable" by comparison. "The main mass of the city looks as if it had been built last week," he wrote.[11] As more and more newcomers flocked to German cities, they came upon a world they felt to be harsh, unstructured, and anonymous. The newcomers struggled to work, to house themselves, to relate to a new world in which class cleaved the city into sections. It was a world that loomed over them, in which they were thrown to navigate as best they could, with all the old bonds of extended family and traditional community increasingly frayed. And ruling over this increasingly industrial world was a German government that remained allied to aristocratic, military, and rural interests. At a time when Britain, France, and the United States had representative government, the German Empire remained a fortress of authoritarian rule. Munich's middle class remained fiercely loyal to the empire, but this loyalty belied anxieties. Many felt buffeted by the pace of industrialization and yearned for older times, for "old Bavaria."[12] They would lament the trials of modern times, the precarious lives, the struggling tradesmen. And in this city that would later be the center of Hitler's power base in Bavaria, they would blame the Jews. The contradictions played out in Munich's bars and variety halls: the people would drink the beer from the city's proliferating breweries and watch clowns and jugglers, or listen to folk singers and comedians recall past times. When the night was over, they would step outside into streets lit by electric light, wired for telephones, trafficked by streetcars and automobiles.

Just as ordinary people had to navigate these contradictions in their everyday lives, so artists tried to make sense of them in their art, and the dominant style in Germany in the early years of the century, the dominant mode through which these responses were filtered, was Expressionism. It was a broad movement affecting the full spectrum of culture, from art to literature, cinema to architecture, and it had centers in various cities across Germany. The movement is too various for any one figure to encapsulate it fully, yet Kandinsky's attitudes are emblematic of its ideas, and he became a key representative of the style in Munich. First, his outlook on the modern world was characteristically Expressionist: he felt it was a marvel, but that it also bred a materialism that was starving people's inner selves. As he put it, "Our souls, when one succeeds in touching them, give out a hollow ring, like a beautiful vase discovered cracked in the depth of the earth."[13] He was, down to his bones, an artist and an individualist, one who believed that artists had a special role in healing the world. He looked at the chaotic interior of the modern cities, at the atomization it brought, the loneliness amidst the crowd, and he hoped that art could transcend this and create a spiritual communion.

Since my focus is on artists who strived to put an end to art, Kandinsky would seem to be a red herring, for he clearly cherished art as a redemptive force. Yet he deserves a place here not only because he shaped the ideas of so many avant-gardists, but because he appears again and again in their stories, now here, now there. Also, his commitment to art in so many forms suggested another way in which it might be integrated into life. Kandinsky believed that creativity didn't need to be confined to the highest spheres of painting and sculpture, it could be lavished on ordinary items as well. He likely absorbed this idea from the Art Nouveau movement that was approaching its height in Munich when he arrived. It meant that his early output was remarkably eclectic, including jewelry, ceramics, fashion design, and embroidery. Kandinsky didn't necessarily view these forms as secondary to art because he believed that the path to a spiritual, abstract art might lie through geometric ornament, and if so it might well resemble a tie or a carpet.[14] He saw no one form of art as satisfactory. In fact, he aspired to create a *total* work of art, an idea the composer Richard Wagner had spoken of as the *Gesamtkunstwerk*. This ambition was shaped in part by his experience of peasants' houses in Russia: he described them as "magic" houses, where the furniture was decorated and the surroundings enlivened with votive candles and pictures. They taught him "to move in the painting, to live in the picture."[15] In a sense, Kandinsky wanted to convey in his art what his synesthesia led him to experience in everyday life, a cacophony of sensation. If he could achieve that, he might encourage the great spiritual communion that would heal the abrasions of modernity.

By 1912, Kandinsky had become a key figure in Munich's Blaue Reiter group, and he had just published the widely read treatise "Concerning the Spiritual in Art." He was a leader, and one who came to regard him as such was Hugo Ball, who at the time was an increasingly influential theater director and poet. Ball spoke of Kandinsky as a colossus, believing that just his presence in the city would have made Munich modern. They shared similar preoccupations. Ball enjoyed the liberties that the modern cities afforded him: Bohemian enclaves like the Schwabing district were some of the only places where people like him could speak their mind and criticize the authoritarianism of the German Empire. Feelings like this were further nourished by his study of Friedrich Nietzsche, who celebrated individual freedom.[16] So while some saw a socially corrosive chaos in the modern city, Ball valued it—at least to some degree. Nietzsche fed his fascination with irrational forces, teaching him that the true nature of the world was to be chaotic, and that an overemphasis on powers of reason can prevent us from perceiving this truth.[17] Nietzsche also encouraged him to believe that social change could come from the artistic expression of pent-up energies. Artists could be social reformers, sweeping away conventional morality in an outpouring of creativity. Notions like this were slightly distinct from the more redemptive, spiritual, and communitarian rhetoric of Kandinsky, but they were common enough among German Expressionists in the prewar years.

Whatever Ball's differences with Kandinsky, he was happy to promote his work, and in spring 1914 he was planning a stage production of one of the artist's abstract compositions for theater. *The Yellow Sound* would embody what Kandinsky understood by a total work of art. It is an operatic composition in color, sound, and motion, and it consists of six "images" and an introduction. There are characters designated as "coworkers," and that included five "giants," a child, a man, and some "indefinite creatures" that Kandinsky felt should "vaguely recall birds, have large heads and a distant resemblance to men."[18] There was no dialogue as such, merely sounds and phrases, and accompanying them were constant changes in color and light, moving objects and figures. The play reaches a climax with an image of a cross formed by one of the yellow giants holding his arms outstretched, an image that gets bigger and bigger until it reaches the height of the stage.

The Yellow Sound isn't a Christian parable, but Kandinsky was drawn to apocalyptic imagery. He spoke of an "epoch of the great spiritual," during which the world's cracked soul would be healed. None of this was going to occur without a huge struggle, and the scale of the violent conflict necessary is hinted at by the original cover design for *Concerning the Spiritual in Art*, which featured a scene of the Last Judgment. When this particular battle would arrive was unclear, but on August 1, 1914, Germany declared war on Russia. The city was convulsed with patriotism. There were rumors of spies—seventeen were said to have been shot dead in the suburbs. There was a panic that the water had been polluted with cyanide. Kandinsky fled Munich, and *The Yellow Sound* was never performed.

APOLLINAIRE WAS IN DEAUVILLE, on the northern coast of France, when war was declared in August 1914. He had journeyed there in the chauffeur-driven car of a fellow writer, who brought along two pet toads called Di and Do. He was in a casino when he heard about the mobilization, and he immediately rushed back to Paris. He sensed that something larger than peace had ended. In an article he penned on the way back to the city he wrote that it was "the end of the party," and he recalled a portent he had glimpsed the previous morning. "A marvelous Negro dressed in a robe of . . . silvery blue and dawn pink, bicycling through the streets of Deauville . . . towards the beach. At last he reached the sea and apparently dived in. Soon, all that was left of him was a sea-green turban, gradually engulfed by . . . waves." They drove back into Paris as if into "a new epoch."[19]

Apollinaire never had to fight. Friends offered him ways to sit out the war in Switzerland or Spain. But he was determined, and being a Russian national, born in Rome with a Polish name, he needed to be. On his first attempt to sign up for the French army, he was declined, so he left for Nice, started smoking opium again, and had an affair. "This war is becoming an artificial paradise," he wrote to a friend. Eventually, he enlisted and was accepted into the artillery, and thus began what seemed at the time an adventure—as it did to so many. He fired off letters, "enough to kill the postmen."

He was in trenches near the Belgian border in March 1916 when a splinter of shell shot through the air, pierced his helmet, and lodged in his skull. He was reading the *Mercure de France* at the time. "I didn't think I was hit," he wrote to his friend André Billy, "and I was going to go on reading when suddenly my blood pissed out." He was taken to a nearby hospital, then to another in Paris. Billy went to visit him and found the helmet and bloodied newspaper sitting on his nightstand. He was alive, and yet he soon came to seem lackluster and irritable; his memory failed him, he was melancholy, he flew into rages: He would never be the man he was. Two years later, Spanish flu consumed Paris, and he was easily felled. The fever burned him up for five days and he died at 5:00 a.m. on November 9, 1918, two days before the armistice brought an end to the war.

BACK IN JULY 1915, there was still joy among crowds packing the streets of Milan. Women handed out flags, flowers, candy, and cigarettes. Three airplanes took off from Malpensa Airport and unfurled tricolor banners. And six hundred Italian soldiers on bicycles paraded past the Castello Sforzesco and down the Via Dante. These were the troops of the Lombard Battalion of Volunteer Cyclists and Motorists, and among them were the Futurists Marinetti, Ugo Piatti, Umberto Boccioni, Mario Sironi, and Antonio Sant'Elia.[20] Having completed a brief training, they were headed for Peschiera, on the shores of Lake Garda, close to the Italian front lines, where they would remain until September.

The whole experience was a tonic to Marinetti. A trumpet roused him at 4:00 a.m. He cleaned his bicycle and performed drills with the other troops. Then they would clamber up a hill in the hot sun to simulate an assault and come back down to a chorus of military anthems. There were also diversions. A celebration was arranged to commemorate the Capture of Rome in 1870, which had concluded Italian unification, and amidst this was a bicycle race under "enemy fire," which consisted of a hail of vegetables. "Energy is not lacking," he was proud to say. Boccioni, too, was thrilled. "I'm not working, I don't think, I'm living a rough and physical life that intoxicates me."[21]

But when September arrived, the battalion was informed that they were to leave their bikes behind, and with them the sunshine, and head into the Alps to fight on foot. By this stage, the novelty of training had worn off for Marinetti, and he was itching for real action. Some glimmers arrived in mid-October, when he joined Boccioni and Sant'Elia on reconnaissance, and they ended up taking an abandoned Austrian trench. A week later, Marinetti's battalion joined regulars to help capture a position at Dosso Casina. The volunteers staged a distraction and the troops maneuvered around the Austrians, who retreated. Marinetti was not at the center of fighting but he tasted the violence he craved, with nearly a week spent under fire. Fear and suffering notwithstanding, Marinetti pronounced the action at Dosso Casina to be "absolute Futurism."[22] It was a consummation. "All the bloody sunsets of my adolescence . . . have been satisfied," he wrote.[23]

But it came at a price. The Italian forces had entered the war poorly prepared and underequipped, and conditions on the front were miserable. Marinetti's battalion walked for days in dense fog and plunging temperatures. Nights were spent huddled in pitch-black trenches, bayonets fixed. "[We] live the tragic life of rabid dogs," he wrote.[24] Boccioni recalled that enduring the cold and the hunger were far worse than combat itself, that war was mostly insects and boredom. Disease spread easily through the trenches, lice infested their bodies, and Marinetti complained of rats with feet like elephant's. Inevitably, there were casualties, and Marinetti estimated that 60 percent of the Futurists suffered in some way, being wounded or killed.[25] Luigi Russolo received a severe head injury in December 1917 and spent the following eighteen months in various hospitals across Italy.[26] Antonio Sant'Elia received a medal in one action but was then fatally shot in the head by a machine gun in 1916. In the same year, while training, Boccioni fell off a horse and was killed. When he heard the news, Marinetti was devastated.

THE GREAT WAR made such a powerful catalyzing impact on Europe's artists that it is tempting to suppose that, without it, there would have been no avant-garde at all. The activities of Marinetti and Duchamp prior to the war might suggest otherwise, yet the war was undoubtedly crucial, acting in some cases to encourage new endeavors, in others to bring tendencies to fruition, and in others to encourage new directions. It touched everyone. Walter Gropius, the future director of the Bauhaus, saw protracted, violent action; when he was demobilized, in 1918, he was more than ready to build a new world. Piet Mondrian, being a citizen of neutral Holland, was spared fighting; nevertheless, the proximity of the conflict bore down on him. We'll meet him soon, standing on the shores of the English Channel in the early months of the war and looking into the night skies in search of order, pattern, logic—some kind of universal that might transcend the chaos sweeping Europe. André Breton, who would later found the Surrealist movement, spent part of his war as a junior doctor treating wounded and traumatized soldiers at a hospital in Saint-Dizier. He would assess the depth of the soldiers' injuries, then ask them who France was fighting and what filled their dreams. He recalled encountering a young, well-educated man who had been fighting on the front lines and had lost all sense of danger. The soldier would stand on the parapets in the middle of bombardments, waving his fingers as if he were conducting the barrage. In fact, the man did not appear to believe the war was real, since despite the violence he had never been wounded. The war was a fiction, the bombs were harmless, the injuries makeup. It's true there were corpses—he'd stepped over them—but they were there to furnish the illusion. The dissection rooms were full of them. Actually, there were so many that some were surely made of wax.

No one expected the war that arrived in 1914. As the historian Eric Hobsbawm argues, it had grown increasingly likely since the 1890s, and by 1910 many spoke of it as inevitable. Yet Europe had experienced so many decades of relative peace, that the outbreak of hostilities took many by surprise.[27] The causes were complex, and have been reassessed by each following generation, but Hobsbawm sees them as a consequence of the formation of new and opposing power blocs in Europe. France, Britain, and Russia faced off against Germany and Austria-Hungary. Military buildup along those lines made any likely confrontation increasingly dangerous, and a succession of crises for those powers—both foreign and domestic—made the whole edifice very fragile. What famously ignited the bonfire was the assassination of the heir to the Austrian throne, Archduke Franz Ferdinand, by the Bosnian Serb Gavrilo Princip, but Hobsbawm dismisses that as "irrelevant" in the face of the larger issues.[28]

The avant-gardists were not unusual, either in how they reacted to the onset of war or to its astonishing destructiveness. Marinetti's enthusiasm captures the surprisingly widespread excitement, particularly among middle-class men, across Europe. Most expected the war to be thrilling and brief; it would blow away the torpor of bourgeois life, it would demolish the tedious administrative bureaucracy that so many found themselves toiling at. Even among intellectuals it was welcomed: Nietzsche had applauded growing militarization in the late nineteenth century and happily predicted that war would "say yes to the barbarian, even to the wild animal in us."[29] German intellectuals hoped war would correct any disharmonies in society and produce a renewal of community, along with primitive experiences that would revitalize young men's vigor. Marinetti felt the same in regard to his fellow Italians, that war was what the country needed to truly unite and find purpose. Many others appeared to agree: French authorities had expected between 5 percent and 13 percent of its conscripts to desert, but in 1914 only 1.5 percent did so.[30]

But disillusionment soon followed. Marinetti's own sobering experiences, along with the number of Futurists lost during the war (according to their leader, the conflict claimed thirteen of them), effectively killed the movement that had begun by promising to glorify war.[31] After that, Marinetti turned to politics. He edged closer to fascism (Mussolini would praise him as a "fervent fascist"), and early in 1918 he founded his own Futurist Political Party that promised a "free and strong Italy," one free of the past, and of the influence of tourists and priests.[32] As a cultural style, Futurism's strident embrace of modernity would ensure that it continued to be influential after the war, but as an avant-garde it was a spent force.

If there was one avant-garde movement that arose directly from the experience of the trenches, it was Dada. Without the irrational spectacle of the war there would have been no impetus for its passionate protest. Dada is surely one of the most complex, many-faceted, and misunderstood of all the century's avant-gardes, and it is one without which later groups like the Surrealists are hard to imagine. It's hard to comprehend, to really digest in its entirety, in part because its output was so diverse, issuing material in all manner of media, and a multitude of periodicals. It also sprang forth in disparate locales across Europe and beyond—in Berlin, Hanover, Cologne, Barcelona, Paris, and New York—with each center shaping its mood: Berlin political in the unstable aftermath of the First World War, Paris more playful and satirical. Dada was anarchic, acidic, preoccupied with a violent, politically turbulent, mechanized world, one in which it was difficult to believe in any stable ground, or in any force of authority worth respecting. As one of their number, the artist Hans Richter, put it, Dada wasn't a movement so much as "a storm that broke over the world of art as the war did over the nations."[33]

Legend has it that the name was selected at random by Hugo Ball and his friend the artist Richard Huelsenbeck, by leafing through a dictionary. It was nonsensical and means "hobbyhorse" in French. Some took up its quest with avidity: writer Tristan Tzara, a child of Zurich Dada, would be hot for the role of avant-garde impresario that had been carved out by Marinetti before him. But others, like Duchamp, simply floated in and out of association with the magnetic fields of Paris and New York Dada, it claiming them more than they claimed it. The movement was born in 1917, and it commanded the fealty of a multitude of avant-gardists for several years until Surrealism superseded it. It began in Zurich with a bizarre variety show called Cabaret Voltaire. And it began there because the war had sent Emmy Hennings and Hugo Ball fleeing from Germany.

Ball began the war with the same excitement as many others. It was going to be a cleansing fire, he believed. It would destroy the decadent Wilhelmine society of the nineteenth century, and it would usher in a newly spiritual modernity. Germany's blood was up. Looking back, Ball's partner in life and in Dada, Emmy Hennings, felt that he had been swept along on "the intoxication of mass suggestion."[34] He rushed to volunteer, but before basic training was complete it was discovered that he had a weak heart.[35] He was determined, though, and he tried to sign up twice more, and again he was refused. Soon enough, Ball talked his way onto a train full of troops bound for Belgium. He reached Dieuze, a small town in what now is France. He would stay there for two weeks before he was arrested and sent home.

What he witnessed was enough to break him. He saw the first soldiers' graves, and he saw the weapons that killed them. "It is the total mass of machinery and the devil that has broken loose now," he wrote in utter disillusionment. "Ideals are only labels that have been stuck on. Everything has been shaken to its foundations."[36] Huelsenbeck began to hear of friends who were killed in action. Then the man who was soon to be his brother-in-law was nearly torn to pieces by a grenade and gave an account of what had happened: "It was like a great wind, a howling that turned into a screaming. The howling came from the projectile, and the screams, I realized next, came from the wounded. They were lying around all over the place, with arms and legs ripped off and stomachs split open, and the chaplains sniffing around them with their crucifixes so that they wouldn't go to heaven without the blessings of the church."[37]

HUGO BALL WAS BORN IN 1886, in a small town in the German Rhineland close to the French border, the fifth of six children. His father was a shoe salesman and couldn't afford to fund a university education, so the boy left school at fifteen and apprenticed in a leather factory. He would work there for four years, studying in his free time, writing poems and plays. Eventually, the pressure of work and study, compounded by Ball's natural intensity, induced a nervous breakdown, and his parents relented and allowed him to gain an education. In fall 1906, age twenty, he left for Munich to study philosophy, but abandoned that before finishing a degree and headed for Berlin. There, he threw himself into theater.[38] Huelsenbeck described him thus: "He spoke in a quiet, clear voice, and he often had an ironic smile on his face. He was tall, his hair was black, and his complexion bad." He was ever attentive; he "leaned slightly as he walked," Huelsenbeck recalled, "his head bent as if he were listening to something." He had a "reckless imagination."[39] And it was an imagination given to extremes. Emmy Hennings believed he was given to holiness too. To her he was like St. Lawrence, his tears like shooting stars.[40]

Hennings was born a year before Ball, in 1885, in the north German coastal city of Flensburg. She described herself as "a seaman's child."[41] When she was twenty, she married. Her first child died, and she discovered she was pregnant with a second when her husband left her, after just a year and a half of marriage. She left the child with her mother and embarked on several years working as a performer with touring companies of various kinds. She was versatile, comfortable in theater as much as nightclubs. She traveled across a broad swath of Europe and as far east as Moscow. Finally, she settled in Munich and worked in cabarets, and it was while performing at a venue called the Simplicissimus that she met Ball. He was a regular in the crowd, and between numbers he'd invite her to his table to talk, and soon enough they were inseparable. "It seemed to me," Hennings recalled of those years in Munich, "as though life was offering me its abundance and beauty from all sides."[42]

The arrival of the war changed all that, and when Ball returned from Dieuze, shattered, he made for Berlin, where he was joined by Hennings, and together they began to organize antiwar events. But that didn't last; dismayed by the same prowar sentiment they had found in Munich, they decided to leave Germany for someplace where they could speak their mind. They arrived in neutral Switzerland at the end of May 1915. Neither had much of a plan. As one of their friends recalled, "[They] came to Zurich without a cent and they left fate to chance."[43] They were not alone, joining an influx of those fleeing the First World War or exiling themselves from other lives. Lenin arrived in September 1914; James Joyce, in June 1915. The city was soon teeming with a multilingual crowd of draft dodgers, pacifists, millionaires, spies, and war profiteers. Ball described it as a "birdcage, surrounded by roaring lions."[44] The mix lent a liberal atmosphere that Ball found enlivening, even if it was somewhat curtailed by police surveillance. The Zurich authorities were careful to maintain the country's neutrality by controlling political activity, so not everything was permissible, though Ball found he could get away with a lot more than he could in Berlin. He remembered New Year's Eve 1914, when he was in the apartment of one of Marinetti's translators, and they stepped onto the balcony to holler out into the silent night, "Down with war!" Such liberties, and the pleasant change of scene, all boosted him. "The city is beautiful," he wrote in his diary. "The Limmatquai is especially attractive.... The seagulls are not artificial or stuffed, they really fly in the middle of the city. The big clockfaces on the towers by the water, the landing places with their green painted windows—everything is so beautiful and pure. It is genuine."[45]

But while there were some things in Zurich to encourage them, others were going wrong from the beginning. Ball entered the country under the false name of John Höxter, one of Hennings's former lovers, and while the pair managed to reach Zurich, soon afterward Ball was arrested and briefly jailed. Neither had papers to work. They rented a cheap attic room under another false name, and Ball found some work in a button factory. But it wasn't enough to live on, and by the summer they had sold their possessions and most of their clothes and were out on the streets, sleeping on park benches and rummaging through trash for food. Emmy, weakened from hunger, began to hallucinate and sunk into spells of sullen apathy.

Ball's experiences in the early months of the war profoundly changed his broader outlook. Whereas previously he had welcomed what he perceived as the irrational forces in the modern world, now he regarded the war as a sign that they had become violently unmoored. It made him cool to the freedoms promised both by anarchism and by the liberated life of Bohemians. He also became pessimistic about the possibilities of theater, and art itself. Not so long ago, it had meant everything to him. It bound things together: "life, liberty, love, morality" meant "inconceivable freedom."[46] But by the time Ball arrived in Zurich, he wasn't sure. Commerce had cheapened everything, he feared: "The poet, the philosopher, and the saint are also becoming commodities." Literature was nothing but a "safety valve" for society. "I feel about theater as a man must feel who has suddenly been decapitated. He stands up and walks a few steps. But then he will fall and lie there dead."[47]

While Ball pondered his disillusionment, the couple's fortunes began to change when Ball found work as a pianist and playwright for a touring vaudeville theater called the Maxim Ensemble. It certainly wasn't the kind of thing he was accustomed to: the group was known for snake charmers, sword-swallowers, fire-eaters, and tightrope walkers. Hennings joined it as a "female humorist, comic, and goblin." Soon enough, it rankled, so Ball and Hennings set up on their own. They wrote some skits and added some yodeling for the home crowd. Again, it wasn't the career they had in mind, but it started them thinking.

Hennings's recent livelihood had been in cabaret, a form that had first blossomed in Bohemian quarters of Paris in the 1880s. Venues like the Chat Noir (Black Cat) were partly intended as platforms to promote the work of local artists and poets, and while they exemplified Bohemia's spirit of satire and disdain, it's *fumisterie*, they consciously sought out a bourgeois audience.[48] At the Chat Noir, the staff of the cabaret presented themselves in the green robes of French academicians, they greeted audience members with exaggerated politeness and addressed them with noble titles. The audience was never in doubt that they had crossed over into another social world, and they loved it. Indeed, after being exported from its birthplace in Paris, cabaret quickly become a popular diversion in Bohemian areas across Europe, one that thrived on a polite audience's taste for something artistic and risqué. Its mainstays were a mixture of popular song, modern verse, and classical music, but in Germany its repertoire included the music of local folk singers, and it was increasingly influenced by folk arts like puppetry and shadow plays. Karl Valentin came up through Munich's beer halls and variety theaters. The great folk comedian is sometimes described as Germany's Charlie Chaplin, and began by doing short skits for what one writer calls the "Weisswurst patriots," who thumped the tables, locked arms, and threw back their ale.[49] But unlike most who found a popular audience, Valentin also appealed to the bourgeoisie and the artists. He could derive humor from the humiliations of everyday life, but he could also have riotous fun with the conventions of popular theater, mixing up stock characters in skits, having them all collide onstage at once. It was self-conscious, inventive, modernist, and after the war Valentin would attract fans like Berthold Brecht.

The other thing that cabaret had to recommend it was that it tended to escape the notice of Munich's assiduous censors. In fact, it was in response to a particularly restrictive censorship bill, the Lex Heinze, that Germany's most famous cabaret, Elf Scharfrichter, or "Eleven Executioners," was born in 1901. Elf Scharfrichter was the invention of an eclectic group that numbered among them an attorney, a theater director, a critic, an architect and set designer, and some painters. They took to the stage with a pillory adorned with a skull, a judge's wig, and a huge axe. Their victims would be the country's authoritarianism, its bourgeois, and the artistic trends of the day.

So, if Ball had once preferred high theater to low cabaret, by the end of 1915, he had reason to reverse his thinking. He had lost faith in theater. Meanwhile, Hennings was a star in cabaret and Ball had lately obtained crude training in its ways. And he thought maybe cabaret could be more than easy, popular entertainment; maybe it could be complex, abstract, and political, maybe it could be a version of the total work of art that Kandinsky had imagined for the stage. Only this total artwork would be one shaped for wartime. In this way, art wouldn't necessarily end, it would just be shifted into a different register.

It was around that time that Jan Ephraim, the owner of the Holländische Meierei Café (the Dutch Dairy Café) in the Niederdorf came to them with the idea for a cabaret. He had a back room with a piano and a small stage and seating for maybe forty or fifty. It was something the café had already had success with in the past, becoming the city's first literary café in 1914 when a group of Swiss poets gathered around the Cabaret Pantagruel. Ball started to dream of a cultural challenge, while Ephraim wondered if he might sell more beer and sausage. And so Cabaret Voltaire was born. It seemed appropriate to dedicate the cabaret to that great eighteenth-century satirist of French life and culture, one who had done his part calling for freedom and hastening his nation's revolution.

It opened on February 5, 1916, a Saturday night, at 6:00 p.m., and even as the small crowd jostled to find seats, Ball was meeting figures who would soon be vital to Dada's future. He remembered greeting "an Oriental-looking deputation of four little men": a young Romanian named Tristan Tzara who was fleeing military service, Tzara's friend Marcel Janco, an architecture student, and

Janco's brother George—and also someone else whose name he didn't catch. In time, he would also be joined by Huelsenbeck, a friend he summoned from Berlin, and the artists Hans Arp and Sophie Taeuber. Together they formed what Ball described as a "wobbly little rabble of . . . wandering prophets."[50]

The plan was for Ball to play piano and Hennings to sing. The stage consisted of no more than a ragged canvas screen behind which Hennings would go through numerous costume changes. Things began in a fashion that was fairly familiar for cabaret audiences of the period. The initial offerings were mostly from high culture. There were readings from Chekhov and Turgenev and, on the opening night, from the cabaret's namesake, Voltaire, as well as music by Beethoven, Brahms, and Liszt. There was poetry by contemporary modernists like Max Jacob and André Salmon. In keeping with the cabaret tradition of decorating the wall, Hans Arp contributed a few of his own works and also sourced pictures by Picasso, Modigliani, Elie Nadelman, and August Macke. And there were also rousing diversions like military marches and popular songs. Hennings sang period cabaret standards like Aristide Bruant's "A la Villette" (At La Villette), Frank Wedekind's "Donnerwetterleid" (Thunder Song), and Erich Mühsam's "Revoluzzerlied" (Revolution Song). And to accompany these, there were a few songs written by Hennings with melodies by Ball. Many thought she was the star of the cabaret, with a presence much larger than would be suggested by what Huelsenbeck described as her "meager and boyish voice."[51] Nevertheless, it was noted that time had not been kind to her: one local newspaper wrote of how "years ago she stood by the rustling yellow curtain of a Berlin cabaret, hands on hips, as exuberant as a flowering shrub, today too she presents the same bold front and performs the same songs with a body that has since then been only slightly ravaged by grief."[52]

The crowd was mixed. There were artists and writers, there were a few well-dressed bourgeoisie who might occasionally find their way in, and there was reliably a group of students that wandered in drunk and smoking long pipes. Huelsenbeck remembered that "whenever someone opened the door, thick clouds of smoke would come pouring out like the smoke that hovers over fields during the burning of the harvest leavings."[53] When Ball played dance music, the students would shove the chairs aside and whirl around the room. Accident, and the cabaret's growing renown, also attracted strange acts, and one of the principles of the cabaret was that it should invite contributions from the audience. A twenty-man Russian balalaika orchestra performed regularly, and on one night a group of Dutch youths showed up with banjos and mandolins, and a character they called "Oily Knee" did an erratic dance. By the end of February, Ball announced that an "undefined ecstasy" had taken hold.

Early visitors to Cabaret Voltaire might have been entertained, but they probably didn't notice anything particularly novel in the format. This, however, soon started to change. One impetus was the arrival of Huelsenbeck. By his own admission, he was a "noisy, energetic, and strong-willed character."[54] His contributions came to be among the more impenetrable. On one occasion, Huelsenback, Janco, and Tzara performed a "simultaneous poem," "L'amiral cherche une maison à louer" (The Admiral Is Looking for a House to Rent), which they read at the same time in French, English, and German, the languages of the war's main combatants. And one of his specialties was the *chant nègre*, with verses inspired by what he imagined was the language of African tribes. He would intone these while dressed in black robes, to the accompaniment of a drumbeat. On one occasion he rehearsed them in front of the owner of the bar, Jan Ephraim, who remarked that they sounded nothing like the languages he had heard on his own African travels. Huelsenbeck engaged him to write some verses that he remembered, and apparently the result went down well at the cabaret.[55] The *chants nègres* borrowed from a few recent enthusiasms among the modernists: one for abstraction (in this case abstract language); another for a fantasy of Africa or an imagined, noncivilized world; and another deriving from Futurism, for performance, shock, and confusion.

The cabaret did well for several months, and while Ball was initially exultant at its energy and success, he was eventually complaining of exhaustion, describing the obligation to stage the nightly events as "crippling." But before he had the opportunity to quit, Ephraim called time, complaining that there weren't enough customers. Ball's famous final performance, on June 23, 1916, saw him sheathed in a cardboard costume with shiny blue cylinders for legs, a collar at the neck that flapped when he moved his arms, and a blue-and-white striped "witch doctor's hat."[47] Too constricted to move, he was carried onto the stage, where he recited his poem "Elefantenkarawane" (Elephant Caravan). Its words were nonsensical but rhythmic, and Ball felt the noise they made recalled that of elephants. To his surprise, he found himself chanting as if he were in church; he felt like a child hanging on the words of the priest. "Hollaka hollala," he sang, "anlogo bung, blago bung, bosso fataka . . ." and on and on. "Then the lights went out, as I had ordered, and bathed in sweat, I was carried down off the stage like a magical bishop."[56]

WHEN I WAS IN MY EARLY TEENS, I went on a school trip to see the First World War battlefields in northern France. We visited vast cemeteries whose squared ranks of uniform, white gravestones receded neatly into the distance. We visited museums and memorials and stretches of what now were quiet, unremarkable farmland, but during the war had been fought over furiously at huge loss of life.

I realized one afternoon as we drew up to another cemetery and parked by the side of the road, that I was bored. And I was immediately revolted at the realization. The war had killed so many people and filled so many cemeteries that I could be bored by it. During the same trip, we visited a local museum that had old, stereoscopic slides of the battlefields during the war, and peering into the vivid, illuminated pictures, I saw fragments of bodies lying in mud, blasted trees and barbed wire, and not much more. It struck me that if such things were shown on television so that children my age could see them, there would be a national outcry. Our textbooks had taught us to relate to the soldiers who went to war because they weren't much older than we were, and yet the things they witnessed were beyond my comprehension.

Perhaps that's why it can be difficult to relate to Dada, or at least difficult to think of ways to apply its lessons. Dada emerged from a world in which it was becoming increasingly common to meet people with traumatic brain injuries, or prosthetic limbs, or who had lungs shredded by chemical weapons. A lot of the avant-gardes who emerged after the war had some proposals for what might replace art in an artless world, but Dada had none. In fact, Dada didn't really have a program to end art so much as a disgust for the kind of world that produced art that was refined, beautiful, rational, and thoughtful. Ultimately, the many tentacles of the Dada movement bequeathed us a lot of art, though much of it is so ephemeral that it feels like what anthropologists call material culture. Hans Arp developed a mode of abstract collage that relied on chance, the notion that he would merely drop some square pieces of colored paper onto another sheet and fix them where they lay. Marcel Janco became known for masks that he made from cardboard, string, and burlap. The long faces look fragile and disarranged, by turns modern in their dynamic, angular geometry, and ancient in their reference to traditional tribal arts.

Some of the most interesting and distinctive work to come out of the Zurich group was produced by Sophie Taeuber. She was the only Swiss citizen among the wandering prophets of Zurich Dada, and she was a teacher at the city's School of Applied Arts. She met the German-born Hans Arp in 1915, when he had a show at a gallery in Zurich, and the two later married and often collaborated on work. Most fruitful was their willingness to mix up the categories of fine and applied arts.[57] She produced a series of marionettes, which were surely inspired by the enthusiasm for puppetry that then gripped Germany, She also produced strange sculptures in turned wood that seem to be many things simultaneously: abstract sculptural busts, or tactile toys, or puzzles, or vases. The same kind of ambiguity enlivens her needlepoint designs, which bring the language of high Modernist abstraction to a medium more often associated with domestic hobbies. Some echo the grid designs typical of De Stijl, other similarly geometric compositions seem reminiscent of Russian abstraction, while others are sui generis, looking like little else being produced in Europe in the period.

THE IMMEDIATE CAUSE of Cabaret Voltaire's closure may have been the bar owner's decision, but Ball was also too exhausted to continue, and he seems to have been too exhausted to maintain Zurich Dada in any other form. It's also possible that Huelsenbeck's arrival had pushed the cabaret too far toward the irrational for Ball's taste. He intended an innovative, modernist, political cabaret, one that would shed light in a dark time, not one that would add to the general confusion. Soon after, he and Hennings announced that they were departing Zurich and they began living in a village on the shores of Lake Maggiore, northwest of Milan. There, Ball began writing a book on the Russian anarchist Mikhail Bakunin. He had no interest in perpetuating Dada or in setting down the legend of Cabaret Voltaire.

Ball was much like Duchamp in his disinterest in the positioning and politicking of the prewar avant-garde, and Dada only lived on because the likes of Tristan Tzara had a personal interest in furthering it. From their Alpine retreat, Ball and Hennings probably looked back on Cabaret Voltaire as the end of something that had begun in Munich, with Hennings's cabaret singing and Kandinsky's Expressionist theater, but it retains its status as a beginning because historians like tales of origin. It seems doubtful that the participants or the audience recognized that something distinctly new was happening at Cabaret Voltaire. Maybe they didn't expect the assault unleashed by the likes of Huelsenbeck, or the impassioned nonsense that Ball delivered on the last night, but what Hennings and Ball were staging was squarely within the evolving traditions of cabaret as they then stood. For the historians, however, Cabaret Voltaire is a kind of manifesto, a scheme for a new kind of avant-garde, one that would often be anarchic and sometimes abstract, and one that would find a format in low culture to say the kinds of things that generally only get said in high culture. There was such variety in the later Dada movement, so many artists, so many themes and concerns and tones, that it seems wrong to take Cabaret Voltaire as being emblematic of anything beyond the mood of those particular "wandering prophets" who washed up in Zurich during some of Europe's darkest times.

/

INEVITABLY, THERE ARE a limited number of accounts of what happened at Cabaret Voltaire in the few short months that it was open. The participants' recollections seem fairly consistent, and the accounts tend to highlight similar things, but what are not at all clear and consistent are the broader recollections of Hennings and Ball—Hennings's in particular. I've told you how she had a child, how her marriage broke up, and how she joined touring companies before setting down in Munich to find better times. When she wasn't working, she took on modelling or selling bathroom supplies. Well, there were also worse times. Occasionally, she resorted to prostitution, which she would supplement by robbing her clients. She was jailed in Hanover for theft, and then again in Munich. According to police files in Zurich, she did the same there; they also listed her as a morphine addict who had on one occasion attempted suicide. In Berlin she was jailed for forging the passports of people trying to flee military service. She was also suspected of homicide.[58] Hennings was not easily reformed: at one point, a lover in Munich asked a psychiatrist to supply documentation that she was a kleptomaniac, presumably to offset the risk of her being arrested yet again.

Was she really so wild? It's very difficult to say. Hennings was Catholic, and she seems to have brought Ball, who had been born Catholic, back into the fold. By the time they were living in Italy, they were increasingly devout. As it turned out, Ball didn't have long to live. He died of stomach cancer in 1927. Hennings was left to write the accounts of their early years—accounts that were increasingly in demand as Dada's fame spread. But her religious devotion left her uncomfortable with her past, and so she set about rewriting accounts. Her edit of Ball's diary, *Flight Out of Time*, is assumed to be heavily redacted. Her own memoirs whitewash her life, while some fiction she published likely offers a more honest account. She talked about producing a "written confession of my life"; she found her notes for this entertaining but dishonest, and felt she glossed over "defects in my nature. . . . The result was that the image of my life became unclear and incomprehensible." Incredible, too, in one of her memoirs, she claims that she served a prison sentence in place of a friend who had been convicted of theft because her friend had just had an offer of marriage from a man with prospects. The tale was surely nonsense. Similarly, she later claimed that she was initially attracted to Ball because she felt she could pray with him. Some may find that odd, given that Ball was charged with obscenity around the same time. The contradictions abound in descriptions of Hennings's fascinating life. It may well be that she was already religious in her Munich days. The poet and playwright Erich Mühsam wrote of her in 1911 that "[she has] deteriorated into complete religious madness. She condemns me and almost all of her other friends as heretics and hallucinates about the devil trying to drag her off. There seems to be chaos in her poor little psyche. And yet she is horny as ever, and [Fritz] Bolz, each time after he has coitus with her—which she is the first one to desire—has to listen to the most horrible curses and complaints about him and herself."[59]

And here we come to another reason why we can't come by an honest account of Hennings and her life. Accounts of Hennings tend to fixate on her sexuality. They remark on her figure, her lovers. Mühsam did repeatedly, noting in his diary details of her life with the regularity and precision of a jealous lover: "Everybody wants to sleep with her and, since she is so accommodating, she never gets any rest. Until 3am she has to be at Kathi's place [the Simplicissimus], where she is taken horrible advantage of, and by 9am she is already at art class." "She is singing and screwing like the devil," he added.[60] The costs and benefits of the liberated life were very unequally distributed between men and women. And if we are to account for the lack of women among the avant-garde, unequal freedom is one of the things we must consider. Paradoxically, if we are to look for reasons why there were so few women at the center of the avant-gardes, the accounts of Hennings's life and work are a good place to start. Women were generally marginalized in the mainstream gallery world due to their marginalization and exclusion from the very institutions that trained artists. The avant-gardes might have scorned that training and thrown open their ranks to an eclectic bunch of the trained and untrained, in all manner of disciplines, but even then, the homosocial norms of the period tended to push out women. The stronger the group's sense of cohesion, of group identity, and the stronger its sense of militancy, the more women tended to be marginalized. The misogyny that coursed through Marinetti's writing is ample evidence of that: in the Futurist Manifesto, alongside vowing to "glorify war . . . militarism, patriotism," he promised "scorn for women." Those who did find themselves at the center of the activity could find themselves cast as muses—inspirations, maybe, but not allowed to be the true producers of creation.

Yet Hennings's centrality to Zurich Dada is undeniable. She was the main attraction at Cabaret Voltaire, one of its signal talents, and it's hard to imagine the cabaret ever having happened without her foundational experience in popular entertainment. Just as it's argued that her religiosity drew Ball further into devotion (and not the other way around), so, too, did her talent for cabaret help the couple find a new mold in which to cast high art.

FOUR   The Pope

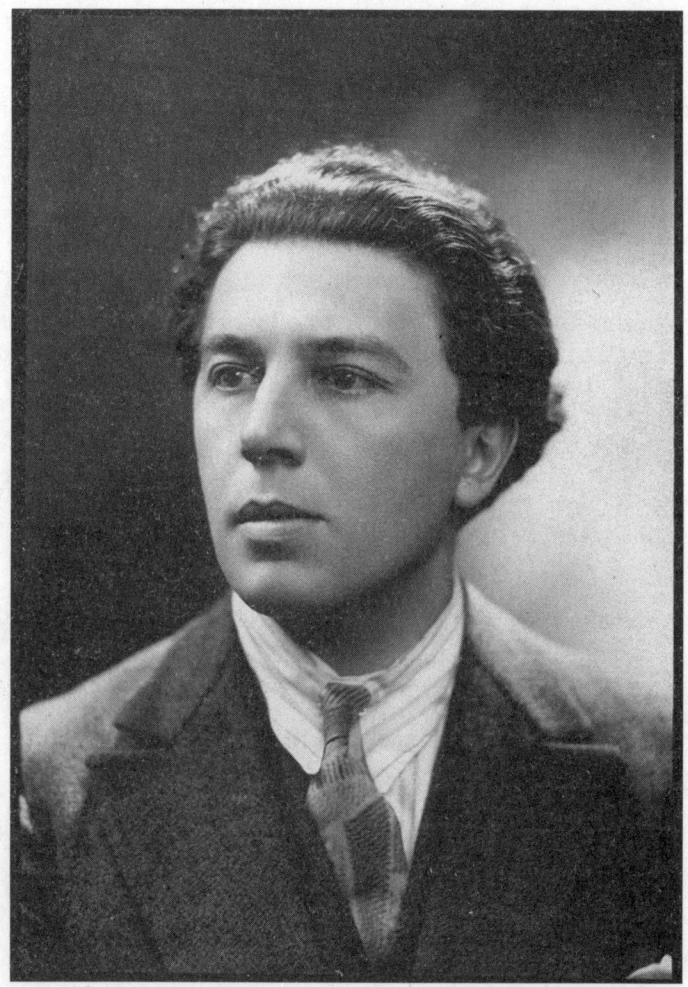

André Breton

WHEN TRISTAN TZARA STEPPED OFF A TRAIN IN Zurich one night in 1915, the city was in the grip of the coldest winter in living memory, and the wind sharpened the edges of a frost that had settled.[1] His friend and Romanian compatriot, Marcel Janco, had arrived in the city a few months earlier, and he was there at the station to meet him. Tzara would later claim (and he claimed much), something compelled him to go to the Altstadt, the city's old town. No matter the cold, or the hour, or his fatigue, something drew him, and the pair walked up and down the same "obscure and tortured" street several times. As if he were channeling some energy in the air, he kept passing by the future home of Cabaret Voltaire, which would open two years after he arrived.

Tzara, raised in a Jewish family, lived in a region of steep hills and forests at the foot of the Carpathian Mountains in Romania. He was short and myopic, often wearing a monocle or a pince-nez. He was bookish and, beyond Romanian, was fluent in German and a little ungrammatical French. Like Marinetti before him, he had run a school literary review. He was sickly and prone to migraines, commonly disappearing for rest cures during the summer. And he was endlessly self-dramatizing. He once wrote a version of his birth certificate that reads as follows:

> TZARA: born at Constantinople, 22 January 1903, 63kg, straight nose, short black hair, round face, broad forehead, distinguishing signs: 4 ears. Took courses in pure philosophy at the University of Sofia, injured in the Bulgaro-Serbian War of 1913. Engaged in the oak trade, has published 220 poems in Paris, 1st floor, 1st door on the right, has won many chess matches, height 1.90 m^2

Not much of this is remotely true, though it served to furnish the myth. Tzara was actually born Samuel Rosenstock, but at some point he decided that a more decorous, more allusive name was required. "Trist" came from the Romanian word for "sad," and Tzara sounded like that language's word for "countryside" or "nation," so his name meant "sad in the country." For one as restless as Tzara, it was appropriate.

Despite being born in the provinces, he got an early taste for metropolitan life when he was sent alone to Bucharest to complete his education, aged only eleven. From there, he would move on to the city's university. But an incident occurred—likely the result of the university's pervasive anti-Semitism—that left him with little choice but to leave. By this point, the First World War had begun and was threatening to drag in Romania, so Tzara set his sights elsewhere. Neutral Switzerland looked like the best place to avoid being drafted, and his friend Janco was already studying architecture in Zurich. Tzara headed there.

He was only nineteen when he arrived, and he would be the youngest of the key figures in Zurich's Dada group. He was somewhat conscious of the fact; conscious also of his relatively thin exposure to modern art. He made up for this by being ceaselessly helpful and throwing himself into all kinds of performances. If he was youthfully bashful when he arrived, it didn't last; Huelsenbeck would later describe him as Dada's "zealot propagandist." In contrast, Ball had always been uneasy with promotion, and uneasy with the growing talk of exporting Dada like it was some kind of product. He disliked the idea that the group would become an official avant-garde, that it would merely add another "'ism'" to modernism's already lengthening list. His plan was to bring down the citadel, not to put up another in its place. Moreover, what he had valued about the cabaret was the intimacy it created with its audience; how could that be reproduced if Dada was to take on international dimensions?

Tzara, however, had other ideas. The young Romanian helped publish an anthology of the cabaret's output, and he helped produce the first Dada *soirée* at an old guildhouse in one of the city's main squares, moving the group out of the seedy Altstadt and into a grander locale. His efforts didn't always draw thanks: one major project was the *Première Exposition Dada*, which was staged in a local gallery situated above the Sprüngli confectionary store. Tzara deliberated over everything, held talks, staged exhibition tours, and at some point afternoon tea was served. Huelsenbeck reflected bitterly that the whole thing had become "a manicure salon of the fine arts, characterized by tea-drinking old ladies trying to revive their vanishing sexual powers with the help of 'something mad.'"[3]

Meanwhile, Tzara was bombarding European and American artists and writers with Dada pamphlets. He printed stationery with a Dada logo and, as if it were a multinational conglomerate, a list of its various affiliated journals and its international outposts in Berlin, Geneva, Madrid, New York, and Paris. Grateful recipients would send back their own avant-garde reviews. And Tzara had a clippings service in Geneva send him updates on press coverage. When the clippings came in, the group would sit around cafés reading the global attitudes to their local antics. They were encouraged but somewhat bemused. Tzara was helped in his export enterprise by the fact that no one could clearly say what Dada was, and the cabaret had never had any clearly defining agenda. Tzara suspected that international success required a little definition—a manifesto, statements of intent—but he left things up to interpretation. The only thing he was clear about was that Dada was new, and it would supersede all previous avant-gardes. Hans Richter claimed that Dada "swallowed Futurism—bones, feathers and all." The Berlin Dada artist Raoul Hausmann said Tzara "wanted to exceed Futurism . . . and marinate Marinetti in his own sauce."

By the time Ball and Hennings had departed for Italy, Tzara had emerged as the de facto leader of Zurich Dada, and with the growing fame of the movement spread the growing fame of its leader. Young, would-be avant-gardists yearned to meet the man, to learn from him. The most imploring invitations came from André Breton in Paris, when Breton was yet no one; he had published a little poetry, that was all, and he had none of the renown he would soon acquire as leader of the Surrealists. Tzara would say he'd come, then he'd change his mind, then change it again: he complained of illness, said he was worried about the weather, he even said he feared rising prices. Breton paced the platforms of the Gare de Lyon no less than five times in two days in anticipation of Tzara's arrival (the Frenchman said this was justified when Tzara was "somewhat like the Messiah"). Perhaps Tzara felt that, in Zurich, he had been a king. What would he be elsewhere? On the other hand, what remained of that Swiss dominion? The end of the war had opened the continent to travel once again, artists were returning from whence they came, and Zurich was changing. By the end of 1919, of the original group that staged Cabaret Voltaire, Ball and Hennings were living in an Alpine village, Huelsenbeck and Janco were in Berlin, and only Hans Arp and Sophie Taeuber-Arp remained.

And so Tzara left. He boarded a sleeper train from Zurich, and on Saturday, January 17, 1920, he arrived in Paris. There was no one there to greet him.

ANDRÉ BRETON WAS DISMISSED from the army in September 1919, and he should have been elated.[*] He was not. He had studied medicine before the war—not out of any particular calling, but because he suspected that other things could be achieved alongside it. Now, age twenty-three, there was nothing to do but return to it. He was thoroughly disenchanted and in this mood was very receptive to the sounds of disenchantment coming from Zurich. He read Dada reviews in Apollinaire's apartment, and enough rumors of its scandals had reached him in Paris to create a sweet anticipation. Breton and the others had already been talking up Dada in French journals. Breton wanted to be avant-garde; he just needed some lessons.

Breton was born in Normandy in 1896 to a policeman and a former seamstress. The couple appeared to be an ill-matched pair, he being affable and indulgent of his son, she being "authoritarian, petty, spiteful," according to Breton.[5] He was their only child, and photographs of him as a young man suggest someone who regarded himself as chosen. His head—which was said to be huge—was set with wide eyes, fat and sensual lips, and a flowing, wavy crown of russet hair that he brushed back from a high forehead. His was a noble demeanor, and it wasn't one fitted to suffering, but when war came to France in 1914, Breton was conscripted along with thousands of others, and in the late summer of 1917 he found himself at the Second Army's neuropsychiatric hospital at Saint-Dizier in northeastern France. British and French troops had begun a new offensive to control positions around the Belgian town of Ypres, one that would ultimately succeed, but with massive casualties. German troops began using mustard gas. Shell-shocked victims streamed into the hospital, and Breton came to feel that the visions and fantasies they entertained, the "madness" they suffered, was more rational than what was taking place beyond the hospital walls. In some sense, they had been traumatized into sanity.

Breton had written poetry throughout his late teens and was drawn to Symbolists like Stéphane Mallarmé, whose writings could feel like broken strings of disjointed images. Here, however, from the jarred minds of ordinary soldiers came lines more shocking still, words that had the power to satirize the war and its absurd rationales with the poignancy of naïve illusions. Words that could take the upturned world of the war and set it right. Moreover, these words were in no way "literature." Even Mallarmé, who had once shocked the literati, was now being swallowed by the prestigious golden maw of "literature." As Breton was beginning to sense—along with so many others of his era who were scattered across Europe—everything modern that had the daring and nobility to talk back to tradition would eventually be nullified by it. Art made everything prestigious and tedious in the end. Authenticity lay elsewhere: it lay beyond poetry—perhaps beyond books entirely—it lay in the kinds of convulsive experience that was felt by damaged soldiers or new lovers or whatever other wild encounters life might greet us with. *That* was poetry.

Breton had ambition and half-formed ideas, but during the war he was still feeling his way through a profession in which he was disinterested and writing poetry that offered no obvious alternative. And it was during this time, in late February 1916, while he was working as a nurse at a hospital in Nantes, that he had one of the few crucial encounters that lit his path. This one was with Jacques Vaché, a handsome, red-haired young soldier who had arrived for treatment of a leg wound sustained the previous fall. Vaché was twenty, the charismatic and flamboyant son of an officer. He had a rich personality and was a cultivated Anglophilia, and this performance was only heightened—for Breton—by the delicious and mysterious emptiness of his origins. He put it about that he had been born in Indochina (in truth he was from Brittany), and it appeared that he no longer had any connection to his family—in fact, no mundane attachments of any kind. He wrote a little, but not too much, just some strikingly dissonant memoirs and a few short stories, an output that for Breton was glorious for its sheer brevity. So while he was familiar with Breton's passions—for Rimbaud, Cubism, André Gide, and much else—and had associated with a group of writers and poets in Nantes, Vaché was scornful of the life of art. He was more interested in men's fashions. He was free from inhibition, bracingly so, and he defended that freedom with a rigorous nihilism. Believing in nothing, he was constrained by nothing.

After his release from the hospital, Vaché worked as a stevedore, unloading coal from the Loire. He spent his afternoons in slums near the port and his evenings in cafés telling lies. Together, Breton and he would meander about, and in a prelude of later Surrealist habits, go in and out of different cinemas, collaging their own narrative from the fragments of each film. When new postings separated the pair, they exchanged letters, until one day Vaché dropped in at the hospital at La Pitié, in Paris, where Breton was now stationed. Missing him, he left a note. Then, so Vaché said, he rescued a girl who was being assaulted by two men outside the Gare de Lyon, took her on a train to Fontenay-aux-Roses on the outskirts of Paris, and walked with her until 4:00 a.m. when they both slept at the home of a man who worked as an undertaker by day and extinguished gas lamps at night. The following afternoon,

Breton arrived at the opening of a play by Apollinaire, and he would later claim that during the intermission he saw Vaché draw a gun and wave it at the crowd. For Breton, such tales served to embellish the legend.

Vaché's philosophy was encapsulated in his concept of "umour," humor with a missing "h," humor that was embittered and absurd. He scorned everything, from patriotism to art to sentiment. In the wake of his encounter with Vaché, Breton decided he was done with poetry.

GERMAINE EVERLING WAS IN HER APARTMENT in Paris one day in mid-January 1921 when a small, portly man in pince-nez arrived at her door unexpectedly. He spoke French with a heavy Slavic accent, and she remembered that "his skin was waxy, like a candle." It was Tzara.

Tzara turned up at Everling's apartment because this was where Francis Picabia now lived. He had separated from Gabrielle Buffet-Picabia after the war, but not before leaving her pregnant. When he took up with Everling, she got pregnant too. The two children arrived within months of each other. It was the kind of situation Picabia created. He was out when Tzara arrived; when he returned home, he was gleeful to meet the visitor. He quickly summoned the others, and before long Breton and his poet and writer associates, Soupault, Aragon, and Paul Eluard, all arrived at the apartment to be underwhelmed. Tzara didn't threaten the dark absurd so much as the comically ridiculous. Breton later acknowledged that Tzara was not what he imagined him to be.

Nevertheless, Tzara brought reputation and know-how, and soon set about devising entertainments that would endure in infamy—or at least until after the press published reports the following day. Breton already had the necessary platform for Tzara, having announced the first of a series of Friday matinees under the auspices of his magazine *Littérature*. These were to comprise music recitals, and readings of poetry, manifestos, and other literary offerings. Into these, Tzara inserted hostile nonsense. At the first event, Aragon was called upon to recite Tzara's poem, "The White Leprous Giant in the Countryside," a verse that begins in nonsense and descends into gibberish. For the second, Tzara took over the publicity and announced from the stage that Charlie Chaplin had joined Dada and would appear live. Those who believed this not-implausible notion and clamored for seats were to be as angrily disappointed as Tzara hoped, but others seemed to be merely amused by how ill-suited the polite and inhibited young men were for causing offense.

The events of the war had brought the idea of high purpose into disrepute, and with it the reputation of the French literary class. How were the children to behave in the wake of their parents' misdeeds? Typical of what Breton came to see as the betrayals of his elders was the career of Maurice Barrès, the Symbolist writer who emerged to fame following the publication of *The Cult of the Self,* a trilogy of novels that glorified individualism, sensuality, and mysticism, and which he published over a three-year period starting in 1888. During the Dreyfus affair of the 1890s, Barrès had aligned himself with anti-Semites and monarchists, and during First World War had been a loud herald for patriots. Breton, Aragon, and others debated Barrès's behavior and determined to put him on trial for "conspiracy against the security of the Mind." A full show was staged, with prosecution and defense, witnesses and jury, and Breton presiding as judge. Barrès was out of town and so conveniently unavailable, but he was represented by a store dummy dressed in evening wear, and the dummy was sentenced to twenty years hard labor.

Events like this one were probably not well known beyond the small circle of the Surrealists. They were intended as performances, and it's likely that Breton invited the press as their purpose was publicity, but they did not furnish the packed theaters that are said to have turned out to hear Marinetti's *serate*. They were investments in future notoriety. And when Breton wasn't pursuing public stunts of this type, he was publishing to whip up other storms. An opportunity to do that arose in October 1924, at the time of the impending death of the literary lion Anatole France. In that case, the poet, journalist, and novelist had not seduced and disappointed but merely stank of establishment virtue and respectable opinion. He was unassailable. So, as France lay dying and the press filled their pages with eulogies in anticipation, the Surrealists published a pamphlet titled *A Corpse*. "With France, a bit of human servility leaves the world," wrote Breton. "To bury his corpse, let someone on the quays empty out a box of those old books 'he loved so much' and put him in it and throw the whole thing into the Seine."[6]

For Breton, books had become suspect, and it was no longer clear why a new generation should add to their number. In 1919, *Littérature* issued a survey to writers, asking, "Why do you write?" Breton concluded that the most satisfactory answer was given by Lieutenant Glahn, a character in Knut Hamsun's novel *Pan*, who said he did so merely because "it shortens the time." Breton particularly reviled journalism—probably because it represented the industrialization of writing, the decline of poetry into dull labor, and for Breton, few things were worse than work ("Let no one speak of work"). In 1923, he announced that he would abandon writing entirely. "Literature allows one never to change anything ... this is why I've never sought to do anything, I repeat, but destroy literature."[7] That, of course, he wrote. For all his good intentions, he could not stop writing.

If books and writing were to be abandoned, Breton felt that some new mode of poetic experience must replace them, and he found the answer in the nascent fields of psychiatry and psychoanalysis, ones that lay outside the respectable literary pantheon. At Saint-Dizier, Breton had been assistant to Raoul Leroy, a psychiatrist whom he remembered as a strange man with blue hair and a "cube-like head."[8] Leroy had learned his trade at the side of Jean-Martin

Charcot, the period's high priest of hysteria. An abiding mystery in the nineteenth century, hysteria was considered a chameleon with many faces, the cause of paralysis, insomnia, sweats, and fainting, generally only in women. Charcot claimed that it was ideas and not damaged nerves that caused it. He could place patients in hypnotic trances and induce hysterical symptoms. By similar means he could make them disappear. Freud would not be translated into French until 1921, but even before this, Breton had absorbed similar ideas and approaches to treatment, such as dream interpretation and free association, and it was these techniques that would be foundational for Surrealist practice in the mid-1920s.

Dada finally ceded its energies to Surrealism in 1924, and Breton wrote the movement's first manifesto, cementing his leadership, or his papacy: for many, Breton would be the "pope" of Surrealism, the doctrinal leader of an art cult with strange transcendental ideas. But it was precisely notoriety and disgrace that were brightening Breton's fortunes as an avant-gardist. His days were now spent serving as librarian and all-round cultural adviser to couturier Jacques Doucet; it was Breton who in 1923 persuaded Doucet to purchase Picasso's *Les Demoiselles d'Avignon*. But the most precious fruits of his labors were harvested after nightfall, among his steadily expanding circle of followers. By the time Surrealism had unfurled its banner across Paris, their number had expanded to include a variety of characters, mostly young men. All were poets, and in the mid-1920s, all were Surrealists who gathered around their high priest, Breton. There was Philippe Soupault, a man given to pranks and flourishes, who would swap drinks with strangers in bars and panhandle for beggars in the street. There was Louis Aragon, the illegitimate son of a politician who was told his parents were dead yet was raised by his mother, who he thought was his sister. And then there was the elegant and mysterious Jacques Rigaut, who was said to be supported by a famous actress. Others included Benjamin Peret, Roger Vitrac, Max Morise, George Limbour, René Crevel, and Jacques Baron, who was only sixteen. A school friend of Breton's, Théodore Fraenkel, was also part of the circle, and occasional guests included Marcel Duchamp and, when he arrived from New York in 1921, Man Ray. Writing, meeting, talking: Breton performed the behaviors of a French writer, yet he was in high revolt against France and writing. Breton displayed his mantle of leadership by wearing a bottle-green suit and carrying an elaborately carved cane.

The group gathered nightly at Certa, a café that stood in the Passage de l'Opera. It was an unremarkable working-class bar with a long counter, barrel tables, wicker chairs, and murky lighting. Its faithful believed it served the best port in Paris. For Breton, alert to the rites of intellectuals, it was a place to plant his flag and gather his confreres. It was the funhouse of Breton's Paris avant-garde and would continue as such until the arcade was razed in 1925 to make way for an extension of the boulevard Haussman, at which time the group moved elsewhere.

Activities like this might be overlooked as after-hours distractions, yet it was crucial for Breton that the Surrealists' output should not arise from the studio, or the library, or some other traditional artistic retreat, but instead from everyday life. Art was seen, in these early stages, as merely a vehicle to access pure, uncensored thought, and not necessarily the only vehicle. Just as Breton disavowed art, so he disavowed the appearance of artistic activity. Hence he liked to think of the group as a band of neutral, quasi-scientific researchers. At one point the group established an office, the Bureau of Surrealist Research, which was open to the public, Monday through Saturday, 4.30 p.m. to 6:00 p.m., and someone was always at the desk. Stationery was printed, along with a line of small stickers that they pasted up around Paris ("PARENTS! Tell your dreams to your children!").[9] And when they published their first journal, *La Révolution Surréaliste*, in 1924, it was modeled on a science magazine, printed with a garish orange cover that Aragon found at the printers, and contained matter-of-fact reports on dreams and accounts of suicides drawn from the newspapers. It was sparsely illustrated, and the group determined that it would contain no art. Whether or not it was widely read, it served to advertise that the Surrealists were not artists in any conventional sense.

Together they began the experiments, the search for new poetic experience, for alternatives to literature. The group tried recounting dreams and entering hypnotic states, and Breton introduced them to automatic writing. As Breton's biographer Mark Polizzotti argues, this discovery came to him as the conclusion of several years spent thinking about the relationship of art and life, and the nature of poetic imagery.[10] The vivid, disconnected thoughts of his wartime patients had stayed with him, as had the formats of Cubist collage and advertising. Contemporary poetry also suggested new ideas: Breton regarded Apollinaire's approach, with its clashing and disconnected images, as a lodestar for modern poetry in France, and ultimately he would borrow a term that the poet had coined, Surrealism, to name his new movement. Eventually, Breton moved from thinking of random images as inspiration, to thinking of them as the basis for an entirely new procedure in writing, and a means of linking the unconscious to the page.[11] His first programmatic use of this was in *Magnetic Fields*, a volume of poetry and prose he cowrote with Philippe Soupault in the late spring and early summer of 1919, and which was dedicated to the memory of Vaché. According to Breton, he would meet Soupault every day after he had finished work and the two would continue with the writing. Each piece followed the others rapidly, Breton recalled, and the only reason they concluded chapters was because they had reached the end of the day. The results were abstract but pungent, and the first lines of the prose chapter "Eclipses" captures its character: "The color of the fabulous salvations darkened until the slightest death-rattle: calm of the relative sighs. Despite the smell of milk and coagulated blood, the circus of leaps is full of melancholy seconds."[12]

This approach to writing would be, for Breton, the foundation of Surrealism, which he defined in the manifesto as "psychic automatism in its pure state." The group would devote themselves to the "dictation of thought, in the absence of any control exercised by reason, exempt from any aesthetic or moral concern." They would achieve this in various ways. One group experiment, the Exquisite Corpse, required each participant to create a fragment of a drawing, fold the paper so as to cover their design, and pass it on to the next person to draw another fragment. But there were many other approaches, and among them particular individuals developed star turns: René Crevel would lead seances and tell fortunes that predicted calamity; Robert Desnos would perform telepathy with Marcel Duchamp, who at this point was going about his life in New York unawares of the ideas being sent to him.

Breton decided that poetry needed to come off the page and become as pervasive as advertising in the modern city. To make that happen, one needed to do no more than decide it had been achieved, and to *read* the city *as* a poem, as a clash of signs and symbols read from streets and shops and monuments and parks. From this, one might spin a series of associations and cross-references—crossed psychic lines. The aim was to break through to the unconscious. By letting his desire loose in the city, he might trace it out as one might follow a route as your finger moved across a map. In the throes of this liberating pleasure, fantasy and reality would merge, dreams and waking reality would intermingle, and real liberation would be glimpsed. One just needed to walk outside. As Breton put it,

> You can be sure of meeting me in Paris, of not spending more than three days without seeing me pass, toward the end of the afternoon, along Boulevard Bonne-Nouvelle between the *Matin* printing office and Boulevard de Strasbourg. I don't know why it should be precisely here that my feet take me, here that I almost invariably go without specific purpose, without anything to induce me but this obscure clue: namely that it (?) will happen here.

ON OCTOBER 4, 1926, Breton was on a walk.[13] He stopped at a stall outside a bookshop. Then he walked in the direction of the Opéra. Next, he crossed an intersection marked by a church. Dusk was approaching and the people from workshops and offices were pouring out onto rue Lafayette. He remembered watching them shake hands as they departed before they filtered into the crowds. They were a gray river of long coats with heads dipped into brimmed hats, shoes kicking up the leaves of chestnut trees. Then he saw her. Her head was aloft, her eyes were darkly outlined, penciled as if in haste, and when they flickered, they shone like shaded lamps in the gloom. "I had never seen such eyes," he recalled. She was almost airborne. She called herself Nadja.

He took her to the terrace of a café near the Gare du Nord, they talked, and Breton was captured by her. She was a "free genius," he decided, a solitary spirit led by desire, and before her he was "black and cold . . . like a man struck by lightning, lying at the feet of the Sphinx." She was on her way to the hairdresser. She was also short on cash.

Breton's chance meeting with Nadja would lead to him writing a short book titled after her. It's a digressive text, concerned partly with his theories and partly with records of their encounters. For a long time, it was really all that we had to account for her, and that led some to speculate that she was pure invention, that Breton fantasized her into existence. He depicts her as the model of a woman with a free mind, one who has little regard for convention, and who appears to have the powers of a seer, one who lives her life according to the dictates of chance and desire.

Breton said that she had come from Lille, where her father was wealthy and her mother devout. She would write to them occasionally telling them nothing of her life. She had left behind a lover, and she wrote him infrequently until not at all. And now she didn't know why she was in Paris. She wandered the city by night, lingering on the Metro and searching the faces of the commuters for their thoughts. They were workers in an everyday world—and she would be, too, if she only could find work. She had tried at a bakery and at various butchers. She smuggled cocaine from The Hague and was arrested at the station upon return. Now her landlord was hounding her for money—she might go to awful lengths to placate him. Her health was poor. "Who are you?" Breton asked. "I am the soul in limbo," she replied.

The couple agreed to meet the next day at a bar on the corner of rue Lafayette and rue du Faubourg Poissonière, and when Breton arrived, Nadja was transformed, finely clothed in black and red with a hat that she lifted to unfold her straw-colored hair. Breton showed her some of his poetry and other writings. "Life is other than what one writes," he assured her. In fact, life is best lived in a rush of violent raging desire, in a total war against the rational and the everyday. Though, perhaps you could put that on pause now and again. So they talked. Eventually, they climbed into a taxi and he left her at his door. She was unhappy. "And what about me now?" she said. "Where shall I go?" And that seems like a fair question, given that Breton had taken himself home and left her hanging, but then *Nadja* isn't a book that concerns itself with practicalities.

They planned to meet the following day at five thirty, this time at another bar, the Nouvelle France. There they talked about a series of encounters that Breton, painter André Derain, and writer Louis Aragon had had with a woman who walked back and forth across the street questioning passersby (Nadja always seems open to listening to Breton wax on about his ideas, which was no doubt part of her appeal). The men decided that the woman was a "sphinx," and Breton tells Nadja that she, too, is such a mysterious beast. But this only served to make her angry. She was in love with him, she said. He can make her think and do whatever he wishes. "If you desired it, for you I would be nothing, or merely a footprint."

In Breton's account, the next day he awakens with a violent headache. He has made no plans to meet with Nadja that day, but he absolutely must. He sets off in a taxi. Suddenly, at the corner of Saint-Georges, he senses her presence on the sidewalk. He tumbles out of the taxi and runs up a street. There she is.

This is what Breton would later call *l'amour fou*, mad love. For him, desire is preordained; it cascades in chains of coincidence. Nadja was its agent. On one occasion while driving on the road from Versailles to Paris, he recounts that she forced her foot down over his on the accelerator, covered his eyes with her hands, and kissed him. Another time they walked the streets until, nearing midnight, they arrived at the Tuileries and sat before a fountain. "Those are your thoughts and mine," she said. "Look where they all start from, how high they reach, and then how it's still prettier when they fall back. And then they dissolve." Then one day they were walking along the rue de Seine when she spots a pointing red hand in an advertisement and imagines it to be tracing a line in the sky. "The hand of fire," she cries. And then one evening they are sitting alone on the terrace of a restaurant on the place Dauphine, and she tells him there are underground tunnels passing beneath their feet. She recalls a time when she was at the hotel across the square with another man. The man was about to leave and return to North Africa and there was a voice saying, *You're going to die, you're going to die.* She points at a darkened window. *In a minute it will light up. It will be red.* Moments later, a red halo radiates on the curtains.

ONE AFTERNOON, WHILE MY HEAD was full of Breton's adventures with Nadja, I walked out of my apartment and just kept going. I opened myself to the possibilities of chance and hoped my unconscious would unburden itself and connect with the world. Meanwhile, I got some exercise. Finding my first outing a pleasure, I developed a routine like his. Several days each week, I would leave the house at around 3:00 p.m., and for maybe an hour would walk in random directions. I began to imagine that anything might happen. I could witness something, I could meet someone, a kind of Bretonian "it (?)" might happen. But if nothing occurred, I could at least feel the freedom of having no purpose and no destination. Paris enforces direction on us, with its straight streets and its speed and the relentless momentum of its crowds, and merely declining to be carried along with its currents brought me a mix of feelings: freedom, anticipation, and sometimes fear. No one knew what I was doing because I was just walking. I appeared to be a man with a destination, but of course I wasn't, and it felt like a kind of disguise. *Wow!* I thought. And then I reflected that I didn't really know where anyone else was going as they passed me in the street, and maybe they were headed to some extraordinary nowhere too. At times, I would stop and stand at the end of streets for no reason and look at people pass by. I looked like I was waiting for someone, but I wasn't. I was at the intersection of lives! It felt very Bretonian—except for the time I stood at an intersection with a Kentucky Fried Chicken. And then I began to notice that lots of people in my neighborhood were also just hanging around.

Usually, I walked in my dull, suburban neighborhood of apartment blocks and bodegas. Eccentricity on the streets I walked took the form of garden ornaments or clashing color schemes on rented and subdivided houses. I looked for things that seemed to be surreal, but the closest I could find were often religious, like a shrine to the Virgin Mary set up on a concrete patio. I was conscious of there being an extraordinary number of cemeteries in the area, as if the city had for decades decided to bury absolutely all of its dead near where I would later live. I saw them but for some reason I never reached them.

I began to feel that opening myself to the marvelous in the twenty-first century was harder than it seemed. Sometimes I simply couldn't find the flint to make a spark. Then there was my all-too-regular awareness of what might be a sensible direction to walk in a big city and what might lead to encounters that were revelatory in all the wrong ways. I would be walking along some empty street and start to get uncomfortable, and then I'd get a sense that there were some nice houses or a park just over yonder and I might even be able to get an ice cream. I'd then check myself and remember I wasn't looking for nice, and I should probably be heading in the other direction, where I was pretty sure there was a strip club and a few parking garages. But were strip clubs more Surrealist than parks? I wasn't sure. One afternoon, I ran into a neighbor walking his dog on a distant street and I asked him what brought him so far from home. He told me that he just lets the dog decide where to go. I started to think about getting a dog.

I began to suspect that the problem was that I was repressed, that my unconscious was locked up tight, or that I wasn't letting chance lead me. At least one problem might have been that the gates to the unconscious were not as plentiful in my neighborhood as they were in Breton's. The Surrealists were drawn to flea markets, where they would find evocative curios. And there were particular streets and squares where they could expect to come upon the marvelous, generally because they possessed some evocative quality or historical significance. In *Nadja*, Breton said that he experienced the place Dauphine as a secluded wasteland that emptied out his will. He confessed that the statue of Etienne Dolet, in the place Maubert, caused him "unbearable discomfort," but it might well do that to anyone who knows that the sixteenth-century scholar and translator was burned to death for heresy on the very spot marked by the monument.

Louis Aragon, meanwhile, found the marvelous in the old nineteenth-century shopping arcades with their window displays of outmoded fashions and their mannequins that looked vacant and unfeeling, like the automatons that drifted back and forth to work on the boulevards outside. When Aragon walked into the arcades it was as if he walked into the sea, where time slowed and objects drifted in twinkling light. They were "human aquariums," he wrote. "The whole fauna of human fantasies, their marine vegetation, drifts and luxuriates in the dimly lit zones of human activity, as though plaiting thick tresses of darkness."[14] The Surreal was something experienced in the places that were being left behind by the modern world, or else were remnants of its distant past. But in a city less marked by history, like New York, or away from the historical heart of a city, out in the sprawling banality of its suburbs, where I walked, everything can seem equal, everything laid down in the same shallow historical soil with nothing standing out to grasp the imagination.

The other problem was the very basic difficulty of trying to unlock the unconscious. It is one thing to accept the Surrealist notion that the visible world is not real, but it is another thing to penetrate it. What lay so insistently before me as I walked down streets could not be so easily swept away. Breton's notion of the unconscious was shaped in large part by Freud's notion of dreams, and he would seem to scan the street as if he's looking for those signs and symbols. In *Nadja*, he recounts an occasion when a woman came to the Surrealists' offices, the "Centrale," as he refers to it, wearing sky-blue gloves, and the thought of these remarkable gloves sends him on a flight of anxiety about her removing the gloves, and what happened when she returned with a bronze glove.[15] If such motifs felt fresh and risqué in Breton's time, they seem hackneyed today, and if you go about the streets searching for the kinds of symbols Breton celebrated—searching for lost gloves, lost shoes, and extinguished cigars—the whole exercise can seem like a parody.

Breton's ideas always functioned at some remove from the official doctrines of even Freudian psychoanalysis. Freud himself seems to have found Surrealism a little misguided. His therapy was one that intended to reconcile its patients to their reality, but Surrealism was promising a program of radical psychic liberty, with some fanciful, playful, or literary means of achieving it. On the one occasion Breton met Freud, at the sage's Vienna offices in 1921, there wasn't exactly a meeting of minds, and Breton came away feeling spurned.

He spat back that Freud was no more than a "little old man with no style who receives his clients in a shabby office worthy of the neighborhood GP."[16]

Notions of the unconscious have also changed somewhat since Freud's time, and one doesn't have to be familiar with the latest clinical advances to suspect that the methods Breton freely adapted from Freud—which have nothing to do with clinical practice—are questionable. Yet if the Surrealists' antics sound ridiculous today, they surely had more persuasive power in the very different world they emerged in. Breton invented Surrealism for a world with a far starker difference between public and private selves. In this world, when men went out to work (and it was mostly men), they put on the uniform of a public world, the blue coveralls or a white collared shirt, and they shut the door on their private worlds of family and love and fear and desire. They became part of the mechanics of the world, or its bureaucracy, and maybe that gave them a creeping sense of anomie, alienation, or anxiety. Freud's model of the unconscious was almost a map of that world, with its public world in the conscious light of day, its private world plunged into the darkness of the unconscious. The problem today is that the public man has gone. He's probably showing up to work in a hoodie and sneakers, he's posting on Instagram about his kids, and maybe he isn't the married patriarch of old, maybe he's a woman and she's gay, or it's neither man nor woman, and neither Breton nor Freud have much that's plausible to say about any of them. Modern man is dead, and whatever we call the person who has replaced him, that person isn't riven by the same fissures of old.

Of course, Breton wasn't suggesting we take his strolls around the city as the basis of a new clinical practice in psychoanalysis, but rather as the basis of a new kind of poetic prose, the kind he wrote in *Nadja*. When he and Soupault sat down to write *Magnetic Fields*, they did not enter a trance and access their unconscious, whatever they might have claimed, but they used that idea to guide how they devised and combined poetic images. Breton's notion of walking in the city is much the same. It is a framework for how a writer might draw on the random sights and images of the city and combine them into a compelling tale.

/

ULTIMATELY, BRETON WAS AN AESTHETE through and through, and he held so fast to the promise of poetic experience that he could put the disappointments of reality aside. For all his repeated claims to be renouncing writing, he never could. He poeticized his life and lived among its lyrics. In the apartment of the proclaimed enemy of art, pictures jostled on the walls—paintings by Max Ernst, Picabia, Picasso, Duchamp, and Giorgio de Chirico, and African and Oceanic masks and dolls clustered on shelves. Breton was also canny enough to recognize that art was good for promotion. While Ball departed Dada as soon as it was in danger of becoming Tzara's bandwagon, Breton was happy to build Surrealism up into a cultural juggernaut and ride it as far as it would go.

Breton would tolerate a lot for the purposes of promotion. Over the years, he expelled multitudes from his inner circle, always working to lead the group in his chosen direction, but the one character who suspiciously survived was Salvador Dalí, and the only explanation for that was that he was good for publicity. Breton admitted him in 1929, announcing his arrival with a preface written to introduce an exhibition of Dalí's paintings in Paris. Dalí had much to recommend him, being already the cocreator, along with Luis Buñuel, of the film *Un Chien Andalou*. It's a brief silent movie, only around twenty minutes long, and it borrows some of the conventions of the period's romantic comedies, yet it begins with a sequence in which a woman appears to have her eye sliced open with a knife, and thereafter it continues to veer off course as the protagonists encounter a series of terrifying visions. Over the coming years Dalí's paintings would attract notice, his interest in Surrealist objects would yield some of the movement's most popular and memorable motifs, and his flair for theater would bring attention. For all that, Breton tolerated the excesses of his behavior, his elitism and his greed and, even, ultimately, his preoccupation with Hitler.

All the time, no matter what he had once said about literature, art was at the center of Breton's promotional efforts. In no time he was writing a manifesto on Surrealist painting to justify the new disciples he was welcoming into the fold. It's fair to say that Surrealism's greatest legacy lies in the visual arts, despite Breton's intentions for the group. It put forth a striking language for unconscious and sexual life that inevitably became popular with advertisers. Yet that is not to say that the world is now more transparent about desire and its mechanics. On the contrary, the regularity with which sex and desire are slyly referenced in our culture surely only serves to encourage the illusion that we are more in touch with ourselves than were our parents. Some figures associated with the Surrealist movement suspected that its acceptance of art was always ludicrous. For how can the unconscious govern the creation of something that requires conscious thought? Pierre Navaille, an early member of Breton's troupe, after turning skeptical, wrote, "No one can still be in the dark about the fact that there isn't any *surrealist painting*. Neither pencil marks deposited by aleatory gestures, nor the image retracing dream figures." Navaille felt that Breton had simply betrayed his own insights. What there are, however, are "spectacles. . . . The street, the kiosks, cars, streetlamps bursting against the sky."[17] The Surreal could be found in the street, just where Breton claimed it was to begin with.

Inevitably, Navaille was later purged from Breton's circle. He was probably content to be so dismissed. But one who was not was Nadja, and she was a lot realer than Breton liked to admit. He scooped her off the street, turned her into art, celebrated her as an oracle, then cast her aside. She was barely twenty-five. The pair saw little of each other after December 1926. He drew away, uncomfortable with her erratic behavior, and she sorrowfully struggled to accept the relationship's end. In January 1927, she wrote him one of the many imploring notes she would send him during this time: "I feel lost if you abandon me. . . . I'm like a dove wounded by the lead she carries in herself. . . . Alas, you've only come by 2 times, and my poor pillow has seen much bitterness, many dried tears or tears held in, calls, moans. . . . Ah, my André, know that everything is finished for me. But I had you, and it was so beautiful."[18]

It sounded like acceptance, but Nadja was unwell. She moved from one poor hotel to another one that was worse, and soon after she was found wandering the hallways. "It's raining," she wrote, "My room is dark / Heart in an abyss / My sanity is dying."[19] She was committed to a psychiatric hospital with hallucinations and feelings of persecution, and Breton was left to explain his behavior—at the very least, to himself. She had become a projection of his own desires, his own quest for mental freedom, yet in encouraging her, he had only loosened her grasp on reality and sent her into an institution. His response was to scorn psychiatry and its asylums: "Madmen are *made* there," he spat, "just as criminals are made in our reformatories." Breton never visited Nadja during the months she was hospitalized in Paris, and in May 1928, she was moved to a hospital in her native Lille, where—after almost thirteen years—she died of typhoid in January 1941.

FIVE
The Monument without a Beard

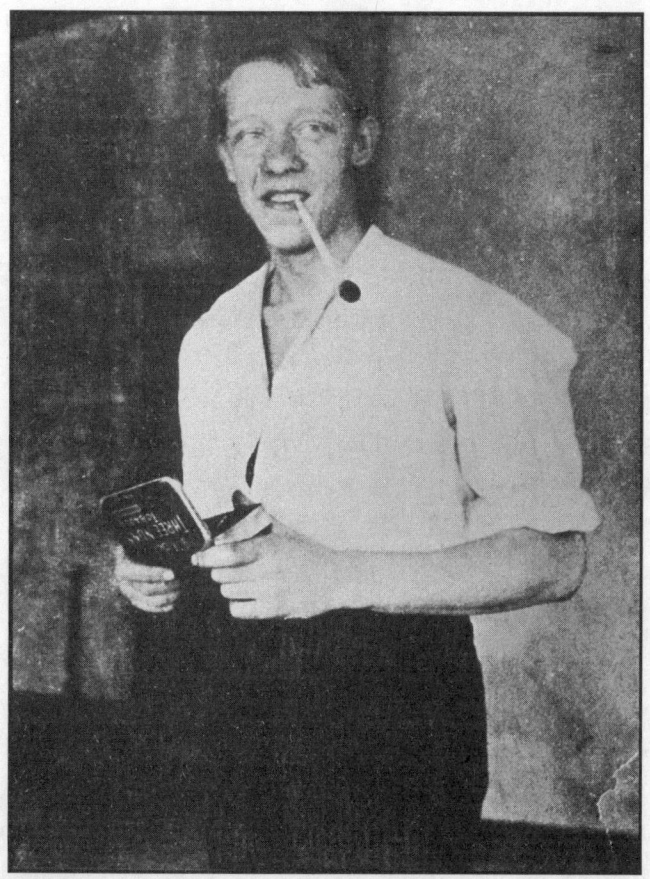

Vladimir Tatlin

THE FIRST WORLD WAR NOT ONLY REDREW THE MAP in Europe, it reshaped minds, decisively forming the outlooks of artists and writers whose most important work would only come in the years following the war. That's why the history of the avant-garde always seems to return us to these years, even when the lives of its protagonists lead us decades hence.

The same is true if we're to tell the story of the Russian avant-garde, though in this case the tale begins just a few months before the hostilities, in the spring of 1914, when Picasso got an unexpected visitor in his Montparnasse studio.

He was a Ukrainian man by the name of Vladimir Tatlin, and he was brought along by one of Picasso's recent friends, the Latvian-born sculptor Jacques Lipchitz. Picasso's circle included a surprising number from Eastern Europe and beyond. When he moved to Montparnasse in 1912, he met several artists who kept studios in La Ruche, a sprawling complex known to many as "The Hive." Its residents—the "bees," as they were called—included the likes of Fernand Léger, the poet Blaise Cendrars, and a number of Eastern Europeans like Marc Chagall, Chaim Soutine, and Lipchitz. His circle also included Baroness d'Oettingen and Serge Jastrebzoff, two Russian artists about whom almost everything was a little mysterious, from their real names to their relationship to their parentage. And if all these individuals were not enough to give Picasso a good impression of the East, there was also the fact that his greatest collector to date was the Moscow cloth merchant Sergei Shchukin, who had been buying an average of ten works every year—and some of the best pieces Picasso had painted.

Tatlin had already seen many of these pictures because Shchukin had thrown open the doors of his palace to the public. He undoubtedly arrived at Picasso's studio full of admiration for the man, yet Picasso may have been a little nonplussed by his guest. Tatlin had started life as a merchant seaman, then switched to painting Russian icons, but it was his talent as a musician that had brought him overseas. He played the bandura, a Ukrainian instrument something like a zither or lute. He had just come from performing at an exhibition of folk art in Berlin, where he had played before Kaiser Wilhelm and was complimented for his performance. And he didn't speak French, so when Lipchitz wasn't translating for them, the visitor had to communicate in gestures. Tatlin thought to make himself welcome by playing the accordion.

Over the past eighteen months, Picasso had been working on a new series of works depicting guitars. Their growing fame was attracting artists to his studio from throughout Europe, and it is said that Tatlin would visit Picasso several times over the coming weeks. He was captivated. The reliefs brought the image and the idea of a guitar to vivid and amusing life. It's said that Picasso sought advice from Julián Gómez Rámirez, a renowned guitar maker whose workshop was so small that he worked out on the street.[1] They were unlike anything the Russian had ever seen. They weren't paintings anymore, for they sprang into three dimensions; but they weren't sculptures either, for they hung on the wall. And they used all kinds of new materials—newspaper, wallpaper, sheet music, and sand—all brought together in disjunctive compositions as if there were no laws governing what the artist might use. Imagine that. A painting that wasn't a painting. A sculpture that wasn't a sculpture. You could do anything.

Tatlin begged to stay. He said he would make himself useful sweeping floors and stretching canvases. But Picasso had no use for him. He gave him some tubes of paint and sent him on his way. Soon enough Tatlin was back in Moscow.

VLADIMIR TATLIN'S LIFE SPANNED some of the most sweeping changes of modern Russia. Born in 1885 in the Ukraine, when it stood under the domination of the Russian Empire and its tsars, he rose through the ranks of the modernists and, just as the Bolsheviks took power, he inspired the Constructivist style that was revolutionary Russia's greatest achievement in the realm of avant-garde art. He helped lead Russian artists in their attempts to abandon art and start work instead on buildings, products, and useful "constructions." But he would be buffeted by the realities of Soviet rule: many of his early, experimental artworks were lost; of his great flying machine, the *Letatlin*, only a single wing survived after his death; his products were never manufactured; and his most famously ambitious project, the Monument to the Third International (1920), was never built. He did, however, survive, and would live to see the passing of Stalin before he died in 1953. Not all would be so lucky. The poet and playwright Vladimir Mayakovsky also rose to prominence among the modernists, he relished freedom and change, and he came to believe in the Communist cause and supported it when few did—he even went to work writing advertisements to support it—but eventually the state bureaucracy wore him down. He shot himself at the age of thirty-six.

Western avant-gardes almost accepted defeat as a premise; they knew they were paltry in number and pitted against the ranks of the bourgeoisie. Dada's nihilism, its chaotic and anarchistic accents, was fueled by hopelessness. But in Russia, the ground moved with the avant-garde, and for a short and extraordinary time seemed to align with their ideals. Here it seemed as if the avant-garde might finally destroy the idea of bourgeois art. They set about redefining it and then many abandoned it entirely. This extraordinary and rapid succession of events has made the story of the Russian avant-garde an exemplary one in the history of modern art, a freak occurrence, a single moment when turmoil in art and turmoil in politics coincided to produce new possibilities. None of this was apparent at the outset. Just as Russia tumbled rapidly and unexpectedly from a bourgeois revolution in February 1917 to a proletarian and communist revolution in October of the same year, so the artists tumbled from one situation to another, with all the problems and possibilities of those moments forcing new changes upon them. So, the tale of the Russian avant-garde is a play with several acts, and I don't think I'll be spoiling it if I tell you now that it doesn't have a happy ending.

BUT IT BEGAN WITH EXCITEMENT and adventure, and Tatlin found that from his earliest days.[2] His mother, a poet of some repute, had died when he was two, and he was raised by a stepmother he disliked. His father, a railway engineer, often traveled. So when he was seventeen, in 1903, he left his home in Kharkiv and made for Odessa. There, he joined the Merchant Marines and found a job as a cadet, then set sail on a boat bound for Bulgaria, Turkey, and Persia. In time, he would sail throughout the Mediterranean. Even when, upon his return from his first long voyage, he decided to pursue life as an artist, he would still find work in the summertime as a sailor (and when that wasn't paying his bills, he worked as a wrestler and an extra at the opera).

Outside Paris, there was probably nowhere better to see French modernism than in Moscow. Prominent merchants like Shchukin had significant collections, which they opened to the public. This only encouraged artists to travel: when Tatlin went to Paris he was following in the steps of two friends, Liubov Popova and Nadezhda Udaltsova, women who had gone to Paris a few months previously to study under the Salon Cubists Gleizes and Metzinger.[3] The Russians were often acutely aware of their regional heritage: Tatlin's first work as an artist was at an icon painting studio near the Kremlin. Yet the attraction of such work is probably best explained by the sheer quantity of Western influences they were also drawn to, and that they felt necessary to parry. Tatlin's painting *The Sailor: A Self-Portrait* (1911–12) is a representative example of how he united the Russian tradition with the modern. It has a dynamic quality, the sailor's face shaped like a bright blade of an axe, with dark figures swirling around it in the background. But it also has a simple, schematic quality, and a monumentality that is reminiscent of icons.[4]

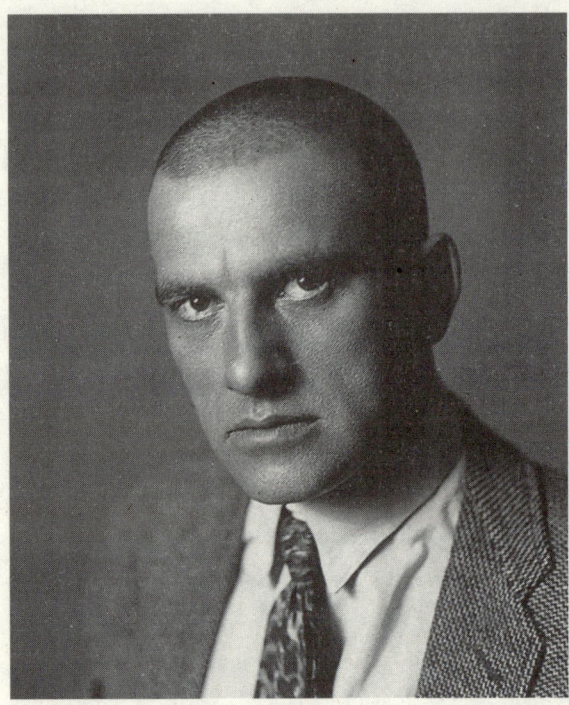

Vladimir Mayakovsky.

The landscape of Russian art seemed to promise more and more in the years leading up to the revolution. The scene increasingly resembled that of the West, with its myriad splintered factions, and in that regard it had clearly absorbed the habits and attitudes of the avant-garde that had taken shape in Paris. The World of Art group pioneered modern styles in Russia at the turn of the century, importing aspects of Symbolism and late Impressionism. As said, the nation's folk art was also a significant influence on some artists, religious icons being particularly popular as a source of inspiration. But so, too, were Cubism and Futurism after they emerged in the West. One distinctive Russian amalgam of those modern styles, Rayonism, offered a highly abstract imagery of light, patterns, and reflections. Many Russians spoke of Futurism as the leading force in Russian art, and one artists' society, the Union of Youth, to which Tatlin was allied, invited Marinetti to St. Petersburg in 1914. The Italian's manifesto had been published in one of the city's newspapers in 1909, barely a month after it had been announced to Parisians on the front page of *Le Figaro*. But Marinetti's arrival only touched off fighting among the Russians. For them, "Futurism" meant a broad range of modern styles, not merely the Italian export.

In fact, just as one group of Russian artists was feting Marinetti in St. Petersburg, another one was touring a different, eclectic version of "Futurism" around the provinces. Mayakovsky joined the poets and artists David Burliuk and Vasily Kamensky in a series of talks and performances in which they discussed Western modern art and showed lantern slides of their latest work and that of other modernists like Picasso. They also larked about. They wore radishes in their buttonholes and they had planes and dogs and kabbalistic signs painted on their faces. They attracted notice. Mayakovsky claimed that in Odessa they were pelted with flowers, candy, fruit, and several boxes of herring. He also claimed that their performance in Kiev brought the governor-general to the theater, along with the chief of police, eight police commissioners, sixteen assistant commissioners, twenty-five police supervisors, sixty constables, and outside the theater, a crowd of fifty mounted police.

/

VLADIMIR MAYAKOVSKY WAS INCLINED to exaggerate, but he was also inclined to impress. His friend, the writer and critic Osip Brik, claimed that he "was not a human being but a happening."[5] Born in 1893, in a village near the provincial capital of Kutaisi, in Georgia, his father was a forester, and family legend had it that their name was earned in tribute to their long line of tall and powerful men, "mayak" meaning "lighthouse" in Russian. A photograph of the family shows the poet's father to have been a sturdy, bewhiskered tower of a man; the boy Vladimir sitting beneath him already had an intense gaze. But when Mayakovsky was twelve, that tower, while sewing some documents together with a needle and thread, pricked his finger, contracted blood poisoning, and died. He was forty-nine. The family packed up and moved to Moscow.

It's likely that the loss of his father at the beginning of his teens loosened the reins on the young Mayakovsky and shaped his character into the energetic, combustible, and unruly adult he soon became. He gambled on cards and billiards, he was arrested several times for disseminating illegal literature, and in his student days, he presented himself as a shambling vagrant. He stood six foot three with long hair, and was commonly arrayed in a black shirt, black cravat, frayed pants with shiny backsides, and a broad-brimmed hat pulled down over his eyes. His teeth were hideously decayed. David Burliuk's wife, Marusya, remembered that when he spoke or laughed—and his laugh was said to be abrupt and peculiar—"all you saw was some brown, corroded and crooked, spiky stumps."[6]

Nevertheless, Mayakovsky was imposing, and shortly after the success of the Futurists' jaunt around the provinces, he could be seen strolling St. Petersburg in a black overcoat and top hat, with a cane. Women were drawn to him, and he could be promiscuous. Students were swept up along with country wives, wives who, Burliuk said, cuckolded their husbands "in hammocks and swings." The tale of Mayakovsky's romances could fill its own chapter, but I won't let it detain us here. Suffice it to say that in the years after the revolution it led to an unusual situation in which he behaved much as if he were married to another man's wife. Lili Brik was a sculptor, her husband, Osip, a lawyer with an ever-growing interest in literature. Shortly after the Briks set up together, they met the poet. Osip was bowled over by him, and recognized him as a young writer with an extraordinary talent; Mayakovsky was bowled over by Lili. Soon after, Mayakovsky was living in a one-room apartment on the same floor as the Briks. Not long after that, he gave up his apartment and moved in with them, and everyone regarded Lili and Mayakovsky as the couple.

Mayakovsky found himself to be very impressive: at age twenty he debuted a tragedy for the stage entitled *Vladimir Mayakovsky*, and in his early verse epic on his own grand struggles and sufferings, "A Cloud in Trousers," he sang:

Of grandfatherly tenderness I'm devoid
there's not a single grey hair in my soul!
Thundering the world with the might of my voice,
I go by—handsome,
twenty-two-year old."[7]

It's typical of his style, one that refuses to linger on tender feeling, as the previous generation of Symbolists were considered all too ready to do. Instead, Mayakovsky is happy to use colloquial syntax and vulgarisms, and to break up any rhythmic regularity in his lines.

WHEN TATLIN RETURNED from Paris to Moscow in 1914, the Russia he found was happy and prosperous—superficially, at least. Liberals were gloomy, frustrated in their attempts to unseat the monarchy, but the economy was booming, and in the villages, where the nation's one hundred million peasants resided, all was peaceful. By the end of 1917, Russia was a very different place. War had shaken the country, and in February a revolution toppled the tsar, and an experiment in democracy began. In October, another revolution brought the Bolsheviks to power. The pace of change was dizzying.

Mayakovsky could breathe the freedom in the air. One day, he and the poet Nikolay Aseyev were wandering about Moscow marveling at all the signs for new political parties that had been established in February's wake. It seemed as if anyone could launch themselves on the public square. Mayakovsky wondered out loud whether the Futurists should stand for office. Aseyev pointed out that no one would vote for them: "The devil only knows, the way things are just now." Mayakovsky replied, "Just think if I was elected president!"[8]

Osip Brik was similarly excited. When Lenin returned from exile in Zurich in April, arriving at the Finland Station in the famous sealed and armored train, having glided across Europe under the protection of the Germans as if national borders didn't exist, Brik went to witness the spectacle. Lenin arrived and stood atop the train to address thousands. "The people need peace," he bellowed, "the people need bread, the people need land."

"Seems crazy," Brik reported, "but dreadfully convincing."

Yet while Russia's intellectuals had been enthusiastic about the February revolution, most were skeptical at the prospect of Bolshevik rule. Russians had become so weary of war and hunger and political upheaval that there was little optimism that a change in rulers would make much difference. The situation was also highly confusing. The reports of the American journalist John Reed vividly capture the fog of the situation in St. Petersburg. He described a divided city in which some areas saw people in furs, drinking champagne and gambling, while elsewhere there was fear and hunger. He watched a soldier beaten to death in the streets for stealing. And he saw crowds descending on piles of newspapers whenever they appeared, desperate for any clearer picture of whatever was happening, wherever it was happening.[9]

Soon enough, however, changes came that spelled out Russia's direction—at least in the short term—and for artists, the individual who held the most power to decide their fate was Anatoly Lunacharsky. Shortly after the revolution, Lenin named him as head of the People's Commissariat of Enlightenment, commonly known as Narkompros, a sprawling ministry overseeing education and the arts. Lunacharksy had been involved in politics and the arts for two decades. In 1917, he was in his early forties, and he was swept up by the drama of change, calling it "colossal in everything, tragic and significant."[10]

The scholar Sheila Fitzpatrick describes him as "a large, untidy man with pince-nez and a benevolent expression."[11] Regularly he would be seen walking about Moscow in the kind of huge fur coat favored by the rich merchants in an earlier time, his arms waving about, his scarf flapping, his coat unbuttoned and trailing in the snow. He was a prolific playwright, and one drawn to philosophy. Lenin referred to such interests as evidence of his "lightmindedness," nevertheless, he believed him to be a "splendid comrade." Also, artists seemed to respect him, and in the wake of the revolution, this was valuable.[12] While many artists had welcomed the freedom promised by the democratic revolution in February 1917, few were enthusiastic about the arrival of the Bolsheviks, though few had any clear idea of what that might mean

So Lunacharsky decided he needed to offer an olive branch, and in the days after the revolution, he had put out a widely publicized invitation to Russia's leading artists to join him to discuss collaboration with the new government. To signal his appreciation, he invited them to the Smolny Palace, an ornate classical building on the banks of the River Neva in St. Petersburg. It had once been a school for the daughters of the Russian nobility, but since returning from exile, it was where Lenin had stationed himself. Now the halls thundered with the sound of heavy boots as workers carried bundles of newspapers and proclamations to and fro. To be invited to the seat of power was an honor, but of all those invited, only Mayakovsky, Brik, and four others turned up.

In time, however, the artists began to find their place in the new Bolshevik realm of art. One notable change had already begun: a matter of weeks after the February revolution, the Imperial Academy of the Arts had been closed. Now it was formally abolished; the academic era was over. Change also came to modern art: the myriad factions of the 1910s disappeared and were replaced by an array of government-sponsored agencies with bland-sounding names like those of divisions of municipal government. And these government agencies were often directed by individuals of extraordinary artistic talent that no sane individual would place in charge of a government agency.

Even Wassily Kandinsky found a role. After the First World

War was declared, he had fled Munich for Switzerland, and there he moved among the homes of friends, hoping to wait out the conflict. But as the months passed and that seemed unlikely, he reluctantly returned to Moscow.

Kandinsky's time back in Russia seems to have been an unhappy one on several fronts. His years in Germany had been gloriously productive, but back home, he hit a slump. He struggled to get back to work, and he produced few paintings. When the Bolsheviks came to power, he became a college administrator leading Inkhuk, the Institut Khudozhestvennoi Kul'tury, which opened in 1920. This might have seemed the wrong appointment for an artist who, in Munich, had been an advocate for a spiritual abstract art, but Kandinsky proved talented in this area, and Inkhuk blossomed into a remarkable college, one that embarked on projects that no institution in Western Europe would have contemplated. Its goal was to direct research into modernism in art, and it held debates over materials, texture, color, space, time, form, technique, and the psychological and physical responses of viewers. It was here that artists confronted new questions that had arisen as a consequence of Bolshevik rule. What should an artist do in a Communist society? What was their responsibility to the people, to the state, to themselves?

Questions like those were frequently asked in the new Russia, and the changes that had come over Russian art in the few years before the revolution put it in a powerful position to answer them. Artists were more than ready for change and challenge. Tatlin's work was exemplary in this regard. He had been to Paris, he had met Picasso, and upon returning to Russia his work had transformed. Probably the first conclusive sign of it was *The Bottle* (ca. 1913). We don't have a lot of information about this work because its whereabouts are unknown. It's believed that when Tatlin died, the concierge in his building was impatient to clear his room and discarded many of his belongings.[13] But the single grainy photograph that survives suggests that it wasn't a naturalistic illusion of a bottle; it was an analysis of the thing, a description in fragments, combining a silhouette of its profile, a circle describing its base, and an arcing curve outlining its exterior shape. Wallpaper, wood, metal, and glass were all used to evoke its facets, and critics believe that what Tatlin was trying to achieve was less a visual representation than an exploration of its contrasting materials and textures. This was not something then done in the West. In subsequent works, like *Corner Counter-Relief* (1914–15), Tatlin would go even further, abandoning description for abstraction, and abandoning the traditional forms of painting and sculpture for something entirely new, an arrangement of metal sheets and wires that would span the corner of a room. It is as if Tatlin had sought to tear the canvas, the materials of old-fashioned painting, from the wall and leave them in midair. Or, as the historian John Milner puts it, as if Tatlin had imagined himself grappling with ropes and sails, just as he had done during his days at sea.[14]

So when revolution came, and Lenin spoke, Tatlin was more than ready. Lunacharsky informed Russia's artists that their leader had had "one of those fortunate and profoundly exciting ideas with which he has so often shocked and delighted us."[15] Lenin wanted a grand campaign of monument building to celebrate the revolution, valorize its heroes, and educate the people. Lenin wanted statues, lots of them, all over Moscow and beyond. And he wanted tsarist monuments toppled.

And he wanted it done now.

Time passed. Lenin made inquiries. He demanded more activity. Then, on May 13, 1918, Lunacharsky received a telegram from Lenin stating, "I am surprised and indignant at your inactivity." He quickly got to work. Statues started to appear. And Lenin, despite his other responsibilities, was happy to be present at the unveilings. Marx and Engels were celebrated, but also the French revolutionaries Danton and Robespierre, the Russian writers Tolstoy and Dostoyevsky, and the French composer Chopin and the Russian Mussorgsky. The statues varied broadly in style, some traditional, some modernist, though generally it was clear who was being celebrated.

And then there was Vladimir Tatlin's idea. His monument would not be a statue, a figure, a hero. His would be a monument-machine building, four hundred meters high (thirteen hundred feet). It would be the tallest construction in the world. It would straddle the River Neva as it snaked through St. Petersburg. It would be a tower that would seem to have thundered out of the ground on a diagonal. It would be like the Eiffel Tower, a crowning symbol of modernity, but taller still. Like old imaginings of the Tower of Babel, it would be coiled, but rather than confusing speech, confounding the world, it would transmit messages of perfect clarity and persuasiveness. It would house a radio station, a telegraph and telephone exchange, a printing shop. It would be what critic Maria Gough has called "a gigantic, mobility-mad, multitasking, spectacle-producing communication device dedicated to revolutionary agitation."[16]

It would be made not of stone but of glass and steel. It would be constructed from elemental forms. A cube, a pyramid, and a cylinder, one atop the other. At its base, a glass cube would house a legislature; above it, a glass pyramid would house executive bodies; above that, a glass cylinder would house information services. And each would rotate, the cube once per year, the pyramid once per month, the cylinder once per day. Elevators would glide up the spine of the building, carrying workers to its different functions.

It would have meeting rooms, gymnasia, lecture rooms. It would have everything implying movement and dynamism. There would be nothing passive, nothing static, no museums, no libraries. It would have a garage, and as one early promoter put it, "standardized motorcycles and automobiles" would pour forth from it, distributing "appeals, proclamations and publications."[17] A giant screen would be affixed to its wings and films would be projected at night. Searchlights would project slogans onto the clouds in a rainbow of colored letters. It would be, as Vladimir Mayakovsky put it, "the first monument without a beard" and, referring to the month of the revolution, "the first object of October."[18]

All they had to do now was build it.

/

TATLIN'S MONUMENT WAS QUICKLY perceived among his peers as an incitement to further advances. He had shifted rapidly from a relatively naturalistic style of painting through a phase of modernist experiment, and had arrived at utility, which was now taken to be the necessary destination for all. Artistic composition was out, art-as-construction was in; artists should no longer be thinking with taste and aesthetics in mind, but instead with engineering. What the terms "composition" and "construction" meant in practice, and whether or not they were incompatible, was the subject of some debate, but the artist Aleksandr Rodchenko put the matter simply: "All new approaches to art arise from technology and engineering and move towards organization and construction."[19] Rodchenko's wife, the artist Varvara Stepanova, was also at the center of these discussions in the period around 1921, and she put the problem in more extreme and final terms: "Technology and experimental thinking will take the place of aesthetics," she proclaimed. "Art will be "purged."[20] A few thought that the only thing left for art was propaganda, but all other traditional uses were over. As one writer put it, "Art ends with us."[21]

Finally, on November 24, 1921, more than twenty of Inkhuk's artists and theorists signed a proclamation renouncing art and applying themselves instead to the production of useful objects. More debates followed over what these objects should be. Was it better to call them "things" or "constructions"? They certainly weren't "commodities," because those were the emptily entrancing things that filled Western stores. They were "products," and so the artists came to talk of themselves as "Productivists." And as these products were akin to tools, they came to speak of themselves as the people's "coworkers," even their "comrades."

Inevitably, Tatlin was in the forefront of the attempts to create these comrades. He developed a host of designs for new products, including a bentwood chair, a sleigh, a nursing cup for infants, several ovens, a wood-burning stove, a linen sportscoat (said to have been both rustic and futuristic), and a multipurpose pot (a combination cooking pot and teapot with a lid that could double as a frying pan). Maybe Tatlin lacked the entrepreneurial, risk-taking gene, and one of his peers claimed he had a "morbid fear of plagiarism," but not one of them made it to production.[22]

The only artists to work in industry with some success—if only temporarily—were Stepanova and Liubov Popova, who in 1923 started working for the First State Cotton-Printing Factory. Before the revolution, the enormous factory on the banks of the Moscow River had been known to all as the Tsindel Factory, after its owner Emil Tsindel. But following years of war, it was struggling, isolated from textile production in other nations and working with outmoded designs and equipment. In the late fall of 1923, its director turned to Popova and Stepanova, who had become renowned in Moscow for their work in costume and set design for theater. They went to work as "artist-productivists." One might have expected them to have carried over the Constructivist language of geometric abstraction directly into their designs, but what they produced instead tended more toward patterns and vibrating optical effects. The factory's rudimentary printing presses weren't very sophisticated, but they did allow layering and interlinking of forms, of stripes and circles. Popova and Stepanova wanted to exploit what the most advanced Russian production techniques could produce and to put forth a language of geometry and dynamism that suggested a style for the modern Russian woman in the new revolutionary state. The scholar Christina Kaier likens Popova's designs to the "flapper" dresses of 1920s America, with their loose-fitting, drop-waisted style. With them, the designers hoped to generate pride in the nation's modernity.

But there were problems. Popova and Stepanova were working at the factory at a time when the field of design was not well established, and those who did design work in industry did not expect to do so at some distance from the factory floor. The management wouldn't let them work in the factory's research lab or its design studio, and they were forced instead to work from home. Critics sometimes conclude that it was the parlous state of Russian industry that stood in the way of Productivism. Most of the country remained industrially backward and stuck with technology that long predated the war. The country simply had no money. The poet Andrei Belyi quipped that "the victory of materialism in Russia resulted in the complete disappearance of all matter."[23] And Kandinsky's exasperation with the country is said to have peaked when it took him two weeks to obtain the necessary documents to buy a pair of shoes, only to find there were none.[24] Yet more than industrial capability stood in the way of Popova and Stepanova; there was also sexism, and the ordinary tensions of the factory floor, the management, and the design office. When in May 1924 Popova died suddenly after contracting scarlet fever from her five-year-old son, the experiment ended.

/

IT WAS A LOGIC that spared no one, not even Mayakovsky. He was sometimes stung by criticism that his work was obscure, which led him to produce what he termed "utilitarian poetry." He decided to be a poet-journalist, reporting on the world and rousing the people to action. He wrote on topical themes—against religious holidays, in lament when Lenin was ill, and three poems to celebrate the workers' holiday on May 1.

And then he went into advertising.

Following the Civil War that pitted Communists against an alliance of their remaining opponents, the so-called White Russians, Lenin decided that the most effective way to revive the economy was a controlled reintroduction of the capitalist market, a phase known as the New Economic Policy, which lasted from 1921 to 1927. It was to affect much more than economics, for Lenin decided that it needed to be accompanied by a new wave of propaganda that would ensure the victory of state enterprises as they competed on the same plane as private companies. Soviet citizens were to be persuaded that they could support the revolution through shopping. And to do that work of persuasion, the Communist government was going to have to turn artists from being engineers of objects to being engineers of minds.

In fact, Mayakovsky had made a start in this field as early as 1919, when he designed around five hundred posters for ROSTA, the state telegram bureau. Then, one day in 1923, he met his friend the artist Aleksandr Rodchenko in a café in Moscow. Rodchenko remarked that he was now also designing advertisements. Mayakovsky saw an opportunity, and so was born the most unlikely advertising agency that ever was, the Reklam-Konstructor Mayakovsky-Rodchenko (Advertisement Constructors Mayakovsky-Rodchenko). By day, Mayakovsky would woo clients and compose slogans; by night, Rodchenko would design ads, arriving with assistants at seven or eight in the evening, collecting Mayakovsky's notes, and working in the studio until morning, when they would take the finished ads back to Mayakovsky. Mayakovsky liked to compose poetry by pacing up and down and beating out a rhythm with his hands. He would do the same for the ads' mottos, marching around the Briks' house, sometimes using Lili's piano to help sustain rhythm. To a modern ear, and in translation, they sound clunky: "Attention proles / Cooking oil / Is three times cheaper / Than butter / But richer / Than all the others / Get it from Mossel'prom." Some seem barely sincere, as if the work were beneath them. An advertisements for pacifiers read "There have never been and are no better pacifiers. You'll want to suck them until old age."[25]

The duo were busy. They created around fifty posters and much else. They produced work for GUM, the state department store, and for the tea directorate, among others. The aim was always to prop up the revolution by promoting its enterprises, and often Mayakovsky was explicit about both goals. He designed a series of wrappers for Mossel'prom's "Red Star" caramels, each of which carried a verse commenting on the Red Army's recent Civil War victory over the Whites. If you got through a packet of caramels, you could gather all the wrappers into a sequence to read the whole poem. Humble labor or not, Mayakovsky was exultant. Advertising was "commercial, industrial agitation," he claimed; moreover, it could be "poetry of the highest order." Rodchenko, too, was thrilled: "All of Moscow was decorated with our work."

Energized by new demands, feted by comrades, courted—or frustrated—by the state, Rodchenko and Mayakovsky were at the center of Russia's leftist avant-garde in the mid-1920s. The apartment of Osip and Lili Brik became their meeting place, the hub for a network of writers, artists, theoreticians, and filmmakers. Occasionally, the crowd would move to a dacha in the village of Pushkin, outside Moscow, and there they would talk art and literature, play croquet, and sunbathe.

The first time Rodchenko and Stepanova visited the dacha, there was a crowd of thirty. "There were people in the rooms, on the balcony, in the garden—everywhere," Rodchenko recalled. After they had dinner, he wandered about the garden and took photographs, and then returned to record the occasion. He gathered everyone on seats, and while they sat in anticipation, he positioned the camera and stacked up several chairs, on top of which he placed an ashtray heaped with magnesium for a crude flash. He extinguished all the lights, struck a match to help him focus the lens, then lit a ribbon of paper that led to the magnesium and rushed back to take a seat. The paper fizzled in the darkness. There was a terrible noise and bleached white light. The windows were opened, and smoke rolled out.

/

NIKOLAI LOSSKY FELT that the summer of 1922 was a fairly unremarkable one. Busy, interesting, but nothing special. The philosophy professor had been staying in Pushkin, where the Briks summered, along with his wife, her mother, and his children.[26]

Around mid-August, at the height of the season when the middle class abandoned the cities for their dachas, a friend invited him around to meet a poet and another writer. They sat around talking, and they listened to one of them give a "a vivid description of peasant life in the north." The next day, Lossky was called into the headquarters of the Cheka, the secret police. He thought he needed to sort out something with his passport. He was taken to the upper floors of the building, told to sit down on a bench, and an armed guard was stationed next to him. He realized that it wasn't about his passport.

Another Moscow professor, Alexander Ugrimov, was out of town when his daughter responded to a knock at the door. Men had come in search of him. His address was sitting by the phone, but they missed it. In the morning, she saw a friend who told her there had been raids throughout the night. She managed to get word to her father, but he concluded that it was pointless to resist. When he returned to the city, he turned himself in.

They came for Mikhail Osorgin in the countryside, and by the time they came, he was almost prepared. He was outside, a short distance from his house. Someone ran out of the house and waved frantically at him. He understood, picked up his fishing rod, and made off down the hill. The remaining experiences, his memories of those last moments in the country, never left him. He recalled "an invisible vapor of mint" that rose from a field; "a primeval pine forest, never logged and completely untended."

Little more than six weeks later, the first group of sixty writers, philosophers, journalists, economists, and literary critics were all deported. The first ship left from the Kronstadt pier in St. Petersburg on September 28, specially chartered and bound for Stettin, a port city in what was then Germany and is now northwest Poland.[27] The Politburo had discussed no less than thirty times the problem of wavering intellectuals. The Civil War was putting pressure on the Bolsheviks, and while Lenin was ready to accept a loosening of economic policies to keep the nation afloat, he would not accept backtracking on politics. The intellectuals had to shut up and fall in line, and if necessary, there would be "preventive surgery" to deal with them. When his officials were done, some two hundred had been expelled, along with their families.[28]

IRONICALLY, MAYAKOVSKY BEGAN TO FEEL the chill soon after he completed "150,000,000," an epic poem in praise of the revolution. As he often did, he gave a reading of his new work at the Briks' apartment. There was a crowd of around twenty there to hear him, and among them was Lunacharsky, who had been invited in the hopes that he could aid its publication. The bureaucrat was supportive, but in truth he wasn't a friend of experimenting ("I never was a Futurist," he said, "am not a Futurist, and will not be a Futurist"), and when Mayakovsky tried to find a publisher, he ran into problems.[29] When it finally appeared, Lenin denounced it. It was "rubbish, stupid, stupid beyond belief and pretentious," the leader wrote, and "Lunacharsky should be horsewhipped" for allowing it.[30]

The problem wasn't the poem's support for the revolution, the problem was its dissonant modernism, what one opponent called its "mayakovskery." Lunacharsky worried about the rhetoric, about whether the poet was in earnest, whether the "150,000,000" of the title, the Russian population, would know he was in earnest. Increasingly, there was no room for doubt. Even his friend Osip Brik had started to work for the secret police. But Mayakovsky persisted, insisting on freedom, struggling against its disappearance. He complained of encountering only a stultifying bureaucracy and new forms of censorship. He complained of red tape, paperwork, and stupidity, and he wrote a poem titled "All Meetinged Out." By the early 1920s, he was the only major poet left in Russia who wholeheartedly supported the Revolution, yet his patience was ebbing.[31] In 1922, as Lenin was contemplating expulsions, he wrote a long poem titled "Fifth International." The Communist Third International had been inaugurated in 1919, but Mayakovsky had had enough of it, and dreamt instead of a spiritual revolution. He wrote a section in which he has become a spirit and converses with a Lenin who has been petrified into a statue locked behind the Kremlin walls. Finally, Mayakovsky decided it was best to leave that portion out, and when the censors had at it, they cut some more. He had taken to speaking of the time since the Bolsheviks took power as a "three-year-long Golgotha walk."[32]

There is no straight line from Mayakovsky's struggles with the young Soviet state in the early 1920s to his suicide in April 1930. His life was always in tumult, and if it wasn't work that was exhausting and frustrating him, it was illness—or his hypochondria—or love. Eventually, his affair with Lili Brik cooled. Other lovers replaced her, the last being the actress Veronika Polonskaya. What happened at the end isn't clear, but Polonskaya came to his apartment one final time on April 14. They argued, and Mayakovsky fell to the floor and wept. In fact, it's likely that the encounter ended with Polonskaya telling him that she was leaving her husband and moving in with him. But then she left the room and heard a noise, and returned to find the poet had shot himself through the chest. He seemed to have done it on impulse, and yet he also seemed to have planned the whole thing, and had written a poem to address those he would leave behind, announcing in it, "Life and I are quits."³³

/

A YEAR EARLIER, IN 1929, Tatlin's early observations at sea started to take him in a new direction. He was the head of a small research group that was housed behind the high walls of the Novodevicky Monastery in Moscow. A journalist once visited him there and described the scene. "A few steps on to the open balustrade of the tower, then you draw back a heavy iron bolt and enter a high, vaulted bell-room, transformed now into a medieval laboratory. High up, shrouded in the twilight of the monastery, hangs in rope a great white bird without a head."³⁴ This bird was Tatlin's flying machine, the *Letatlin*, its name a combination of the Russian verb *letat*, meaning "to fly," and the artist's name.

As a sailor, Tatlin had spent long hours watching gulls circle ships, and now he returned to studying their flight. His team pondered how insects fly; they dissected storks and ducks, swallows and sparrows. They consulted a surgeon and a pilot. "I want to give back to man the feeling of flight," wrote Tatlin.³⁵ His flying machine would be a glider, or as he sometimes called it, an "air-bicycle," but it would also be an "ornithopter," a device that flaps its wings like a bird. On the downward motion, the wings would bend and contract, on the upward they would reach out wide. It would be a wondrous thing, but, Tatlin hoped, it would also be an ordinary thing, one that the Soviet masses might use. He envisaged flying schools for children as young as eight. Everyone could learn the rudiments of the *Letatlin*.

For all the magic suggested by inventions like the *Letatlin*, and all the attempts by artists to turn themselves into engineers, constructors, agitators, the real legacy of Russian Constructivism was an artistic language, a style that spoke of science, technology, and utopia. It was most effectively exported not by those committed to the goal of ending art, but those committed to its furtherance in the more welcoming climate of European galleries and museums. The two brothers Naum Gabo and Antoine Pevsner became the Constructivists' principal disciples, but instead of preaching art as construction, they espoused an intellectualized language of ideal geometry, transparency, and new materials. In sculptures made of translucent plastic we see ideal forms that look like prototypes for some kind of technological perfection. Critics today often describe their art as "constructive" rather than "constructivist," to distinguish it from the ethos of Tatlin and his peers. That work often retained an urge to transcend painting and to become a modern, abstract, public art, yet it found that task increasingly difficult in the postwar period as the leading artists turned toward expressive abstraction. Oddly, however, Tatlin's Monument has had its own legacy in the West. Indeed, it is one of the twentieth century's most cited artworks. His Monument—or at least the proud, striving shape of it—has become shorthand for techno-utopian ambitions. In the 1960s, the American Minimalist Dan Flavin produced a series of sculptural tributes to it, each in his trademark fluorescent light bulbs. More recently, the Chinese dissident artist Ai Wei Wei has produced a version, entitled *Fountain of Light* (2016), that is made of over thirty-two thousand glass crystals, and that seems to make a wry comment on where all the technological aspiration has got us—skylines with buildings that look no better than Christmas ornaments.

It was while Tatlin was working on the *Letatlin* that Mayakovsky killed himself. The poet lay in state for three days. On the day of the funeral, his coffin, draped in black and red, was carried to the crematorium of the Don Monastery on a steel-gray tank designed by Tatlin, the artist David Shterenberg, and "John" Levin. Alongside it lay a wreath made of sledgehammers, flywheels, and screws, and a caption that read, "An iron wreath for an iron poet." Sixty thousand people were said to have followed it, with mourners leaning out of windows and hanging off trees and lampposts.³⁶ Rodchenko described the scene:

> When they brought the coffin, the police could not hold back the crowd, people broke through from side streets the whole time and continually upset the proceedings. They hung up flags and Mayakovsky's verses on the buildings. If Volodya had seen that, he would have understood that he was not alone, that he had a response, that he was loved, that he was needed. But he swayed slowly on the lorry, on the iron platform built to Tatlin's design by Vkhutemas students, dully rumbling and severe. He floated past slowly. The most alive of the living. The energetic commander of the new revolutionary front of the arts. The great proletarian poet of the USSR.³⁷

When the coffin finally reached the crematorium doors, the crush was such that the police had to shoot into the air to clear the crowds.

SIX

Saint-Peter of the Straight Line

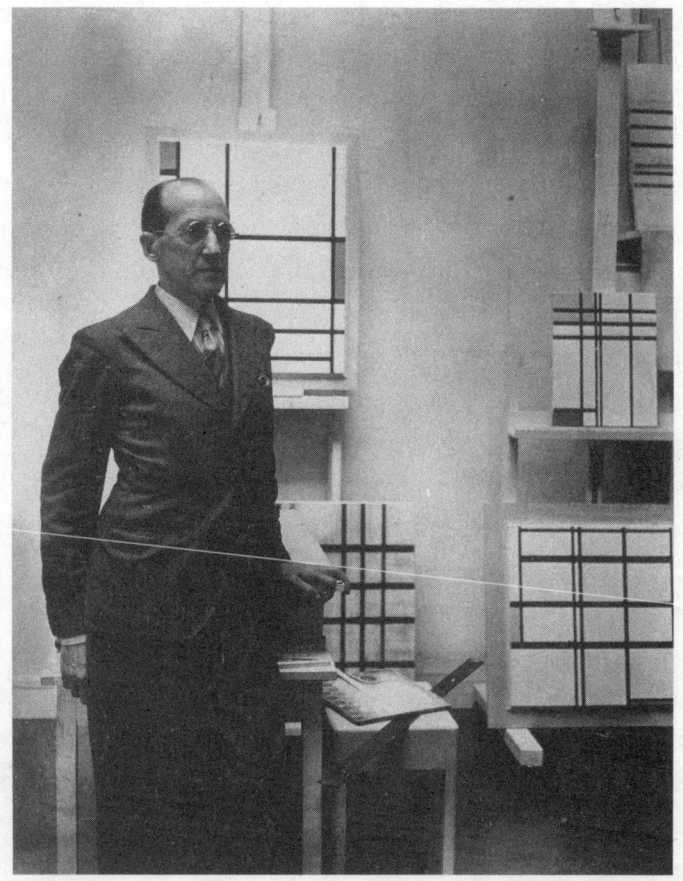

Piet Mondrian

DOMBURG HAD BEEN A POPULAR DUTCH SEASIDE resort since the early nineteenth century. People came for the spa, the broad beaches, and the forests that stretched out from the edge of town. Piet Mondrian had stayed there many times, and over the years had painted a few of its sights, a windmill at the outskirts, and the tower of

St. Gerulfus, a massive, fourteenth-century edifice flanked by thick buttresses at the center of town. But when he arrived in the fall of 1914, it can't have been with great pleasure, as only a few miles south, German troops were driving across Belgium and heading for France. Mondrian had been living in Paris since 1912, but after he came back to see his ailing father in Arnhem, family forbade him to return.[1] Soon enough he found himself staying in the house of an old friend in Domburg.

When he wasn't painting, he liked to walk. A wide beach spilled down to the sea, punctuated by long, paired wooden stakes that helped break the powerful waves from the North Sea. From Hoge Hill you could take in a sweeping panorama: the town behind, the beach before you. And one night when Mondrian went out walking the beach with Mies-Elout Drabbe, an artist friend, he stopped and sketched. The stars were visible overhead; the waves audible below. He took the drawing, reworked it, and reworked it again. Drabbe later recalled that "he worked on that little drawing for days, every morning moving one step further from the reality and one small step closer to its spiritualization."[2]

Stars were objects of particular curiosity for Mondrian. It struck him as significant that, with the naked eye, you could never examine them individually; instead, you could only ever see their position in a much larger totality. It was the relationships that mattered. Yet, glance briefly at one section of the sky and it will appear much the same as another; one handful of stars may seem much the same in their haphazard positioning as those arrayed across the entirety of heaven's dome. The microcosm echoes the macrocosm. As Mondrian paced the dunes by night, and a war began a few miles away, he looked to the skies in search of a lesson. He was forty-two and unmarried. He lived simply. He was known by a few as a rising modern painter, but that was all. Modern life in Paris had seemed transitory; war, hopefully, would be fleeting too. Surely there were some things that endured? Some timeless universals?

PIET MONDRIAN WAS THE ELDEST of five children born to Pieter Cornelius Mondriaan, a driven and outspoken schoolteacher, and his taciturn wife, Johanna Christina.³ His father liked to draw, and it was likely from him that Piet first developed an interest in art. When Piet was born in 1872, his father was the principal of the Christian Reformist School at Amersfoort. To him, teaching was not merely an occupation but a blessed vocation, one bound up with the futures both of Holland and Dutch Calvinism. There is some disagreement about Mondrian's early years. Mondrian's first biographer, Michel Seuphor, characterized the artist's father as a domineering zealot, a "strict Calvinist," a man "not inclined to take moral questions lightly, or to compromise his parental authority." However, a more recent account by Hans Janssen has softened the picture, pointing out that Mondrian's opinion of his father changed over time, and while he always struggled to connect with the man, he eventually came to empathize with and admire the way he lived in accordance with his convictions—convictions that undoubtedly had an impact on his son.⁴

Calvinism had been central to the formation of Holland in the sixteenth century, and over the subsequent centuries the nation's political and religious development remained closely tied, making it an inextricable part of the culture Piet Mondrian was raised in. It would be wrong to attempt to explain Mondrian's art or thought in terms of Calvinism—or indeed in terms of any single system of beliefs—but some of its tenets clearly had a shaping force.⁵ For example, Calvin taught that in every area of life we are forced to reckon with the mystery of the inexplicable, but that a general knowledge of God can be found by studying nature. As Mondrian gazed up at the stars on Domburg beach, that thought must have occurred to him. Calvin also taught that God implanted humans with an inbuilt sense of the divine: if Mondrian couldn't see God, he could surely sense him, sense his presence within nature's order. All these inklings would play a part in his later art.

Many of Mondrian's siblings followed their father into education, though many also grew to be adventurous or nonconformist in their own lives and ideals.[6] Willem Frederik taught for a while until he joined a bank, but then he left for South Africa to become an assistant to the governor of Suriname. Louis also trained to be a teacher, and later became an adherent of the radical humanitarianism promoted by the Christian anarchist Jacob van Rees, which encouraged living in harmony with nature and humankind. Carel was perhaps the most ostensibly conventional, since he later worked in a bank, though he gained a reputation for debauchery.[7]

Piet learned to paint early on, and he took his first lessons from his father, and from an uncle, Frits Mondrian, who was an influential figure in the Hague School, a group inspired by the romantic Barbizon School painting of mid-nineteenth-century France. Piet later trained and qualified to teach drawing, and at age twenty left home for the Academy of Fine Arts in Amsterdam. But there he proved an indifferent student, and his true education would be autodidactic and would unfold over the ensuing decade. His earliest work is somewhat naturalistic, recording a realistic world of landscapes and buildings in Holland, often scenes he knew intimately. Yet already there are stylized elements: *Dorpskerk*, a painting of the village church at Winterswijk, from 1898, borrowed from Art Nouveau to depict the sturdy structure through a hauntingly serpentine tangle of tree branches, and framed by a long hedgerow whose branches seem to curve and reach with an almost human animation. Around 1905–6 he painted several views of the River Gein, on the outskirts of Amsterdam, and these play with symmetry and reflections in a manner reminiscent of the Symbolist painting of figures like Edvard Munch.

But in an account Mondrian penned in 1941, he felt his early work was already shaped by the distinctive perspectives of his mature years. "I preferred to paint landscape and houses seen in gray," he recalled, "dark weather or in very strong sunlight, when the density of the atmosphere obscures the details and accentuates the large outlines of objects. I often sketched by moonlight—cows resting or standing immovable on flat Dutch meadows, or houses with dead, blank windows. I never painted these things romantically; but from the beginning, I was always a realist."[8] Mondrian may be describing a visible world far removed from the abstraction of his later work, yet listen to its emphases: the desire to put details aside and focus on the outline; the density of the atmosphere, the flat planes of blank windows; the high vertical of the moonlight, and the flat horizontal of the meadows. This is Mondrian filtering the world through his own sensibility, preparing it for his language of lines and planes. But for him it won't be subjective, expressive, romantic—it will be real.

MONDRIAN FIRST MOVED TO PARIS early in 1912. His aim was to continue his self-education, but he found himself enlivened by the distractions of city life. He arrived sporting a beard, but soon enough shaved it off and cut his hair short to style himself as urbane. When he had some money—which was not often—he would buy the latest American fashions and dine out and dance. Back in Holland, his friends joked that he was "the dancing Madonna" because of his odd way of shuffling rigidly about with his head held aloft.[9] In later years, when Mondrian had made his reputation, journalists tended to depict him as a dour, distant, and hermetic character. That's a picture formed more by the cerebral abstraction of his later work than by knowledge of the man. It's true that he could be a little odd, sometimes difficult to connect with, brusque—he knew this himself. He could be intensely attracted to women, but while his relations with them tended to be easy and conventional enough, he struggled to settle with anyone. Yet some firsthand accounts describe him as a friendly and engaging man, at times solemn, serious, and dignified, yet at others childlike in his sincerity and naivety.[10]

Like a lot of the artists we've encountered already, Mondrian cycled through a succession of styles in his early years. After his attempts at Art Nouveau and Symbolism, he borrowed from Van Gogh, from Fauvism, and from Divisionism, which advocated the division of color into individual marks or dots. Then, late in 1911, on the eve of the move to Paris, he discovered Cézanne and the Cubism of Picasso and Braque, and his work took leaps forward toward abstraction, his imagery becoming more fragmented and his palette more monochromatic. Over the next two years, while he soaked up the ideas current in the French capital, his motifs, often trees, remained consistent, but just as the branches of that early *Dorpskerk* picture seemed to rival the church as a focal point, so the trees in his Cubist pictures became nothing more than occasions to muse on form, structure, and interconnection. By 1913, Mondrian had put aside any ostensible motif and was painting abstract grids, not in the manner of his mature style, with its rigid lines and primary colors, but in a manner that was highly advanced nonetheless.

So by the time Mondrian was back in Holland and was pacing the beach at Domburg, he had learned a great deal from Cubism, and what he would derive from the experience would not be an old-fashioned topographic landscape, or a study in mood, but instead a vision of something much more fundamental. He produced drawing after drawing, and with each one the arrangement of the beach, the sky, and the receding piers became both more complex and abstract. Everything was being reduced to a notation of short, intersecting horizontal and vertical lines encased in an oval.

Mondrian was in search of the universal. He was never completely absorbed by the concerns of French Cubism because his thought was already shaped by ideas he had encountered a few years earlier in Holland, and central to those was Theosophy.[11] Heir to the American spiritualism of the early nineteenth century,

Theosophy had been established in New York in 1875 by Madame Blavatsky, the Russian writer and mystic, and Henry Steel Olcott, an American lawyer. Theosophy was highly eclectic, drawing on ancient Eastern religions as well as modern, Western ideas. Blavatsky viewed it as a revival of ancient religions that had been passed down to her through mediumistic contact with a secret band of Masters, or Adepts. These Adepts weren't spirits but instead highly evolved, godlike men, chiefly residing in Tibet. She claimed to have gone there to study with them, and that they wrote Theosophy's major texts through her. She encouraged a fascination with spiritual phenomena and the occult laws underpinning them. She didn't speak of an anthropomorphic God but instead an Absolute that was impersonal and immanent in nature. She believed that matter arises from the interaction of universal forces engaged in an evolutionary progression, one that humans encourage by passing through multiple reincarnations. Her ideas could be esoteric, but they were also couched in terms that appealed to the period's liberalism: she promoted the notion that all religions are essentially one, and she longed for a "Universal Brotherhood of Humanity" that would bring people together. Such progressive ideas, along with her optimistic views on science and social reform, had a powerful appeal in the period—perhaps even more so during and after the war, when organizations like the League of Nations endeavored to make this dream of a world brotherhood into a reality. Theosophy attracted some influential adherents—at one point, Thomas Edison was a follower—but it remained an interest of the intellectually curious rather than a movement that attracted a popular audience.

It's thought that Mondrian joined the Dutch branch of the Theosophical Society, and as early as 1908 he seems to have entertained the idea that clairvoyance was possible. Its ideas were crucial to a painting he produced before his trip to Paris, *Evolution* (1910–11), which depicts three schematically drawn female nudes in rigid poses. One looks directly at the viewer, the two on either side have their eyes closed and heads tilted back as if consumed in a trance; bright abstract shapes emanate from behind them. Theosophy's influence on Mondrian's work changed over time and was most often diffuse, but in *Evolution* it was very specific, as what he was undoubtedly describing was the group's belief that humans have auras containing shapes and colors.[12]

In early 1915, Mondrian interest in Theosophy took a significant turn when he left Domburg and moved to Laren, a picturesque village and sometime artists' colony between Amsterdam and Utrecht, where he remained until 1919. There, he encountered Mathieu Schoenmaekers, a former Catholic priest who was trying to combine elements of Theosophy and Christianity and who called himself a "Christosophist."[13] They met regularly at the home of a farmer's wife, who organized evenings to bring together writers, artists, thinkers, and musicians. Mondrian often brought his work to show Schoenmaekers, who appears to have been unmoved, but terms and ideas that the former priest discussed with Mondrian helped him think about his work in new ways. Schoenmaekers was convinced he himself could reveal the absolute that was underlying the structure of the universe. He encouraged Mondrian to think "in relationships" and find "unity in opposites," to contemplate a vertical life force countered by horizontal gravity.

Schoenmaeskers supplied language Mondrian would borrow: the man spoke of a "plastic mathematics," and that phrase no doubt influenced the artist's later term for his own style, "Neo-Plasticism." Schoenmaekers even encouraged Mondrian's belief in the value of painting, since he believed that abstract ideas needed to be visualized to be understood, and that an object of contemplation was needed for us to be truly present to ourselves.[14] All these ideas undoubtedly fed into Mondrian's thinking and sustained his inquiries, even if he was later skeptical of their larger, religiophilosophical claims.

CHRISTIAN EMIL MARIE KÜPPER was born in Utrecht in 1883. When he was young, he changed his name to Theo van Doesburg, taking the name of his likely biological father, who married his mother several years after he was born. Years later, Van Doesburg suggested to a friend that he might use his original name as a pseudonym. In an article with the byline "Sergeant Christian Emil Marie Küpper," he described "Van Doesburg" as his "battle name" (apparently, a name beginning with "Sergeant" was insufficiently militant).[15] By that stage, he was already going by the name "Pipifox" in some magazine articles, and that name may have replaced another. Sometimes he would be Aldo Camini, "anti-philosopher."[16] When another writer, I. K. Bonset, started contributing poems to Van Doesburg's magazine, *De Stijl*, Mondrian asked if he could meet him. Bonset was allied with Dada, and that wasn't usually to Mondrian's taste, but Bonset was interesting. Could he drop by when he was in Paris? Could he speak at a conference? No, and no. Of course, I. K. Bonset *was* Van Doesburg. The name was probably derived from the Dutch *"Ik ben zot,"* meaning "I am foolish." Mondrian didn't work this out until 1923, by which time he felt pretty foolish and somewhat annoyed.

Impersonation had been one of Van Doesburg's earliest impulses, and he wanted to be an actor before he switched to painting and writing poetry and prose. His parents approved of none of these pursuits, so at age eighteen, he ran away and earned a living making copies of paintings in the Rijksmuseum and giving art lessons. He first came to minor prominence around 1912 as a contributor to *Eenheid*, a weekly journal that one writer described as being aimed at "Theosophists, Freemasons, Rosicrucians, Spiritualists, vegetarians, and teetotalers."[17] Those were growth areas in prewar Holland. They were not of the kind that furnished routes to riches, but Van Doesburg always seemed more motivated by the approval of an audience, and he had an energy and style that was reminiscent of Marinetti. By 1916, he had wholeheartedly embraced modernism, and was finding his way to total abstraction. His paintings began to show a gridded, geometric appearance; they retained a sense of the real world as if seen through a filter. Some of the stained glass he made the following year left that real world behind in favor of a rigid, abstract imagery of colored rectangles. He would only advance, never retreat. Michel Seuphor recalled him as "a strange man, with a narrow face, a keen eye, and much aggressiveness; there was in him something of the bird of prey and the parrot."[18] But Van Doesburg had a fierce self-belief and high hopes, describing himself as "an artist sprung directly out of himself, someone *en route* from an obscure point of departure to an unknown place."[19]

Van Doesburg had done several spells of military service, one as early as 1903, and when the war arrived in 1914, he was mobilized. Holland remained neutral during the conflict, but the nation mustered troops for security and the artist soon found himself near Tilburg, on the border of Belgium, within earshot of the bombardment of Antwerp.[20] With little to occupy him, he fell to thinking and writing. His ideas could be odd, sometimes paradoxical. On the one hand he was nihilistic, seeing the war's destruction as necessary, a "shattering of the image of the world" that was essential if it was to be reborn.[21] On the other, he predicted that the age of militarized war would soon end, to be replaced by a new form of struggle fought on spiritual lines.[22] Art, he sensed, would aid in this transition to spirituality, and ultimately to a state of harmony and perfection. The writing of influential figures like Kandinsky gave some credence to Van Doesburg's belief in the importance of spirituality in the arts. Other writers on abstraction, like the British artist and curator Roger Fry, also spoke of a reality lying behind appearances.[23] Everything was trending in this immaterial direction.

In October 1915, Van Doesburg saw an exhibition of Mondrian's work in Amsterdam, and he began to be convinced that he had found a new pioneer in this immaterial realm. He said it gave him a "purely spiritual" feeling, "one of tranquility, the immobility of the soul."[24] Mondrian and Van Doesburg started corresponding in November 1915, and in February of the following year Van Doesburg came to Laren so the two could meet. As Mondrian wandered the shores in Domburg and Van Doesburg penned articles in Tilburg, their thoughts had run along similar lines. Both wanted to see through the unstable, destructive materiality of the war to something they felt was more spiritual and immaterial—yet which was somehow also more stable, more harmonious, and more real. They believed this spiritual realm might be felt universally, by all humankind, no matter their nationality or allegiance.

By 1917, Mondrian and Van Doesburg were laying plans for a new avant-garde. Mondrian began speaking of his own work as "Neo-Plasticism," but Van Doesburg settled on "Der Stijl" (the Style), and the latter's zeal and energy would ensure that his choice became the most widely accepted term. In early November 1917, Van Doesburg published the first issue of the journal and titled it with that phrase. In it he printed a manifesto in four languages and exhorted artists across the world to "work for the formation of an international unity of Life, Art and Culture." Its first statement of belief reads as follows:

> There is an old and a new consciousness of time.
> The old is connected with the individual.
> The new is connected with the universal.
> The struggle of the individual against the universal is
>   revealing itself in the world-war as well as in the art of
>   the present day.[25]

While some avant-gardes, like Surrealism and Futurism, thrived on close collaboration and a group identity, De Stijl was scattered and disjointed. The original signatories of the manifesto included painters Mondrian, Van Doesburg, and Vilmos Huszár; sculptor Georges Vantongerloo; architects Jan Wils and Robert van 't Hoff;

and poet Antony Kok. Over the ensuing years, other associates would be drawn into the circle, including the architects and designers J. J. Oud and Gerrit Rietveld, and the painter and designer Bart van der Leck. The group was dotted across Holland, some in Laren and Voorburg, others in Utrecht, Tilburg, and The Hague. There was never a meeting at which more than three or four were present simultaneously. They communicated by mail, or through their vital nexus, Van Doesburg. In some sense, when we speak of the movement, we're really speaking only of the journal, because that's the only means through which the group truly came together. When Van Doesburg began to publish it, he hoped to print a thousand copies, but ultimately he printed far fewer, and subscriptions never exceeded two hundred, most of those being friends and acquaintances of the artists involved. The circle remained small, loose, and porous, as it perhaps was intended to be. The editorial in the very first issue of *De Stijl* described the movement as a "spiritual community," though one writer has said that it's clear that the community they imagined never existed.[26]

Three central prewar currents fed the idea of De Stijl. Firstly, there was Futurism. The Italian movement had foundered during the First World War, its numbers depleted by the conflict, and its enthusiasm for violence and technology challenged by the realities of war, but many of its ideas, and in particular its embrace of modernity, remained influential. Marinetti was still alert to developments across Europe and eager to assert himself. When he read the De Stijl manifesto, he recognized one of his own and sent Van Doesburg a packet of books and magazines (the Dutchman was thus anointed).[27] The second ingredient was Cubism, which supplied its formal language, its geometry, and its commitment to abstraction. It's also worth noting how profoundly De Stijl rejected the Expressionism that had been so important before the war. The age of the individual was thought to be over: the universal and the collective would be the future.

Thirdly, there was the legacy of the Arts and Crafts movement.

After reading Van Doesburg's manifesto, it can be difficult to believe that the latter played a part, yet the nineteenth-century reform movement was crucial in shaping attitudes to the place of art in modern life throughout the early part of the century. The Arts and Crafts movement sprang from a current of mid-nineteenth-century thought that was critical of industrial society, of the art and culture and living circumstances it produced as much as the factory conditions it imposed on its workers. From those arguments, developed by the likes of John Ruskin and A. W. N. Pugin, sprang the ideas of William Morris, the writer, designer, artist, and poet, whose high ambition it was to bring change to the whole lived environment. Morris fully understood his ideas to be utopian, and borrowing from understandings of that idea by the early sixteenth-century British statesman, scholar, and Catholic saint, Thomas More, he saw people to be inextricably linked together in a "commonwealth." If one was to bring any real change to people's lives, it was necessary to change the whole of that commonwealth. These were old ideas, yet they took on new resonance in the postwar period, when people throughout Europe and beyond were grappling with what individuals and groups could positively achieve.

William Morris not only denounced the conditions of factory work, he also attacked the products the factories produced. He felt they were badly made and encrusted with ornament—ornament that was often false in the way it sought to disguise the purpose of objects. The solution to both problems, Morris believed, was to return to small workshops, and to reeducate craftspeople in the traditional skills of their trade. In 1861, Morris spearheaded his own effort to bring this about by creating Morris & Co., a long-running and successful venture that produced furniture, wallpaper, fabrics, and stained glass. But although the movement found influential followers, it struggled to reconcile its ambitions for a new mode of craft production with its desire to make the fruit of that work available to all. Morris's dream of good design for the people ultimately meant good design for those who could afford it.

Consequently, architects and designers who emerged in its wake, like Frank Lloyd Wright, would emphasize a greater role for the machine in the reform of design. For Wright, the goal was less the workshop revival of the vernacular than a vision of a better kind of mass production, and a mode of design that would isolate the elemental, raise up the simple and unadorned, and create a language for modern architecture and design that reconciled nature and humanity without harking back to a former age. Indeed, Wright's style, with its muted decoration and stress on plain walls and flat roofs—verticals and horizontals—would feed into De Stijl through his Dutch follower, Hendrik Petrus Berlage, a key figure in the pre-war Amsterdam School of architecture.

The influence of the Arts and Crafts Movement also explains the diversity of the contributors to De Stijl. The avant-gardes often attracted a wide range of talent (Futurism boasted the talented architect Antonio Sant'Elia), but the presence of architects and designers in De Stijl was much more central to its logic and aims. A common theme among Dutch artists was *gemeenschapkunst*, "community-art," and Van Doesburg called for a "monumental collaborative art . . . wherein the different spiritual means of expression (architecture, sculpture, painting, music, and the Word) in harmony—that is, each one gaining by collaboration with another one—shall come to the realization of unity."[28] This notion was only conceivable because, in the 1910s, the aims and language of those various mediums appeared to be converging. So while Mondrian was finding his way to a geometric art through Cubism, the group's future architects and designers were exploring the possibilities of a geometric architecture. Robert van 't Hoff built a villa at Huis ter Heide in Holland in 1916 that seemed to be assembled from rectangles, its low, flat roof crowning grids of windows. In the same period, J. J. Oud completed a project for seaside housing that employed flat roofs and repetitive geometric forms.[29]

What De Stijl promised was less a new direction in art and design than an attempt to guide parallel paths toward convergence.

Convergence would be key to how De Stijl hoped to locate *the* Style. However, Van Doesburg and others realized that none of this could happen immediately. Before they achieved union, the artists needed to locate the common denominators among the arts. Just as Schoenmaekers had taught that timeless universals underlie a changeable reality, so it was plausible to believe that universals underlie the arts. A process of purification would have to be undertaken and a new and fundamental language would have to be revealed. Then, when it was brought to light, a new unification could take place. When it did, the group would have discovered *the* style that could be shared by all and through which all the arts could be harmoniously integrated. Everything could then be absorbed and translated by style. As Van Doesburg once put it, "Nature will become idea, and idea is style."[30]

MONDRIAN WAS ALWAYS GOING to return to Paris. It was only the war that had kept him in the Netherlands. He was saving funds and taking French classes for what he hoped would be a prompt return. Yearning for the city life once more, he also took dance lessons. Finally, in the early summer of 1919, he was ready to leave. Van Doesburg was doing the same, having decided it was "impossible to breathe any new life in Holland," and the two met briefly in Amsterdam before going their separate ways.[31] Mondrian's journey to Paris seemed auspicious: he ran into one of his collectors on the train, who bought him dinner and, on arrival in the French capital, put him up for the night at his hotel. Soon enough, Mondrian was back in his old studio on the rue du Départ. It was blanketed in dust, but it was bigger than he remembered and his rent was the same. The roar of the trains from the Gare Montparnasse reminded him that he was back in the city.[32]

During the early days of his return to Paris, Mondrian would edge ever closer to his signature style. He moved from paintings with soft colors and regular modular grids to the distinctive palette and composition of his mature work. From this time, until he moved to New York in 1940, he would paint in planes of primary color (blue, yellow, and red), "noncolor" (white, black, and gray), and black lines. His aim was to lend each element a powerful and distinct intensity while combining them in a whole in which none dominates the other. For Mondrian, conventional, naturalistic paintings established hierarchies of importance, with some things in the background, others in the foreground, some centered, others marginalized. But his Neo-Plasticism would remove these hierarchies by situating all the elements so that they oppose each other: the planes of primary color opposing the areas of white, black, or gray; the verticals opposing the horizontals. If this was achieved there would be a quality of balance and, as he put it, "repose." The universal laws of art would be revealed, and along with them those of a future society:[33] harmony, equilibrium, and freedom in multiple dimensions—material, social, political, spiritual. And when society made those transformations and achieved a similar balance, art would fall away, finally unnecessary.[34]

The ideas that animated Mondrian's art can seem distant from their result, particularly when you're merely glancing at the pictures. They seem too vague to explain either the detailed decisions behind the compositions or how the art might connect with larger social ambitions. Yet, as ever with difficult work like this, looking at them long and hard can help. One feels the concrete world drop away, and in its place a series of simple, fundamental propositions asserts itself. Whatever esoteric ideas drew Mondrian to Theosophy, no code is necessary to decipher these pictures because they do appear to speak a universal language, of up and down, line and plane, openness and closure, light and darkness.

The simplicity itself is persuasive as a foundation for a new society. The elements in the pictures are not arbitrarily arranged: they are not a series of random arrangements of harmony. When the pictures are placed in the sequence in which they were made, we can see Mondrian working through different formal problems, trying out how different parts of the image might be managed. The fundamental ideas informing these pictures also shifted. In the 1930s, he put aside the quest for "repose" in favor of establishing "dynamic equilibrium."[35] At that point we see the lines in the pictures asserting themselves more powerfully against the planes of color, sometimes animating the canvases without any color at all. And when he arrived in New York in the 1940s he would talk of seeking "mutual oppositions," and then he would seek to do away with lines entirely.

Painting was highly valued among the ranks of De Stijl, but in some sense that was only because it was considered to be the medium closest to architecture, and therefore the medium most likely to be successfully integrated with it. It was the easiest to purify and distill, and therefore the most likely to disappear into architecture. Once that had been achieved, other art forms would follow. Ultimately, artists would integrate every aspect of the ordinary house, exterior and interior, "right down to the writing paper."[36] Mondrian generated some ambitious and eccentric plans for this integration. He loved music, and at one point he decided that the modern world needed some kind of fusion of jazz and classical (he believed the waltz had "round lines," whereas the new age called for straight ones). This new form of music would be based on three tones and three nontones, which would be analogous to the color palette of three primaries plus black, white, and gray. "Music as art will come to an end," Mondrian confidently predicted. "The beauty of sounds around us—purified, ordered, brought to the new harmony—will be satisfying."[37] He even had an idea for a new kind of dance hall entertainment, with a meandering audience and repeat performances of music in a hall decorated with neo-plastic paintings.[38] And then there was dance: One Dutch critic recalled meeting Mondrian in a ballroom full of dancing couples and asking him how he would represent the scene. "Well," he replied, "I would abstract it into vertical and horizontal lines." In another interview, the painter remarked that "dances like the tango and foxtrot reveal something of the new idea of equilibrium through opposition."[39] The foxtrot seemed particularly promising since it encouraged the dancers to place their feet parallel to each other, rather than facing outward, and the attention to lines pleased Mondrian.

The notion of some consummate, singular style makes it sound as if the goal of De Stijl was a kind of aesthetic victory in the realm of fine art, the latest fashion to end all latest fashions. Instead, however, Van Doesburg wanted it to deliver the absolute end of art. Art couldn't be fixed, he complained, and the effort to produce so much of it had led to the neglect of life: "Art has poisoned our life," he complained. It was everywhere, in "post-cards, stamps, pouches, railway-tickets, pots, umbrellas, towels, pajamas, chairs, blankets, handkerchiefs and ties. How much more refreshing are those articles which are not called art: bathrooms, bath-tubs, bicycles, automobiles, engine-rooms and flat-irons."[40] Art must end, Van Doesburg declared, instead life must be paramount.

/

I WAS IN A REALLY GOOD MOOD when I got home from the library that day—books had been read, ideas had sprung forth, even a few words were typed. And my wife had barely walked in the door when I was telling her that Mondrian had painted abstractions on his studio walls.

"Wild, yeah?" I said. "I didn't know he did that. But he just covered the studio with rectangles."

She put down her keys.

"I mean, we could do that," I went on. "I could work out how he did it and turn our apartment into a Neo-Plastic utopia!"

She looked at me.

"It would be great for the book, we'd actually be recreating an avant-garde interior! Mondrian's actual studio! Crazy!"

"I'm just going to get changed," she said. "Okay?" And she walked off.

I'd been in the height of enthusiasm for De Stijl for a few weeks by this point, and things at home were already on their way to Neo-Plasticism, albeit in a more modest way: I had recently bought my wife a pair of socks woven with a design from Mondrian's paintings, and she did seem quite genuinely happy with them. A fully Neo-Plastic interior was maybe a big step, but in my defense, Mondrian's rue du Départ studio is a legend. It was not only the place where he painted some of his greatest canvases, it was also the place where he first began to pursue the logic of De Stijl and radically transformed the interior to unite painting and architecture.

It was on the third floor of a building with a crumbling courtyard. In the recollection of Michel Seuphor, who was a frequent visitor, to find it you had to labor up a dank, foul-smelling staircase, past dirty windows and "a dark hole: the water closet." For the last few steps, you were plunged into darkness:

> Then everything changed. The room was quite large, very bright, with a very high ceiling. Mondrian had divided it irregularly, utilizing for this purpose a large, black-painted cupboard, which was partially hidden by an easel long out of service; the latter was covered with big gray and white pasteboards.... He had two large wicker armchairs, also painted white, and, on the scrupulously clean floor, two rugs, one red, the other gray.[41]

I don't think I read Seuphor's description too closely, but then I was just too excited to get started. I had assumed that what Mondrian had done in his studio was to extend his paintings onto the walls, and that he'd done that in simple, predictable, and wholly pleasing ways. So, perhaps a rectangle of yellow bled off the canvas to fill a huge sunny expanse across one wall, and a sliver of red moved out diagonally to bloom on the ceiling. Black lines would arrow out of the canvas to encompass the room in dynamic movement. A neo-plastic interior with a neo-plastic palette. So, I assumed, I could copy a Mondrian, I could mock up one of his simple frames, and I could make my own freestyle extensions. It was going to be, like, totally harmonic.

But I hit a problem when I got back to the library a few days later. I found at first only black-and-white images of his old Paris studio, and when I found color images that some diligent researcher had constructed, I saw that things weren't as predictable as I'd hoped, nor so charming. There were some gray rectangles in weird places, and canvases shoved together, and bits of square mirror; even the furniture and the windows played a part. I realized that I wasn't going to be able to make these larger changes without risking marital breakdown, and besides, by that time my determination to create my own neo-plastic utopia had gotten far ahead of me. I had purchased paint samples, I had rejected some reds, splashed some yellows on the wall.

I decided I would keep it simple. I was going to reproduce *Composition C*, from 1935. A large square of red stood sentry on the left-hand corner above a sliver of yellow and another square of blue. Black lines divided them and carved out a channel of white through the middle. But then I had to contend with the dining-room table, and I decided that if the red was not to overpower the wall, I would have to invert the design. Was anyone really going to notice? I made calculations. I discovered that the wall wasn't as square as I'd thought. I fudged it. I made calculations, laid down masking tape, levered open some tins of paint, and set to work.

I don't have the space here to look at the intricate decisions that Mondrian made in modifying his studio, but it's fair to say that the whole has an appearance of an unfinished experiment, of thought in process.[42] While he had some sophisticated ideas about architecture, ones that were informed by current debates, they remained more theoretical than those of the architects in the group, like those of Oud. Some critics also find them somewhat contradictory or unworkable, and in a certain way they were hostile to architecture itself. Mondrian's theory was premised on an opposition to separation of any kind: painting might be extended into architecture to unite interiors, but architecture itself still established separation with the environment around it, and therefore it needed to be dissolved into "architecture-as-environment." Elements that separated themselves were "things," and they needed to go. They claimed their own individuality against the needs of the whole—they stuck out, in other words. "Unique beauty is the opposite of what characterizes things as things," Mondrian announced.[43]

The more persuasive efforts at integration came from the group's architects and designers. However, those took a while to appear, partly because of the caution of the architects, who understandably had more to lose than the painters in risking a bold new style on large commissions. In the group's early years, Oud was their most significant architect, but when, age only twenty-eight, he was named Rotterdam's city architect, he pulled back from the group and he would sign none of their manifestoes or petitions.[44] The architect and designer who brought about the most successful version of De Stijl was Gerrit Rietveld. He found his calling after he started working in his father's furniture workshop at age twelve, and in 1917, when he was in his late twenties, he established his own. It was not long afterward that he created one of his most famous designs, the *Red/Blue Chair* (1917–18). It consisted of a long, red, rectangular back, a blue rectangular seat, and a grid of black struts to supply legs and arms. All the elements appear to float independently of one another. It looks as if Rietveld had anticipated Mondrian's mature style and applied it directly to design. It was a unique, handmade object, yet in its geometry, simplicity, and rationalization, it had all the appearance of a prototype for machine production. What Rietveld wanted above all was less a seat than a lucid articulation of form, space, and volume.

It was only the beginning, and by 1923 he was working on the most famous example of De Stijl architecture, the Schröder House in Utrecht. He first worked with the client, Truus Schröder, when she asked him to refurbish an apartment she shared with her husband, Fritz, and their three children. Fritz was a lawyer, and the family lived above his offices—but not happily, as the two regularly argued. Fritz was a Catholic, but Truus had broken with the faith, and they quarreled over how they would raise their children. Hoping to appease his wife during one of these difficult spells, Fritz encouraged her to rearrange the apartment in the manner of her choosing, and so she engaged Rietveld.

The architect couldn't change Truus's circumstances, but he could bring a new sense of freedom to her daily life. To open up the space, he moved a dining table from the center of the main room to the edges; he made the hearth less obtrusive; he allowed for diffuse lighting, and he applied simple blocks of color to the walls. These might sound like cosmetic gestures, but they suggested liberation from the conventions of traditional domestic life. The dining table was where the patriarch was given his throne, the hearth was that symbol of the home as refuge, which his wife was supposed to maintain. Schröder was thrilled with the changes. Soon after, she divorced Fritz and commissioned Rietveld to build her a house. This time, the architect gave her something much more striking that, still situated today at the end of a dull row of suburban housing, stands out as an extraordinary formal play of lines and layered rectangles, each element sharply distinguished in color and shape from its neighbor.

The parallel with Mondrian's painting is striking: there is none of the symmetry that ruled traditional Beaux Arts buildings in the nineteenth century; instead the entirely asymmetrical ensemble seems to be held together in a dynamic tension. Inside, the design is equally striking, and elements of it may have been suggested by Schröder herself, particularly the open plan live/work area on the second floor, with its built-in furniture. By day, the space was wide open and afforded views over what then was flat countryside (today the view is sadly obscured by a highway). By night, partitions could be moved to create private bedrooms. In explaining the design, the architectural historian William Curtis points to the importance of

Rietveld's work as a furniture maker, and likens the whole to an intricate cabinet.[45] It is perhaps the closest the group came to their dreamt-of "total work of art," one in which all the elements are seamlessly integrated and consistent expressions of the same idea.

AT THE OUTSET OF THE 1920S, Mondrian and Van Doesburg were broadly aligned in their beliefs, and things looked promising as the former headed to Paris and the latter began what would be an odyssey around Europe, lecturing and agitating for their movement. Like Marinetti before him, Van Doesburg became less a man than a phenomenon. When he arrived to give a lecture in Barcelona, the crowd stood and chanted, "Doesburg! Doesburg!" In the process, he attracted some key figures to the group, like the Russian artist El Lissitzky, whose involvement formalized the kinship between De Stijl's technological utopianism and that being pursued in Russia. A more surprising entrant was Hans Richter, an artist whose association with Dada should have put him at odds with De Stijl's rationalism, yet whose openness to its ideas shows how persuasive Van Doesburg could be, and indeed how varied were the ideas and personalities within Dada itself by the 1920s.

Key to De Stijl's international success was the way Van Doesburg used it to draw together ideas that were current in a diverse range of other styles. But he was also touting a popular idea in postwar Europe, that of rebuilding the world in spiritual as well as in concrete terms. As the 1920s wore on, with Communism gaining ground in Russia and capitalism recovering in the West, the political landscape seemed to offer opposing routes to achieving it. In that situation, De Stijl could seem all the more persuasive as a neutral middle ground, a technocratic approach in an age of political polarization.[46]

The critic Reyner Banham captures some of the movement's appeal when he writes of its "inexplicable mystique."[47] It had the power to draw together somewhat ineffable ideas and become a rallying point for all those who shared an interest in universalism, abstraction, and machine production. In doing so it would advance what would be a long-running ambition in midcentury art to transcend easel painting and create a modern, abstract art in the public realm. We can see those aims shaping the vogue for geometric abstraction that swept Latin America in the postwar years. De Stijl held out the consoling ideas that underlying all the conflict and turmoil in the world lay some unshakable fundamentals from which to rebuild. Indeed, one can see the appeal of this in Mondrian's life: the First World War had kept him in Holland when he wanted to be in France, and then the Second World War sent him away once again. He fled Paris in 1938 "without thought of return"; arriving in England he announced, "I'm on my way to America," where he arrived in October 1940.[48] Persisting throughout all this change, all this political and culture shock as he moved from place to place, was his art and its style.[49] In an upturned world, only "the new spirit is characterized by certainty," Mondrian wrote in the sixth issue of the *De Stijl* journal, "it does not question, it offers a solution. Human consciousness ... expresses itself in art in such a way that—by creating equilibrium—it excludes every question."[50]

Unfortunately, the new world would also have to contend with egos and their rivalries. The broad, collaborative nature of De Stijl's project made those nearly inevitable from the beginning. Since the group's official doctrine made all the visual arts subservient to architecture, a number of painters were not happy taking orders from architects. Bart van der Leck even left the group when he found out there were architects involved, and he claimed he had been deceived into joining in the first place.[51] Tensions like this quickly eroded the membership, and by 1922 many of the core Dutch group had officially left, including Vantongerloo, van 't Hoff, Oud, and Kok. Soon after, De Stijl consisted of little more than Van Doesburg, his aliases, and whoever he could summon up to write for its journal.

It didn't help that, for all his galvanizing energy, Van Doesburg was quarrelsome and inclined to cause rifts. In some sense he was at war with himself and the various apparently conflicting ideas he advanced under his different pseudonyms. But Mondrian, his great discovery, was a particular focus of irritation as the years passed. He accused his friend of dogmatism and apostacy. One lingering argument was the use of diagonals. Around 1918, inspired perhaps by religious or theosophical ideas, Mondrian had proposed their use, and he created a few "lozenge" paintings that hung on the wall in a diamond shape. At the time, Van Doesburg had been opposed, arguing that they would disrupt the natural perpendicular lines of architecture. Later, however, they seemed to swap positions. Van Doesburg decided that verticals and horizontals merely reflected the increasing mechanization of the world—not its underlying spirituality. The spirit cried out against these conditions, and so painting should express that urge with oppositions, and therefore with diagonals.[52]

Their arguments were arcane, and at some level, the pair recognized that themselves. The source of their final breakup, in the mid-1920s, was more a matter of personalities than anything else. Things deteriorated. Mondrian wrote a text for the magazine in which he tried to excuse himself for the dozens of pretty flower paintings he had recently produced to pay the bills; below it, Van Doesburg added a note: "The editors decline all responsibility for the statement."[53] On another occasion, Van Doesburg accused Mondrian of intercepting his mail. Finally, "I. K. Bonset" authored a poem titled "Saint-Peter of the Straight Line," in which Mondrian was mocked both for his interest in Theosophy and for the fact that he wasn't getting any sex.[54]

What all this concealed was the uncomfortable fact that one after the other, Mondrian and Van Doesburg were concluding that the grand project of De Stijl, to distill a single modern style for all the arts and thus to end art itself, could not be achieved. Mondrian decided that the world wasn't ready for it: the prevailing state of technology and the economic conditions made it impossible. By 1922, he could write that "what was achieved in art must for the present be limited to art. Our external environment cannot yet be realized as the pure plastic expression of harmony."[55] At first, Van Doesburg couldn't accept this impossibility, but not long afterward, he seems to have come to the same conclusion.[56] As he became more interested in technology, he saw the world as dynamic, ever moving, and in a world of such constant transformation, it was going to be impossible to locate a stable universal. Moreover, mass production was going to do much more to shape the object world than a mystical universal ever could.

Van Doesburg once complained that, for the Theosophists, spirituality was an abstract concept; the proper task was to integrate it into reality. Yet, De Stijl could not achieved this merger. Spirituality remained something just out of grasp. In 1927, Van Doesburg wrote a manifesto for a new endeavor called Elementarism. He prefaced it by saying that it was needed to correct dogmatic ideas (and everyone would have known whose those were). And in his final comments he said that the artist's studio should resemble a medical laboratory with the thin atmosphere of high mountains where cold kills microbes. Perhaps a higher spirituality, purity, harmony could be achieved, if only the conditions were right. But by that time, the difficult conditions were not just in the world but in Van Doesburg's body. His dream of a mountain studio was a dream for his own better health. Finally, hay fever developed into severe asthma, and he died of a heart attack in Davos, Switzerland, in March 1931, at the age of forty-seven.

/

THE ARC OF MY OWN SMALL PURSUIT of De Stijl was somewhat briefer and more tentative than the group's leaders, but it, too, ended in disappointment. I let paint dry; I smoothly removed masking tape; I applied more tape and, with it, new coats of color.

It was looking nice. Meanwhile, I gave some thought to the rest of the room, and I tidied up a bit. Mondrian said it was okay to own stuff, even stuff that was curved, so long as you could put it away, and I did my best. He also said in the Neo-Plastic interior, non-Neo-Plastic pictures would have to be turned toward the wall, so as not to be, I suppose, "things." One step at a time, I told myself.

Meanwhile, it was summertime, and it was hot. I was in the habit of opening windows throughout the apartment, and I began to notice, approvingly, how they were broad rectangular panels of glass that I was moving back and forth. I threw them open, eager to further dissolve architecture, to be radically open. It was noble, by day, but then at night couples returning from local nightclubs would pause to have ugly arguments outside my window. When they had passed, the trash collectors arrived with a grinding roar of machinery and breaking glass. Opening up the studio to the world may have made sense to Mondrian, but he wasn't living in Queens.

While all this was playing out, my wife started to sport her Mondrian socks on a regular rotation. There was a family dinner discussion of Neo-Plasticism. A child asked if we were going to have a totally neo-plastic apartment. My wife paused with her fork in the air. "No," I said, "Wouldn't it be great?! But it's too much work." Her fork resumed its journey to her mouth.

When the work was done, and all the masking tape was removed, and the dining table was back in its place against the wall, I sat on the sofa and looked at it. I decided that I liked the color, the dynamism, but I was troubled. It looked daft. I couldn't decide whether I had radically opened up the space or just put kitsch on my walls, some dead, congealed, and hollowed-out sign. Sometimes pictures die for you. Whole styles and languages of art can do that when they are reproduced again and again, and when they proliferate outside the museum. Certain works by Monet and Van Gogh can feel dead, and maybe Jackson Pollock's entire late style. It's possible to wind the clock back and see all this afresh, but it takes work, it takes careful looking. I decided that was what I was going to have to do with Mondrian. I could make him live again.

Meanwhile, however, my wife would be wearing her socks, and I was starting to notice Mondrian in other places. He was on shirts, shoes, bags, throw pillows, water bottles, board games, blankets, mugs, aprons, necklaces, cabinets, men's briefs, and earrings. Mondrian—or some empty and generic "Mondrian"—has become his own really bad universal. This isn't entirely new, since Van Doesburg was complaining about it in his own time. What irked him was embellishment, but what has brought about the tidal wave of Mondrian kitsch is a new moment in the commercialization of art. It is, if you like, art's revenge against those who would seek to kill it, and it is a high irony that the style of artists so committed to ending art should end up appearing everywhere as some empty sign of taste and refinement.

But the world of art and design is much more commodified than it was in the day of De Stijl, and it deals in brands and co-branding, signs of prestige and status that have little to do with the objects they decorate. In such a world, it's easier to imagine Louis Vuitton or IKEA as the magicians of a total environment than it is to envision some brandless utopian language showing the way.

SEVEN

The School, the Cathedral, and the Whitewashed Die

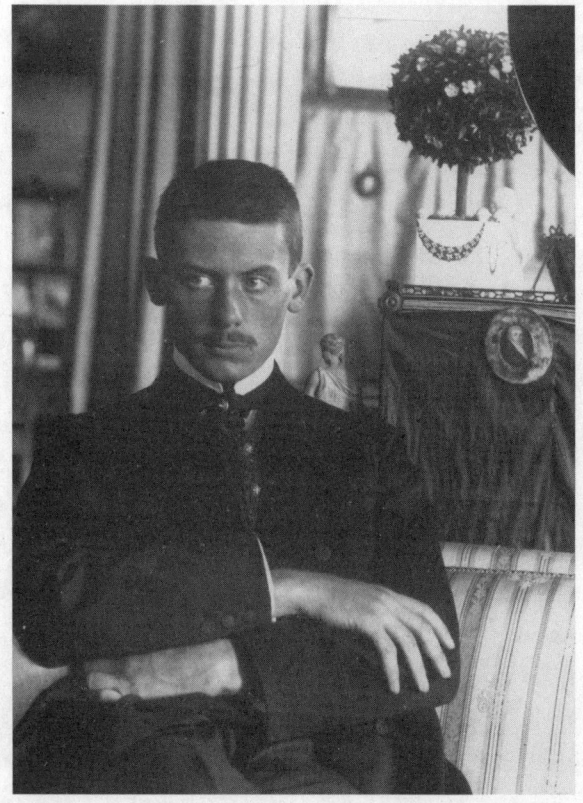

Walter Gropius, ca. 1903

A SSIGNED TO FIELD RECONNAISSANCE DUTIES IN the mountains of Alsace in fall 1914, Sergeant Major Walter Gropius of the 9th Wandsbeck Hussars would ride about on horseback trying to establish the location of French positions. On one occasion, he was sent to clear the way for machine guns. He clambered up a thickly wooded hill and looked out over the valley near Senones. Finding it clear, he posted sentries and proceeded on his way, bellying up another slope nearby. Here, he was stopped short. The valley of the Meurthe stretched out before him, and its roads were packed with Allied troops. Shots came from the bushes and forced him back. He returned, only to be fired on once again. Not long after, he was woken in the night and sent to do reconnaissance near Celles. Moving through a forest, he was confronted by French troops hiding in the darkness. The Germans moved their horses to safety and advanced. Eighty men were lost within an hour, and Gropius was left to lead those remaining, dug in among the trees, for the rest of the day. The following night, he led an infantry troop almost straight into the enemy's positions, and they were fired on and spent the rest of the night in pouring rain. Weeks passed. He was sent to retake a hilltop position. He and his men fought their way up the hill over four days and nights, until a mortar exploded in front of Gropius, covered him in earth, and rendered him unconscious for several minutes. On another occasion, an officer was shot in the heart in front of him. Another day, a shot flew through his cap; bullets would later lodge in his shoe and his coat. Finally, in June 1918, he was buried in debris when a German stronghold collapsed. He was the only one among the group to survive. He breathed the air that filtered down a flue into the rubble and lay there in darkness for three days, shouting for help until by chance he was found.

When the war ended a few months later, Gropius said that it came upon him, "as in a flash of lightning," that "the old stuff was out."[1]

/

WEIMAR HAD A REPUTATION as a quiet, cultured, aristocratic city. It was the capital of the grand duchy of Saxe-Weimar Eisenbach. It was renowned as a poet's city, "the German Athens," once the home of Goethe and Schiller. Bach and Liszt had both lived and worked there; Nietzsche had died there in 1900. When Gropius arrived early in 1919, Weimar still had a medieval character, with winding streets and pretty squares, a castle, and a marketplace surrounded by houses with high-pitched gable roofs.[2] The population had doubled in the last fifty years, but little had changed over that time. It was conservative—chauvinistic, some thought—and while it usually appealed only to tourists, its quiet reputation recommended it from the turmoil gripping Berlin, some 170 miles away, in the months after the war. Kaiser Wilhelm II had abdicated, unrest had followed, and to avoid the fighting Germany's constituent assembly relocated to Weimar and declared the nation a republic.

Gropius was only thirty-five when he moved to the city, yet he was already a widely recognized architect. He had been born into Berlin's comfortable bourgeoisie in 1883, and into a family that had long and impressive associations with architecture. His great-grandfather had been close to the great early nineteenth-century architect Karl Friedrich Schinkel. His great-uncle was Martin Gropius, who ran one of the largest architectural firms in the city. And Walter's father had had thwarted ambitions in the same field. Gropius himself had a relatively brief training in architecture, and one that was split between short periods in technical schools and practical experience in architects' offices. His most consequential early work was in the office of Peter Behrens, one of Germany's most versatile and influential architects and designers, a man committed to the union of art and industry. Gropius described himself as nothing more than Behrens's "factotum," yet that understates his personal friendship with the man. By the age of twenty-seven, Walter Gropius had established his own office.

He had been shy, withdrawn, and correct as a young man. He had a plain appearance, a prominent nose, and protruding ears. When he was younger, he wore a moustache. Later, he shaved it off and combed his short hair forward into a thick, imposing fringe that disguised his thinning hair.

But success in work gave him confidence to disregard whatever other shortcomings he might have worried about. He developed sophistication and charisma, so much so that, just as he was opening his office, he began a long love affair with Alma Mahler, the socialite and wife of the composer Gustav, a liaison that opened up to him the world of Viennese high society. They met in 1910 at a fashionable clinic in the Styrian Mountains. He was there to relax after opening his office, she didn't seem to want to be there at all, but they fell in love immediately, and a few years after Gustav's death, they married. Although Gropius was likely tolerant, Alma Mahler's waywardness was probably too much for him. During their relationship, she also had an extended affair with the painter Oskar Kokoschka, which she described as "one fierce battle of love."[3] She had had affairs with the painter Gustav Klimt, with Mahler's doctor, with an eminent experimental biologist, with another composer, and with Arnold Schoenberg's music instructor. Alma liked sophisticated company, and when Gropius introduced her to his mother, a somewhat stolid example of Berlin's bourgeoisie, things went badly. Gropius's biographer, Fiona MacCarthy, dates the decline of their relationship from that point. Their union would bring them a daughter, Manon, who was named after Gropius's mother, who died in her teens. The couple divorced five years after marrying.

Gropius was prominent enough by the time of the First World War that, in the middle of it, he was summoned from the front to meet government officials about running a new art school in Weimar. Henry van der Velde, a Belgian architect, had been the director of the Kunstgewerbeschule, the Grand Ducal School of the Arts and Crafts, but when he was forced out, he suggested Gropius as a replacement. With that opportunity confirmed, Gropius then lobbied to be made director of the Hochschule für Bildende Kunst, the Weimar Academy of Art, and for the two schools to be amalgamated. He won that as well, and when his appointment began, on April, 1, 1919, it was as director of the new entity that we know today as the Bauhaus.

/

THE BAUHAUS WAS NOT AVANT-GARDE in the conventional sense. It wasn't a coherent movement; it wasn't a dispersed network of like-minded souls. It was an art school. But it came to represent an institutionalization of the avant-garde. Gropius staffed it with legends of the art world: Kandinsky, painters Paul Klee and Joseph Albers, architect Ludwig Mies van der Rohe, multifaceted artist László Moholy-Nagy, and designer Lilly Reich. The Bauhaus would produce legends too: among its students were artists, architects, and designers like Marcel Breuer, Anni Albers, Marianne Brandt, and Herbert Bayer. The Bauhaus pursued a similar quest to that of the De Stijl group, and it borrowed substantially from Arts and Crafts ideas. It deserves a place in these pages because it faced the same questions about the validity of fine art as did other avant-garde movements in the period.

We tend to remember the Bauhaus as one of the most important origin points of modern industrial design; the building Gropius designed for the Dessau campus of the school, in 1925–26, has become synonymous with it. It's a confident arrangement of connected rectangles, a building with the aspect of a manifesto, one that seems to argue that a school can be like a factory, and creativity can be utterly logical. But the Bauhaus did not start out like this; it didn't even seem to start in a spirit of confidence. It opened in Germany in the wake of the abdication of the Kaiser and a failed revolution, and in that same year Gropius had these thoughts on the place that he and others might occupy in this shaken world:

> Today's artist lives in an era of dissolution without guidance. He stands alone. The old forms are in ruins, the

benumbed world is shaken up, the old human spirit is invalidated and in flux towards a new form. We float in space and cannot perceive the new order.

Gropius must have been surprised to find himself writing such words because before the war he seemed to know exactly what place the artist had, and that was at the center of a modernizing society. The kinds of beliefs he held during those years can perhaps be summed up in those of the German writer and architect Hermann Muthesius. He shared the beliefs of figures like William Morris, that good design had a moral power to shape people's lives, that there was integrity in the honest use of materials and the frank expression of function, but he was certain that these ideals could be realized through mass production. Muthesius believed that the artist should not strive for pure expression, as the Expressionists had contended, or hone craft skills, as the Arts and Crafts Movement believed; instead, the artist should create "type forms," prototypes for industrial design, for building, or even for urban planning.[4] In the years leading up to the war, this goal had taken on the tenor of a nationalist campaign to modernize Germany. The artist was a mediator, in other words, bringing creativity to the needs of industry. Architecture and technology could work together, and Gropius came to believe that by working alongside wealthy, enlightened clients, designers like him could bring change to German society.

The war shook Gropius's faith in all of that, and it made him look toward some eccentric ideas. Some of the most remarkable were those of Bruno Taut. Prior to the war, the German architect and theorist had been a proponent of glass architecture, and he had designed a prismatic glass dome for an exhibition in Cologne, a structure that resembled a flower ready to bloom. A pacifist, the war only confirmed his belief in the necessity of such work, and in 1919 he produced a series of bizarre watercolors titled *Alpine Architecture* that advocated that mankind should set to work establishing crystalline temples in the mountain peaks and launching glass satellites into space. Here the earth's population would live in peaceful anarchy in a natural world free of sickness and sorrow. He had also worked on designs for a huge garden city for three million inhabitants, at the center of which would be a *Stadtkrone* (City Crown), a towering crystal building consisting of a single, symbolic glass room.

When Gropius set out to establish the Bauhaus, he hoped to collaborate with Taut. It never came to pass, but Taut's spiritualized quest for utopian community strongly marked the first iteration of the school. Gropius hoped it would be more than a mere school, that it would give rise to a new *Siedlung*, a settlement with public buildings, theaters, music venues, and "as culmination, a house of worship."[5] It's striking that Gropius, a man who never showed any significant religious engagement, should feel it so important that his new community would have a religious space. It's symptomatic of the widespread interest in unconventional modes of spirituality that gained strength after the war, but it was also a revival of the Arts and Crafts Movement's interest in the "great building" as an envelope in which all the arts were united. Gropius believed that painting, sculpture, and architecture were once united in the "great building," but had since become separated and siloed. And in two statements that Gropius published in 1919, and which are now taken to be the school's manifesto, he argued that the Bauhaus would heal that separation and revive lost craft traditions, and in so doing would end "arrogant class divisions between artisans and artists."

All these are notions that William Morris could have endorsed. Gropius had left behind his prewar faith in industry and the taste of the German elite, and he had taken refuge in a purer version of Arts and Crafts ideals. Gropius had a vision that teachers and students would "desire, conceive, and create the new building of the future," one that would unite "architecture and sculpture and painting." Lyonel Feininger, Gropius's first faculty hire in Weimar, provided a woodcut to illustrate this imagined building, and it is a gothic cathedral. Again that echoes nineteenth-century ideals of how communities should be anchored and bound together. Yet aspects of the way Gropius and Feininger represented this building point to more contemporary sources. Feininger's image shows the building enmeshed in vaulting bands of lines, and Gropius evoked a day when it would "rise towards heaven as the crystalline symbol of a new and coming faith."[6] Taut's vision, and Feininger's, were one.

The teaching at the Bauhaus was not entirely new as it did borrow ideas that were increasingly common in arts education in the prewar period. The influence of the Arts and Crafts Movement had already substantially changed the way teaching was approached in schools of applied art, and Gropius maintained many of those practices. The Bauhaus would stress workshop craft skills and the study of materials. Gropius was skeptical that any schools could teach the skills necessary to create great art, an opinion that has endured in art schools up to this day, but he was insistent that students maintain high ambitions for their work—they were not to think of themselves as *mere* craftspeople. So, while he arranged teaching around a system of workshops that focused on particular media (sculpture, metalwork, woodwork, and so forth), he determined that they would have two leaders, a *formmeister* (form master) and a *handwerksmeister* (master craftsman), who—in theory at least—would enjoy equal status.

There was one entirely new element in the Bauhaus's teaching, and that was the *Vorkurs*, or Preliminary Course. Gropius believed that, in addition to training in craft skills, the students needed an introduction to modern theories of color, form, and materials. This fundamentally broke with older divisions between fine and applied arts because in the Preliminary Course all objects were equal in the quest to analyze and understand them. In shunning the old conventions and models of academic teaching, it was also in step with the postwar desire to start anew. The course became the defining feature of Bauhaus teaching, a requisite for every student, and one that, after beginning in fall 1920, was maintained throughout the school's lifetime.

In its early years, the Preliminary Course was led by one of the dominant personalities in the early Bauhaus, Johannes Itten. He had won some renown for opening his own art school and been drawn into the orbit of Alma Mahler, Arnold Schoenberg, and the modernist architect Adolf Loos. Mahler said he had a "finely modelled face" and an "eloquent, somewhat Egyptian mouth."[7] He was certainly charismatic, as no less than sixteen students followed him from his painting school in Vienna and enrolled at the Bauhaus, and others soon became his devoted adherents too. Itten became more than a teacher at the Bauhaus; he was something approaching a cult leader. He was an adherent of Mazdaznanism, a belief system that bears comparison with Theosophy, not least in its eclecticism, since it borrowed from Christianity, Hinduism, and Zoroastrianism (the ancient pre-Islamic religion of the Middle East). Like Theosophy, it was also a recent creation of the United States, having been founded in New York in 1902 by a German-American typographer who called himself Dr. O. Z. A. Ha'nish. It was monotheistic, holding faith in Mazda, the good creator, and seeing man's purpose as to make the earth a fitting place for God to dwell. It attracted fewer adherents than Theosophy, but its teachings on lifestyle and diet and on the importance of breathing exercises made some of its practices influential, and Itten was fully committed to them. He shaved his head (under Mazdaznan, hair was associated with sin) and wore a long robe and sandals. He advocated a vegetarian diet and a demanding regime of purging, which was effected by fasting and enemas. Further purifications were carried out by puncturing the skin and anointing the body with oil so that the wounds would let forth imagined impurities. The miseries of this were not enough to discourage followers among the students; one reported "months of torment and itching." The men shaved their heads in emulation of their Master; the women were encouraged to wear short hair and short skirts. Itten felt that his followers among the women "radiated true serenity," but in truth all his followers looked bad, felt bad, and smelled bad.[8]

Itten encouraged them to eat a dish of garlic-flavored mush, and one recalled his skin appearing gray or green.[9]

Taking advantage of the disorganization in the school's early years, Itten effectively assumed responsibility for admitting students, and one remembered an interview process in which he was led into empty, whitewashed room decorated with nothing other than a huge wooden cross:

> On a simple iron bedstead sat a haggard young man in a monk's habit. His cheeks were hollow, his eyes burned feverishly ... The young man looked me over while my companion stood in respectful silence, then he said something in an ecstatic singing voice and nodded. He had seen none of my drawings and barely heard me utter a word but I had passed the test and was accepted.[10]

Itten advocated meditation, and prior to his classes students had to go through a routine of gymnastics and controlled breathing. "You must loosen up," he demanded, "get really loose."[11] Before drawing circles, they had to *experience* the circle, had to swing their arms; if they drew tigers, they must roar.[12] And all these preparations were followed by a series of rapid drawing exercises intended to enliven the mind and the senses. This may all sound somewhat childish, but Itten had started life as an elementary schoolteacher, and the course echoed advanced ideas in children's education about the importance of play as a tool in learning. Some students even designed toys. Much of the teaching focused on studying contrasts—thick/thin, long/short, rough/smooth, transparent/opaque, and so forth.[13] And at a time when abstract art had barely emerged from the studios of the most advanced artists, students at the Bauhaus were encouraged to pursue these inquiries by creating abstract compositions in a variety of forms, including reliefs, charcoal drawings, and collages.

Another significant influence on the early Bauhaus was the

Expressionism that had been such a powerful force in German culture since at least Kandinsky's days in Munich.[14] Itten was also important in this regard since he stressed typically Expressionist notions like form and feeling, instinct and empathy. Students would put aside the old conventions of academic teaching, the long sessions of life drawing and copying from the Masters, and they would let instinctive feeling guide their experiments with natural materials and abstract forms. In this way, it was thought, they would give expression to their own deepest feelings while connecting to buried collective beliefs. Rather as Kandinsky's synesthesia had strengthened his belief in connections between feelings and forms, so Itten taught that abstract form could be powerfully expressive.

Some sense of Itten's teaching is provided by the so-called the African Chair, which is the earliest surviving piece of Bauhaus furniture. Little is known for certain about the origins of the object because it disappeared shortly after it was made in 1921, and it was only rediscovered in 2004. However, it's suspected that Itten guided its production, that Marcel Breuer constructed it, and that Gunta Stölzl provided the geometric patterning of its upholstery. Like Feininger's cathedral, the African Chair does not conform to popular conceptions of the modernist Bauhaus. Two of the upright posts of the chair back rise up and cross over one another, giving it the appearance of a throne rather than a prototype for modern mass production. Although it's commonly referred to as the African Chair, it was more likely to have been influenced by Hungarian folk art, German Expressionism, or even Viking architecture, all sources that appealed to the period's artists in their search for authenticity, vitality, and expressive power.[15]

THE SCHOOL DID NOT have easy beginnings. One of the buildings Gropius inherited had been a reserve military hospital during the war and had been looted. Much work needed to be done to make it ready. The students were a mixed bunch. Some came straight from the army, still in their uniforms and looking for a meal in a time of widespread hunger. However, Weimar in the winter of 1919 had such a shortage of food that, according to one account, there was a "flood of obituaries for small children, the sick, and the old."[16] Others were no more than strays looking for a purpose. But some of those who enrolled were already art students when they arrived, and they came eager for the fresh modes of thought that Gropius promised. All soon became allies. They took to wearing a uniform of sorts. Men adapted the uniforms left behind by Russian POWs, dyeing them different colors, and women wore their hair loose.

Periodically, Gropius had to cope with difficult episodes as some new craze enthused the student body. The country was still in the grip of the so-called *Wandervogel* movement, a nationalist youth movement advocating hiking and communing with nature. At one point the school lost several students to the movement when Rudolf Häuser, a self-styled prophet, led them away on a pilgrimage. Another prophet to pass briefly through was gustav nagel, a wanderer who spelled his name without capitals as he believed they should be banned.[17] "The Bauhaus peels one skin after another in mad crisis," Gropius complained in a letter.[18] He responded by declaring that any students who left midway through the term would be refused readmittance. But throughout all these troubles, a school spirit emerged. Parties were held weekly, first in small country inns, with students taking along instruments to provide music. Then there were monthly balls with attendees in extraordinary costumes. There were kite festivals and lantern festivals.[19] The Bauhauslers soon became recognizable around Weimar, and their behavior drew notice. Weimar mothers took to reprimanding their children and threatening to send them to the Bauhaus as punishment.

THERE IS SOME CONTROVERSY over who exactly invited Van Doesburg to spend time at the Bauhaus. No one ultimately wanted to take responsibility. Gropius certainly met him in Berlin and encouraged him to come, but he quickly regretted it and later denied that he had ever offered the Dutchman a position on the faculty. Van Doesburg and his wife, Nelly, arrived in January 1921, and he took to striding about town in a black shirt, white tie, and monocle. (Itten was unimpressed, remarking that "a man who wears a black shirt also has a black soul." [20]) He taught a course on the principles of De Stijl and issued invitations to his home to listen to him lecture, though one student described it as a tirade of shouting and screaming. He "attacked the issues and people with drums and trumpets," she said.[21] Nelly would break up his lectures by playing De Stijl music, which she hammered out on a piano (the artist and writer Helmut von Erffa said it was "practically all in octaves . . . but with a definite affinity to squares and rectangles"[22]). Unconcerned about making friends, Van Doesburg wrote a stream of complaints about the Bauhaus's culture and the quality of its work. He claimed to be "[spreading] the vermin of the new spirit."[23] Paul Klee had arrived in 1920, and the following year, Kandinsky was hired, but neither could put out Van Doesburg's fires. Gropius later described him as "an arrogant and narrow man," and to his profound relief, the Dutchman finally left for Paris in 1923. Yet his assault on the Bauhaus left a lasting impression, leading its director to conclude that changes were needed.[24] Those changes may have immediately begun in Gropius's own office, because soon enough it was looking like a moderated, livable version of a De Stijl interior. All the elements seemed to be along an imagined grid: there was a geometric club chair, a rug with a checkerboard design, a wall hanging whose design resembles a circuit board, and a light fixture strung on a sequence of wires that stretched across the ceiling.

By this point Itten was increasingly out of step with the direction Gropius wanted to take the Bauhaus. He had never had any great commitment to workshop practice or to handicrafts, and he was repelled by the idea of design for industry, so in the spring of 1923 he resigned. The man who was to be his replacement, László Moholy-Nagy, arrived around the same time. He had had a journey. Born in conservative, rural Hungary during the last days of the Austro-Hungarian Empire, his family had been relatively wealthy, but his father had gambled away their wheat farm and disappeared to America, leaving his mother to return to her mother's house. To be discarded by her husband and forced to return home was a crushing shame for his mother, and it was compounded by the fact that, of her three children, she was forced to send the eldest to be raised by wealthy relatives in Germany. László stayed with his mother, and the experience made a powerful impression on him. He felt driven to redeem their name and was nervous from wounded pride; criticism would always leave him furiously hostile, "stupefied almost to the state of death."[25] Such a man would not be restrained.

He began to dream of faraway places, so at the age of ten his uncle took him to visit Szeged, Hungary's second-largest city. Finding it was unlike the New York of which he had read, he was dismayed. When the war came, he held an officer's rank, but the behavior of his fellow officers, their drinking and roistering, disgusted him, so for the rest of his days he remained a nonsmoking teetotaler. As did a surprising number of artists, Moholy-Nagy found his vocation through illness. In late 1916, during a battle along the Isonzo River, in what is now Slovenia, his whole battery was wiped out. He sustained a shattered thumb, which deteriorated into a raging infection, and he began moving among hospitals seeking a cure. He had always been a quiet child and something of a dreamer, and at first his feelings poured forth in poetry. While convalescing he turned to drawing, and it's said that he filled every surface he could find—

fever charts, postcards, field orders, and dossiers—with drawings of the scenes he encountered. He had never had any formal art training. In fact, prior to the war he had begun training as a lawyer, and a sense of obligation made him complete his studies at the end, but ultimately only art and politics would motivate him. He was attracted to the Hungarian Soviet Republic, the Communist state that ruled Hungary for little more than four months following the collapse of the Austro-Hungarian Empire. He was said to think of its leader, Béla Kun, as a messiah. But the landowning status of Moholy-Nagy's family, and his rank as an officer, didn't recommend him to the revolutionaries, and eventually he left, first for Vienna and then for Germany. By that time, he was penniless, and he would travel his way across the country by working as a sign painter and letterer. He would stay in a town long enough to earn the money for the train to the next town. And slowly, steadily, he made his way to Berlin, arriving in January 1921. During the journey he contracted Spanish flu, which was then ravaging Europe, and by the time he found a hotel he could go no further and collapsed in the lobby from exhaustion.

As an artist, Moholy-Nagy was entirely self-taught. He absorbed the Cubist and Futurist influences that shaped avant-gardes emerging in Hungary, and when he arrived in Berlin he encountered aspects of Dada, De Stijl, and Constructivism. Like many during the period, he was attracted to geometric abstraction for its apparent novelty, its suggestion of renunciation and renewal in the wake of the war. Being self-taught and having worked as a commercial artist, he had more eclectic interests than most. The student Lucia Schulz, whom he met in Berlin and who would become his wife, drew him toward the same Mazdaznanism that had inspired Itten. In line with its emphasis on exercise, she encouraged him to go hiking, and while doing that he began to explore photography, which would be a lifelong interest. The pair was frugal and comforts were sparse. In the winter of 1922, a gallery gave him an exhibition of his work. Looking back on the work he did during that time, he remarked, "One gets frightfully spiritual on crackers and apple butter."²⁶

Gropius hired Moholy-Nagy in the spring of 1923, after meeting him in Berlin. His German was said to be abominable, and he would make up for mangled adjectives with wild gestures. The students would refer to him as "Holy Mahogany." But teaching became what he called his "life task," and he cut an impressive figure.²⁷ One student remembered him "bursting into the Bauhaus circle like a strong, eager dog."²⁸ And he did the boss's bidding: Oskar Schlemmer called him "Gropius's faithful drummer-boy and teeth chatterer." He strode about the school in a coverall, peering through nickel-rimmed spectacles. He took over the Preliminary Course from Itten, stopped the breathing exercises, meditation, and gymnastics, and instead stressed the study of materials and their practical use. He also took over the metal workshop: under Itten, one student described it as producing "spiritual samovars and intellectual doorknobs"; under Moholy-Nagy, they would design modern light fixtures and teapots.²⁹ And alongside him in the *Vorkurs*, Gropius appointed Joseph Albers, who had arrived at the Bauhaus as a student in 1920, age thirty-one, and had recently graduated. And so began the academic career of another of the century's most influential teachers.

An example of Bauhaus design that is today synonymous with the school is the table lamp designed by Wilhelm Wagenfeld and Carl Jakob Jucker in 1923–24, and it is symptomatic of the school's thinking at the beginnings of its new enthusiasm for technology. It is a rigorously logical use of the same motifs, circles and spheres. The base is a metal circle, and the shaft, which is circular, reaches up to a hemisphere that has the same diameter as the base. The pull chain ends in a tiny circle that seems to elegantly summarize the geometric ideal from which the rest of the lamp draws its logic. The scholar Frederic Schwartz argues that it also shows evolving understandings of the meaning of light and clarity.³⁰ Prior to the war Bruno Taut, that architect of crystal buildings, could claim that "colored glass destroys hatred," but by the early 1920s an artist in Moholy-Nagy's circle was talking about the "socialism of vision," something that would be even and leveling in its clarity, and this is what the Wagenfeld lamp would seem to aspire to. We might think of the lamp as an example of Bauhaus style, yet it would seem to reject the very notion of style since it is the product of a series of logical, geometric transformations.

Such designs would have been unthinkable at the school only three or four years before, but the key forces in the school had shifted, and with them Gropius's outlook. By 1923 the school was ready for a new statement of purpose, and the occasion for that arrived when the state authorities demanded a report on the Bauhaus's activities—and no mere written account but a full exhibition. Experience had taught Gropius to be cautious in opening the school to the world, but now he had no choice, and he moved into crisis planning. The result was unveiled in August 1923, with the beginning of several weeks of exhibitions that displayed every facet of the school. Gropius launched the proceedings with a lecture, "Art and Technology—A New Unity." The title would form his central message to the world. Gropius was keen to stress that the Bauhaus radicals had not abolished that old reliable, traditional thing called "art." He stressed, too, however, that they were practical sorts: "technology" would be a guiding light. Previously, crafts skills had underpinned the school's teaching, now the machine would find a place.

The resulting exhibition comprised multiple parts, including exhibits of the masters' and students' work. But the centerpiece represented a remarkable advance from the aims and ideals that the school began with. While the school's original manifesto had carried the image of Gothic Cathedral, and Gropius had dreamt of the school creating its own bustling *Siedlung*, the centerpiece of the exhibition and the culmination of their work was a small white box, a modern family home that was known as the *Haus am Horn*, named after the street, Am Horn Strasse, on which it sat.

The painter Georg Muche was the house's designer, his plan being selected from the school's internal competition. Gropius had contributed a design, but it was rejected as being too conventional. (It was a disappointment he took in his stride. As he put it in a letter to the glass painter and photographer Lily Hildebrandt, the choice of a painter "is the sense of the Bauhaus . . . that other artists might begin to tackle architecture."[31])

Muche's house was simple and geometric, with one raised cube containing the central living area, set within a lower square of surrounding rooms. The structure employed new materials and construction processes. The arrangement of rooms was also novel in eliminating corridors and uniting spaces together that were normally separated, so a mother could work in a kitchen while supervising children in their bedroom. The kitchen had the newest standardized elements, along with a hot water boiler, which was a novelty. The children's room, furnished by the designer Alma Buscher, had walls on which the children could write, cabinets that could become a puppet stage, benches that could be taken apart and reassembled into boxes, a stool and table, or even a rolling car.[32] She also devised a toy made from different-shaped blocks painted in bold colors, with which children were encouraged to build a ship, or a slope, or a gate, or whatever else they could devise. In all these designs, the lessons of the Preliminary Course were to be brought to ordinary children. There was no conventional art on the walls of this house, indeed those walls were conspicuously empty. Art was not to be a focal point; instead, the house was to function as a total environment.

The *Haus am Horn* represented some significant successes for the school, but it is undeniably underwhelming from the outside. Critics likened it to "North Pole Station" and a "whitewashed die."[33] They tended to be more positive about the interior, but still skeptical, likening it to a factory or a laboratory. One critic complained that "tall standard lamps of iron and glass tubes, severe, undimmed by silk shade, recall physics instruments; seats look like looms,

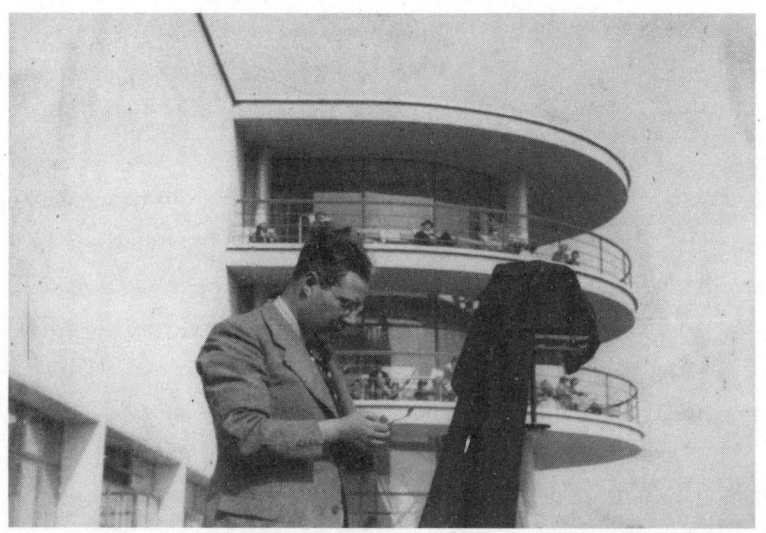

László Moholy-Nagy in London, 1936

furniture recalls printing presses, teapots water gauges."[34] But such criticism seems typical of the attacks on what was an emerging style of modernist design, and one that banished so many of the traditional associations of home.

SO WHAT WAS THE PLACE of art at the Bauhaus? It's not an easy question to answer, and there are all manner of contradictions. Although the workshop ethos of the Arts and Crafts schools would be central to the Bauhaus, Gropius hired several painters in the early years. In placing their avant-garde work amidst a school of craftspeople and designers, he helped to change both, encouraging artists to think about utility and designers to think about modernity. There were also figures like Itten and Kandinsky, who were drawn to spirituality and for whom art was the most open and logical field of work. Yet the Arts and Crafts inheritance of the school worked to undermine art's lofty position. In Gropius's very first address to the students, he warned them that he would "fight vigorously against an exclusive occupation with pretty little salon pictures."[35] Such old-fashioned pursuits were tolerated, but they weren't encouraged, and it was many years before the school began to introduce classes in "free painting and sculpture." The role of such work only became more uncertain as years passed and the school's focus shifted. At certain times, artists at the Bauhaus were made to feel the same pressures as their peers in Soviet Russia: at one point Communist students, seeking a more utilitarian art, even protested the Preliminary Course because of its focus on abstraction and experiment.

We've encountered a lot of avant-gardes in which art had an uncertain or unstable place, but of all of them, the Bauhaus seems to offer the greatest obstacles to defining art's place. For the Bauhaus was never one thing, but instead an evolving institution whose changing outlooks, and changing leaders, gave it a new cast every few years. It also inevitably contained more diversity in its faculty than an avant-garde would in its members. Itten and Moholy-Nagy were polar opposites, yet both were Bauhaus faculty. It seems tendentious, therefore, to pick any one figure as representative of the school's final opinion on art, but I'll opt for Moholy-Nagy. He led the school's transition toward technology; he took the reins of the all-important Preliminary Course; and his own work spanned painting, film, photography, and sculpture. Most symptomatic are surely the series of paintings he devised in the year he arrived, a series of pictures he simply ordered from Stark & Reise, an enamel sign factory. They are geometric abstractions with a predominantly white background, a wide strip of black running down the left of them, and two sets of intersecting vertical and horizontal lines. The colors were selected from the factory's own color chart. They differ only in size: small, medium, and large. Remarkably simple though they are, I'm conscious of the inadequacy of my description of them, and that's partly because Moholy-Nagy wanted their designs to be fully communicable in language. In principle, he said, you could just order them over the phone, which led critics to speak of them as the "telephone paintings." Years later, as if taking his cue, Moholy-Nagy claimed that that was exactly what he had done. These might forsake handicraft, and utterly reject the notion of art as an expressive act, but they remain artworks, conceived for the wall like traditional paintings. When you peer at photos of the *Haus am Horn*, and of Gropius's office in the wake of Van Doesburg's visit, it's these types of objects you see decorating the walls. This is what art meant at the Bauhaus.

There are many exceptions, for sure, but they often prove the rule. For example, the curator Leah Dickerman points out the poignant and telling paradox that one of the most famous Bauhaus paintings, Oskar Schlemmer's *Bauhaus Stairway*, was painted in 1932, three years after the artist had left to take up another teaching post. Unusually for the Bauhaus, it is figurative, a mode that was likely encouraged by Schlemmer's work in the school's theater workshop. He set to work when he heard that the school was to be evicted from its Dessau building, and it depicts students walking up the famous double staircase in the building Gropius designed. While it's hard to imagine such a work emerging from the Bauhaus's teaching, when remembrance was the aim, only figurative painting would suffice.

THE BAUHAUS WAS ALWAYS being watched by authorities, pestered and harassed, and this amidst a national mood that was unstable and politically polarized. Gropius had always feared that if the school became "a playground for political games, it will collapse like a house of cards." He said he was ever vigilant, "like Cerberus," the mythical three-headed dog, "to keep politics of any kind out of the school."[36] In 1919, a Bauhaus student by the name of Hans Gross appeared at a meeting and called for a new leader of German art, "a man of steel and iron" who could express "the German spirit." Gross was kicked out, but he left along with thirteen others, and a subsequent report felt it needed to reassure the local authorities—even at this time, long before Nazis rose to become a national force—that the Bauhaus was a German institution, and that only seventeen Jews worked or studied there.[37] Yet he didn't always heed his own advice, and in the period just after the war, Gropius seemed to believe that Bolshevism was Germany's only hope. In March 1923, Wolfgang Kapp, a German political activist and nationalist, attempted a coup in Berlin, and this sparked nationwide protests during which nine workers were shot dead in Weimar. Gropius joined the long funeral procession for the workers, and many among the Bauhaus faculty did so too. And he went further, subsequently winning a competition to design a memorial to them, which took the form of a jagged, geometric stone abstraction.[38]

As Gropius tried to stabilize the school and steer it through the instability of the postwar years, it's fair to say that the school's changes were a reflection of the nation's wider shifts. When the Bauhaus opened, as mentioned, the kaiser had abdicated and a subsequent revolution had failed. The nation was hungering for community. A version of the school nurtured on Arts and Crafts and Expressionism answered such a desire, while nurturing the individual. But only four years later, Germany was a fragile republic with raging inflation and the need to modernize. Then, the Bauhaus responded with a focus on technology.[39] Gropius could weather these storms, but those stirred up by national politics were harder to manage. In 1923, a new government in Berlin touched off demonstrations across Germany, and soldiers were sent to Weimar to keep order.[40] The whole of Thuringia was placed under martial law. In the ensuing months, Gropius's house was searched.

The Bauhaus moved to Dessau in 1925, and the industrial setting of the city seemed much more appropriate to the school's new direction. Here, Gropius designed the building that is best remembered as the school's home, and the one that encapsulates its ideals at the height of its enthusiasm for technology. It remains an impressive statement, a linked arrangement of clean rectangular volumes. Gropius was given a large amount of plate glass when he began the design, and he used it sumptuously, sometimes employing it in such a way that it appears to wrap the building like a skin, at other times allowing breaks in it to accentuate the floor plan.[41]

While there is a logic at work, a sense of utility and purpose, one can still sense echoes of the immediate postwar period, when Gropius was influenced by the idealism and utopianism of figures like Bruno Taut. This is the crystal building he had struggled to envisage just a few years before. Approaches like his would lay the foundations of the International Style of modern architecture that would rise to global dominance after the Second World War. It might not erase the divisions of class, nation, and creed, as Gropius's generation had hoped, but it would transform architecture. Sadly, however, when you remember how much the Nazis would emphasis blood and soil, race and region, you can see very clearly how statements like the Dessau building enraged the school's opponents, and while the school seemed to have found a more welcoming home amidst Dessau's industry, it didn't last.

Today, now that the Bauhaus's products are such familiar and well-loved examples of modern design, it can be shocking to learn the strong terms in which the school was criticized. One critic complained that their work was "so far beyond the pale" that it could only be understood in "pathological terms." They were accused of cutting themselves loose from society, of experiencing "the deepest spiritual isolation and disintegration." Most were "foreigners," "sky-storming Socialists," and they were "[suffocating] the healthy mass of youthful German art students."[42] Time was up.

In spring 1928, Gropius finally left, worn down by new political battles. As he put it then, "Until now ninety percent of my work has been devoted to the defense of the school."[43] It's possible that Gropius felt that he had become a liability to the school, that having become the lightning rod for the political attacks, the school might fare better without him. Though it's also significant that, with an improving economy, his architectural practice was improving. Gropius announced his resignation during a dance in the Bauhaus canteen, and the band refused to go on playing. His choice of successor, Hannes Meyer, has puzzled some writers. Meyer was a Communist, and his promotion was surely going to make the school's problems more difficult, which it duly did. Moholy-Nagy immediately resigned, and Marcel Breuer followed soon after.

Yet the Bauhaus actually enjoyed a brief spell of success under Meyer. He made architecture preeminent at the school—though he also pointedly changed the department's name to "building": for Meyer, building had no pretensions since, as he put it, it was simply the result of the equation "function x economics."[44] He made almost all the other departments subordinate to it, and in so doing he achieved something that Gropius had always spoken of but never achieved. He encouraged his architecture students to focus on social housing and had design students focus on goods for mass production. In the early 1920s, the few sales the school had managed —mostly of furniture, fabrics, and toys—were generally to private individuals, but by the end of the decade, the increasing prosperity of the German economy helped make the Bauhaus increasingly profitable. The mural painting department was selling wallpaper designs, the metal workshop was selling lighting, the furniture department was producing designs for exhibitions, and a new advertising department was working for the chemical and pharmaceutical conglomerate I. G. Farben.[45]

Eventually, however, Meyer's politics became a problem; it didn't help when the students at a carnival in 1930 broke into songs celebrating the Russian Revolution. Attacks picked up again; one critic referred to the school as the "State Garbage Service."[23] In August 1930, Meyer was replaced as director by Mies van der Rohe, but by then it was too difficult to keep back the forces threatening the school. In October 1931, the Nazi Party ran on a platform that included a vow to shut down the school and demolish it. When they won the election in 1932, they were able to close the Bauhaus for three months. Mies tried to meet with the authorities, but without success. And so they moved again, this time to an abandoned telephone factory in Berlin. But when Adolf Hitler was appointed chancellor on January 30, 1933, the Bauhaus was doomed. On the morning of April 11, 1933, police arrived in trucks and students who didn't have identification were taken away. The Nazis laid down terms under which the school could reopen, among them being the insistence that Kandinsky be ejected, along with the architect and town planner Ludwig Hilbersheimer. This time, Mies was cornered. The masters met one last time in the studio of the designer Lilly Reich. Mies explained the school's financial situation and the Nazi's demands, and he proposed dissolving the school. Everyone agreed.

AVANT-GARDES FUELED THEMSELVES on determination and purpose, and when those things ebbed, for whatever reason, the movements tended to die with them. But the Bauhaus was an exception: it fought to a close, even while there was still will and strength to continue it, yet its end only ushered in new beginnings. Those new beginnings would be in the United States, and one Bauhaus figure after another found refuge there and spread the school's ideas to influential effect. Joseph Albers stayed on at the school until its final days, and he would have the longest association with it, having arrived as a student in 1920 and becoming assistant director under Mies van der Rohe. But he was the first to leave Germany. He arrived in the United States in 1933 when he was invited to teach at Black Mountain College in North Carolina, and he would go on to teach at Yale. Gropius left Germany in 1934, and after a stop in the UK, he would go on to teach at the Harvard Graduate School of Design. In 1937, Moholy-Nagy came to Chicago to establish what became the New Bauhaus. His fortunes were in certain ways symptomatic of the afterlives of all the Bauhaus figures, for he was attracted to Chicago by an association of local businessmen who wanted to create a prestigious design institute in the Midwest. A year later, Mies became the head of the architecture school at what became the Illinois Institute of Technology in Chicago, and in 1958 he built New York's Seagram Building, one of the seminal office towers of the postwar age.[46]

What these teachers brought to the United States was a focus on vision and design, one that is encapsulated in the phrase "visual arts," which suggests that artists are not concerned with divisions between high and low, this medium or that, useful or useless art, but instead with vision itself and all it might include. If there were politics at the Bauhaus, they were left at the Bauhaus, and what arrived in America was a style of modern design and a concern with visual analysis. To the extent that the various fields of contemporary design now enjoy considerable prestige, the legacy of the Bauhaus must deserve some credit. Yet the huge difference in the size of the markets for fine art and for design suggest that the leveling the Bauhaus attempted to bring about has not had a lasting impact with the collectors. This would not have come as a surprise to Moholy-Nagy. When his new bosses in Chicago asked him to organize an exhibition in 1945 on modern art and advertising, he felt the opening celebration summed up the problems with his situation. "The provocative statement is constantly annulled by checkbook and cocktail party," he complained.[47] But he never went back to Europe.

EIGHT

Situations

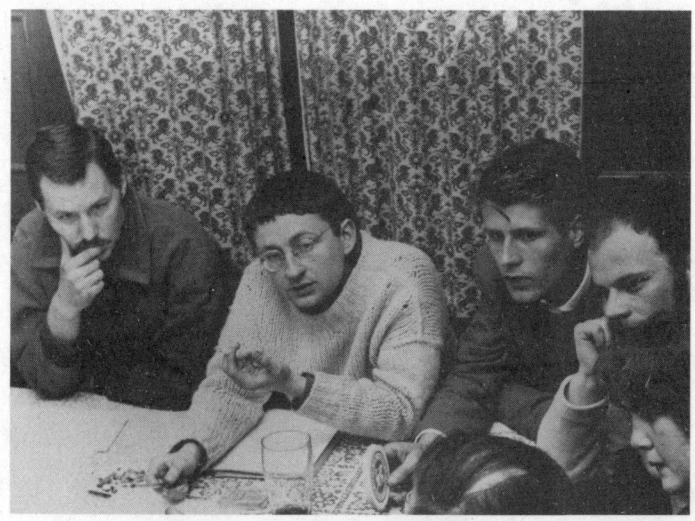

Guy Debord (second from left) at the Third Congress of the Situationist International, Munich, 1959.

THERE WAS A RAIL STRIKE IN PARIS IN THE SUMMER of 1953, and for many, the only way to get around was to hitchhike. Guy Debord was twenty-one at the time. He'd come to Paris a couple of years before and attached himself to a minor postwar avant-garde called the Letterists. They gathered around Isidore Isou, a charismatic and handsome Romanian poet who strode about Paris in an American-style sports jacket. But they didn't have a lot to do, so during the strike he and his friends decided to flag down cars and ask the drivers to take them in whatever direction drivers were already going. After about fifteen minutes, Debord would ask the driver to stop at the nearest bistro so they could buy bottles of wine, and when those were finished and the group was loosened up, they would head off in another entirely random direction.[1]

They started to refer to this as *dérive*, or "drift," and a definition of it was later set down: "experimental behavioral mode linked to the conditions of urban society: technique for passing rapidly through varied environments."[2] To drift was to negate the built purpose of the city and hijack it for different ends, for those who disregarded work and necessity and made pleasure their purpose.

Debord eventually decided that Isidore Isou was an obstacle, so he ousted him from his own avant-garde (Isou would later say that Debord was "worse than a Nazi") and established others with himself at the helm.[3] The most renowned of those would be the Situationists, and for them the idea of *dérive* would remain central. Debord's city wasn't that of the Surrealists; he wasn't attracted to traces of history or curiosities or shop signs or window displays. He felt that the postwar city of consumer society had become a kind of machine, one that had been built with the miserable purpose of bending its dwellers to its will. By drifting through this machine, treating it as a labyrinth and getting lost in it, one might somehow oppose it. Debord and his friends debated how long such a drift should take place; he concluded that the optimum period was a day. Others argued that it should last three or four months.[4] Either way, the key for Debord was to use these experiences to generate a "superior passional quality," a feeling of heightened intensity, one that would counter the deadened force of the modern city.

Debord's own preparations for *dérive* continued to begin with a drink—generally two or three liters of wine shared with a friend on the steps of the cours de Rohan in the Latin Quarter. When adequately fortified (this was considered an aperitif), he would move on to Chez Moineau, a Rive Gauche dive that had survived more or less unchanged since the German occupation. Done there, he might move on to the Vert-Galant, a tiny sliver of garden on the tip of the Île de la Cité. Here, separated from the hubbub by the branching waters of the Seine, he and his friends could drink and smoke hash undisturbed. As his later wife, Michèle Bernstein, recalled, "We were completely free there. The city of Paris was our playground and we were invulnerable."⁵

Debord would probably be fairly blitzed by this point—though one of his fellow drinkers recalled him getting through twenty beers with rum chasers without too much disarray.⁶ It was now time to *dérive*. Hungry, drunk, stoned, he and his friends would launch in search of cheap cafés in a Chinese neighborhood behind the Gare de Lyon, or in a working-class and Jewish district in the Marais, or in the Spanish bars and bistros of Aubervilliers. Debord would be in the advance—for in this as in much else he was a leader. They wouldn't take the straightest route; they probably wouldn't walk straight either. As Debord put it, "among the small number of things that I have liked and known how to do well, what I have assuredly known how to do best is drink. I have written much less than most people who write, but I have drunk much more than most people who drink."⁷ He felt it elevated him, sent him crashing through a gate into someplace else. "First, like everyone, I appreciated the effect of slight drunkenness," he recalled, "then very soon I grew to like what lies beyond violent drunkenness, when one has passed that stage: a magnificent and terrible peace, the true taste of the passage of time."

THE STREET WAS QUIET, with sunlight piercing the rich canopy of trees and patterning the brownstones. I stopped for a moment and scanned the numbers across the street. Then I saw it: Sixty West Ninth Street, a tall townhouse with classical details. The glow from a strong bulb pierced the gloom inside. It was a fine address, expensive now, otherwise unremarkable, but it was here that André Breton had spent his first few months in the United States.

Unlike many avant-gardists who fled Europe in the years leading up to the Second World War, Breton held on until 1941, when conditions under the German occupation of France made life too difficult to remain.⁸ The December prior, he had been swept up in a mass arrest that preceded the visit of France's puppet leader Marshal Pétain to Marseilles. Breton spent four days in detention. In March, he, his wife, and daughter boarded an antiquated boat to the island of Martinique. The writer Victor Serge, who was also on board, described it as "a can of sardines with a cigarette butt stuck on it." From there, they moved on to New York, and an old friend from Paris, the printmaker William Stanley Hayter, met the family on the dock when they arrived in June, bringing them to these temporary lodgings.

I had decided that I would spend a day touring a few of the sites in New York that had hosted the avant-garde, and in following Breton through the city streets, I hoped that I might finally ignite the sparks of the Surreal, that maybe he had brought some of that fire with him from Paris. But I was skeptical, for by the time Breton arrived in New York, something in him and his movement had died. His standing was already diminished by the end of the 1930s. In his quest for orthodoxy among the Surrealists, he had expelled so many that only a dozen loyalists remained in his inner circle, and few of those had been at his side during the great early years of the mid-1920s. And in departing France, the artist Georges Hugnet believed that Breton "dishonored Surrealism," since he left others behind who would have to endure the Occupation, or fight and die. If his stature was reduced, however, Breton's natural *hauteur* was not: the Surrealist painter Dorothea Tanning described him as a "proud man, such a royal man." He maintained this bearing in defiance of his new circumstances, refusing to learn English, dismissing everything as "imbecile."⁹

Guy Debord had admired the younger Breton, but he wasn't alone in feeling that old man Breton was a pale imitation. He felt that Breton had led his followers into little more than spiritualism and the occult, and now the man's movement was decrepit. In 1956, Debord had had some fun at Breton's expense by announcing that the great man, on the occasion of his sixtieth birthday, would give a talk on "the eternal youth of Surrealism." It all made me suspect that, being in New York, I was following the wrong Breton, but I couldn't rectify that in an afternoon.

Apparently, after taking the family to their lodgings, Hayter took them for a drink at the nearby Brevoort Hotel, which at the time was the only café in the city to offer open-air tables in the French style. I checked the location on my phone and headed toward it, but the hotel had disappeared and been replaced by a multistory apartment block that remembered the hotel only in its name. There was simply nothing to register, just lines of windows. So I set off for Breton's next address, 265 West Eleventh Street, where his family settled for their remaining time in the United States. It was a brick townhouse, its tall windows dressed with curved stone heads that resembled arching eyebrows, as if the whole façade was a little taken aback. It was expensive, but again, otherwise unremarkable. I stood looking at it; a figure moved inside. I felt nothing, no tremors or premonitions, absolutely nothing.

Could it be that Surrealism was impossible in the New World? A few appeared to think so. Several Surrealists landed on American shores during the war years, including the artists André Masson, Max Ernst, and Joan Miró, and many of them were disappointed.[10] For Masson, part of the problem was his strange preconceptions: he admitted that his notions of America were mainly formed by an eighteenth-century French novel about Mississippi. And then there were clashes of culture: one of his drawings—best described as a landscape with vagina—was impounded as pornography by U.S. Customs. He couldn't settle in and claimed to find the city's squirrels frightening.

Of course, it wasn't America that closed down Surrealism: it was the war, and the world that emerged in its wake. In fact, the conditions that had brought all the great avant-gardes into being were now passing into history. This is not to say that avant-gardes vanished. On the contrary, they proliferated, and Guy Debord's adventures brought him into contact with several of them. Aside from the pressures in the world at large, it was in large part the character of the modern *art* world—its small galleries, its diverse styles, its lack of centralizing forces—that forged the avant-garde over several decades. It established certain conventions by which artists organized, exchanged ideas, and promoted themselves. That world didn't fundamentally change between the 1930s and the 1950s, so avant-gardism resumed after the war like a series of old habits. Yet the era of the great, enduring avant-gardes, their so-called heroic era, was coming to a close. The world was already hostile to them in the 1930s, when fascism emerged across Europe and Stalin solidified his hold on power in Russia. As we've seen in both Germany and the USSR, avant-gardes were shut down and its members scattered. And it may only be a biographical detail, but it seems significant: on December 2, 1944, while staying on the shores of Lake Como, Marinetti succumbed to a heart attack and died. His health had been failing for some time, but he was writing until the very end, and the ugliest of his long-held sympathies were unchanged: his last poem was dedicated to a "fanatically fascist" unit whose members would later be deemed war criminals for their actions against the partisans. Mussolini awarded Marinetti a state funeral in Milan in December. Five months later, Mussolini was shot dead by the partisans.[11]

Just as the First World War had been a catalyst, creating new conditions that encouraged avant-gardes, the Second World War changed the landscape and narrowed the possibilities. The era of postwar reconstruction in Europe, and the political and economic dominance of the United States, created a new normalcy that spread across the West. Most significantly for artists, modernism emerged from the Second World War as a more widely accepted part of mainstream culture, no longer a fringe activity. And this changed the relationship between the avant-gardes and their audience, turning them from moral and political outliers to subjects of glamor and fascination, and turning their stunts into media spectacles. It all brought a dawning realization that the old modes of opposition had outlived their usefulness.

One who would come to feel this most acutely was Guy Debord. He became best known in his own time for his leadership of the Situationists, a group that endured, despite itself, from 1957 until 1972. But he has become better known to subsequent generations for the book that evolved out of that experience, *Society of the Spectacle*, a dense, aphoristic tract on the postwar times, which he published in 1967, just in time for the Paris riots of the following year. For Debord, spectacle was both the central product of postwar society and the canker at its heart. This society had moved beyond its fetish for goods and had lost itself in images, photographs, advertising, TV, and movies. People now lived in and through the spectacle, and their lives were shaped and manipulated by it. Once, leftists of Debord's stripe had believed that the work of persuasion was carried out in the realm of politics, and that if you wanted to change society, you had to grasp hold of the means of production, the engine rooms of the economy. For Debord, the real battleground lay in the sphere of everyday life; the enemy was everywhere and it was spectacle.

Debord was different from the avant-gardists who had come before him—and very different from Breton. Never a poet or a literary writer, never a painter or sculptor, architect or designer. He was a thinker and theorist of social and cultural revolution, but one who had arrived at that role through the culture of the avant-garde. He knew its history and its limitations. In his "Report on the Construction of Situations," the essay with which he announced his new venture, he nodded to his ancestors among the earlier movements and noted his lordly disappointment in them. The avant-gardes had become little more than playthings of the bourgeoisie, he complained. "At each of these stages one discovers the same totalistic will for change," he complained, "and the same crumbling away when the inability to change the world profoundly enough seems to lead to a defensive withdrawal."[12] A manifesto that followed soon after promised a change: "We will wreck this world."[13]

Art, Debord believed, should play a role in the Situationists' collective endeavor to change the world. Then he changed his mind, and in 1962 he expelled all the artists.

/

GUY DEBORD WAS BORN in a shabby northern suburb of Paris on December 28, 1931, "born virtually ruined," he would later recall. "I never had a childhood."[14] His mother, Paulette Rossi, came from a family that had prospered after her father invested in a shoe factory, but he died young and the business went into decline. Guy's father, Martial Debord, had trained as a pharmacist, and Paulette's mother, Lydie, bought a pharmacy for him to operate when he qualified. But Martial, too, died young, taken by tuberculosis in 1936, so that investment yielded another loss. When Guy was diagnosed with asthma, it was decided that they would leave the smoke of the city and move to Nice. This time Lydie put her money into a fruit and vegetable store, which proved a failure. Meanwhile, Lydie began to care for Guy, and Paulette, still in her mid-twenties, went back to living the life of a young, single woman. Men would come and go, and as they did, Debord's biographer Andrew Hussey surmises, Guy's faith in masculine authority was gradually demolished.[15]

Debord's taste for poetry, and for cultural and political opposition, was nurtured in his teens by the writings of earlier avant-gardists. He absorbed Apollinaire and Breton, and Surrealist favorites like Alfred Jarry, Rimbaud, and Lautréamont. "Throughout the course of my adolescence," he later recalled, "I moved slowly but inevitably towards a life of adventure, eyes open."[16] So by the time he encountered the Letterists, he knew their terrain. He met them for the first time when they were in Cannes for the film festival, where Isidore Isou was trying to get a screening for his film *Treatise on Slime and Eternity*. It was a fragmented and unfinished experiment with three sections: some found footage of Vietnam,

Algiers, and Paris; a love story concerning Isou and a girl called Eve; and footage of Isou walking about Paris with a stylish quiff.[17] Viewers were said to have booed at its first screening, yet the *Prix de l'Avant-Garde* was specially invented and awarded for it. Debord liked the Letterists' style, their Rive Gauche fashions, and insolence, and Isou warmed to his young disciple. When Debord came north to Paris—Isou had found him a room—he went through the motions of applying to study law at the Sorbonne, but it went no further than that. Instead, he spent his days sitting on the balcony of the apartment, smoking and watching the traffic pass along the rue Racine.

In Debord's early days in Paris, Isou was the linchpin of his circle. Born in 1925 as Jean-Isidore Goldstein, Isou had changed his name in tribute to Tristan Tzara, that other Romanian with a nom de guerre. He had worked with France's Resistance during the war, but impatient adolescent that he was, he wanted in on assassination and sabotage, and when those adventures weren't forthcoming, he tired of the whole thing. He decided to board a ship to Palestine in 1945, but changed his mind at the last minute and made his way instead to Paris, and there he established Letterism.

He claimed that the idea had first come to him while walking down a Bucharest street in 1942, when he was seventeen. He decided that the old civilization was dying and a new one needed to be founded. It needed to begin with a new language, one that would be pure noise and transcend all national boundaries. His approach rested on two principles: "ciselant" (chiseling, paring away) and "amplitude" (amplification). He believed that a process led by the former could achieve the latter, and that by applying these principles he could achieve the self-destruction of art.[18] In the field of poetry, this meant reducing verse to its smallest component, the letter, which could be the basis of performances of unintelligible sounds. But the method could also be applied to visual art to create what he called "metagraphics," in which the letter might appear as a graphic element. Or it might be applied to cinema, in which the film is reduced to its barest essentials, perhaps voice and no image, or vice versa. All this suggested a mode of art that was liberating and unconventional, and that paid little attention to the difference between poets and readers, or artists and viewers.

Debord found plenty to attract him in Paris, and he was also attracted by Isou's faith in youth. Isou saw young people as a new sociological category and a potential agent of revolutionary change (it helped that the group were in the springtime of their lives: at one point their average age was twenty-one). With exuberance and bravado valued, wild stunts would follow. On one occasion, members of the group managed to get to the altar of Notre-Dame on Easter Sunday to denounce the church. For Isou, interventions like this one were true cultural activity; an authentic act of courage was "[crossing] a main street on a day of heavy traffic, taking a piss, with your cock out, with no shame, in front of astonished men and women." He felt it took "self-possession."[19]

Although some feel that true Bohemia disappeared in the early twentieth century, that the banquet for Le Douanier Rousseau was its last hurrah, the milieu that Debord found on the Left Bank in the early 1950s had all the appearance of that old eclectic and disordered *demi-monde*, one that united painters with writers with petty criminals with local personalities. Ralph Rumney, a painter from Yorkshire who had fled England to avoid a prison sentence for dodging conscription, would endure for some years in Debord's circle. "I was famously idle," he said, "a runaway, a professional layabout."[20] There was the artist Gil Wolman, who claimed—in his mid-twenties—to already have spent time as a merchant marine captain, a drug trafficker in Algiers, a long-distance lorry driver from Greenland to Pompeii, a Young Communist, a poet, and a knitter.[21] There was Pierre Feuillette, who supplied them with cannabis and who had had his ear torn off by his pregnant girlfriend. There was Vali, Feuillette's sometime lover, and Ghislain de Marbaix, a pimp and small-time gangster who ran a bar. And there was

Ivan Chtcheglov, the brilliant and unstable son of Russian immigrants, who once conspired with the heir to an old, noble Catalan family to blow up the Eiffel Tower because its light disturbed their sleep. The pair were arrested with the dynamite before the deed could be done.[22]

Debord was at home in this milieu. He proclaimed happily that "there was then on the Left Bank of the river, a quarter where the negative held sway."[23] But while making a show of his rejection of conventional life, he was also quite comfortable with its comforts. When he first arrived in Paris, he subsisted on a small allowance that was sent by his mother, who assumed he was committed to completing a degree. Then in 1954, he married Michèle Bernstein, a French woman of Russian-Jewish descent who inhabited the fringes of the circle at Moineau's. The couple seemed to get married on a lark, though the arrangement also provided Debord with someone willing to take care of necessities for him. Bernstein received some income from her father, and she also had a series of part-time jobs that ranged from the bizarre (writing horse horoscopes) to, what were by Rive Gauche standards, the treasonous (writing advertising copy). Yet all this was forgiven when she was supporting Debord and dispersing a little generosity among his friends. Sexism, arrogance, and hypocrisy shaped Debord's attitudes in the home, and when he and Bernstein split up, worn down by the strains of money and the jealousies created by their open marriage, he adopted similar attitudes with his next partner, the French-Chinese writer and poet Alice Becker-Ho, whom he married in 1972. Once asked to explain his domestic arrangements with her, he said, "She does the washing-up, I do the revolution."[24]

Thinking and writing were Debord's central activities. He was never prolific, most of his output being short essays. According to the art historian T. J. Clark, who once visited him, he wrote in a tiny apartment that felt like "an austere cell." While Breton brought his thoughts together amidst the clutter and mystique of tribal sculptures and the paintings and photographs of his associates, Debord had nothing on his bookshelves save "a few crucial texts," works by the likes of Hegel and Marx. Other than that, there was a little poetry, like Lautréamont's *Poesies*, and that was about it. But Clark felt that Debord's activity of writing was a "process that was meant to be seen, and interrupted." Friends and comrades were invited to visit and witness the thinker and leader at his work, and thus his cult was built.[25]

Although Debord found his way to politics and writing through avant-gardism, he sought to stand apart from the artists around him, not exactly as a bystander but more as a thought leader, the philosopher king of misrule. For him, art had political realms, and playing its game meant playing politics like it was a blood sport, making alliances, breaking them, advancing, and always leading. He was barely in Paris six months before he moved against Isou. In July 1952, he banded together with Gil Wolman to break with Letterism and secretly form a new group, the Letterist International. Soon after, he declared Isou to be null.[26] Five years later, he would carry out another takeover when he created the Situationist International.

It can be difficult, even with a close reading of Debord's life and ideas, to discern exactly why he leapt from one avant-garde to another, why he suddenly moved against one faction and embraced another. One likely motor was his evolving ideas. Intellectually, he rarely stood still, and the centrality of small-circulation magazines to avant-gardes meant that they were always havens for debates and changing ideas. The Letterists were no different: the *Internationale Lettriste* appeared four times between 1952 and 1954, and its successor, *Potlach*, twenty-nine between 1954 and 1957. Consequently, Debord was continually absorbing new ideas, connecting new and old together, and moving away from his previous declarations, so it can be difficult to say exactly what any of his groups stood for at any one time.

Of course, another likely spur to the creation of all the postwar avant-gardes was the relentless logic of avant-gardism itself, the need for ever more rounds of agitation, new vanguard maneuvers to win a place in the forefront of ideas. The changing currents of personal friendships also played a part: it's said that Isou was ousted because he had turned into a megalomaniac (at one point he suggested that the central aim of Letterist activity should be the replacement of God as the creative force of the universe). As all these shifts accumulated, Debord likely felt a growing need to draw a line under previous positions, separate himself from former friends, start anew, and make a loud declaration to that effect.

And so it was in July 1957, when Debord was twenty-six, that he went to the remote Italian village of Cosio di Arroscia, high in the Ligurian mountains, and gathered the representatives of two avant-gardes, the Movement for an Imaginist Bauhaus—a handful of artists led by the Dane Asger Jorn—and the London Psychogeographical Committee—Ralph Rumney its only member. Such drinking occurred that tongues turned purple, but Debord never lost sight of his purpose. Jorn wanted to subsume the groups into the Imaginist Bauhaus, but Debord won out, and several days later the participants left as members of a new group, the Situationist International, with Debord at its helm.

Debord had started to use the term "situation" around 1955, though he was never clear about its origin. Hussey believes it came from the artist Constant Nieuwenhuys (referred to always by his first name), who coined the term in 1953 in a small book titled *Pour une Architecture de Situation*. For Debord, the concept was vague and capacious. He said at one point that situations would be "ephemeral, without a future, passageways,"[27] elsewhere that they should take "momentary ambiences of life" and transform them into a "superior passional quality."[28] But being Situationist in the late 1950s meant taking part in a kind of updated, refurbished, and politicized Surrealism. Debord's followers borrowed Surrealist ideas about the city but dumped the preoccupations with the unconscious and sexuality. The role of Jorn's Movement for an Imaginist Bauhaus also suggests how they were drawn to ideas around architecture and design. Jorn's short-lived avant-garde was formed in Switzerland in 1953 after he approached the artist Max Bill about joining the "new Bauhaus" he was planning in Ulm. Bill informed him that the school would be devoted exclusively to design, and had no place for "free artists," so the Dane decided to establish an alternative. The premise was to offer a home for ideas about the place of art in industrial society. After establishing as its headquarters a "laboratory" in Alba, in northern Italy, it attracted some remarkable talents. Jorn was the driving force, along with the Italian artist Giuseppe Pinot-Gallizio, but Constant developed his most influential ideas in the context of the group, and others who passed through it included the renowned Italian designer Ettore Sottsass and the artist Lucio Fontana. Some of these figures would go on to be central to the Situationists' activity, and their number grew as did the renown of the new movement. It soon became genuinely international, staging a series of annual conferences that drew figures from across Europe and North Africa, and its reach was extended by a journal, the *Internationale Situationiste*, which was published from Paris once or twice a year.

By the late 1950s, Debord was preoccupied by the place of art, and of creativity more generally, in industrial society. He felt that art had failed to keep pace with technological change, and indeed that this delay was now retarding society itself. What the Situationists needed to do was build participatory "situations" to challenge the passivity demanded by the world's spectacle. Debord felt that life in the modern world was no longer directly lived and experienced; instead we moved through it passively, shifting from one disconnected fragment of life to another. Workers were alienated from their work; consumers were alienated from the products they consumed. The only thing that made this world appear whole was the enveloping illusion of the "spectacle." The Situationists's goal would be to bring real change to a consumer society and a globalized world that Debord believed was opposed to creative expression and individual freedom. Art could have an important role to play.

In the early years of the group, the artists Jorn, Constant, and Pinot-Gallizio played important roles in pointing to what a Situationists culture might look like. At a gallery in Paris in 1959, Jorn showed his *Modifications*, a series of paintings by unknown artists that he had overpainted with gruesome, comical, or abstract scrawls. Another project that suggested a jaundiced view of modern fine art was Giuseppe Pinot-Gallizio's *Cavern of Anti-Matter*, which was shown at a gallery in Paris in the same year. This was an extension of his notion of "industrial painting," in which he produced abstractions on huge rolls of canvas, nearly five hundred feet long. For the show, he draped the gallery in the canvases and sold them by chopping lengths off the roll. Debord tried collaborating with Jorn on some experimental writing. He also made a loosely structured film titled *On the Passage of a Few Persons Through a Rather Brief Period of Time* (1959), that is partly about a *dérive* and partly an account of the Letterist International.

However, Debord also harbored anxieties about the value of supporting art.[29] It was by no means clear that ordinary art objects could do the work of combating the spectacle, and in one essay Debord stated that "situations are conceived as the opposite of works of art."[30] So while, like Isou, he felt that art should be made by all, he wasn't clear that professional artists could have any role. He suspected that most were interested more in contributing to the spectacle than in combating it; they were devoted to making old-fashioned, sturdy, enduring artworks and selling them like commodities. Moreover, the collectors were turning artists into heroes and neutering their ideas in the process. All this needed to stop.

Debord also felt that that modern art had already achieved some measure of the liberty he yearned to see in life: hadn't Isou's Letterists reduced language to pure noise? The proper task now was to *realize* that liberty, bring it to fruition in everyday life through an anonymous and collective art. As he put it in one essay, "Our time no longer needs to *draft poetic agendas*; rather, it needs to execute them."[31] It was true that this might be difficult to achieve in the existing reality of the world, but if that were the case, there was nothing for it but to wait until it was genuinely possible to construct an authentic experimental *life*.

But what would that experimental life look like? The founding idea of the *dérive* held the key. It had seen some changes since Debord picked it up from Isou. In the mid-1950s he began to connect it with a new, adjacent idea of psychogeography. As Andrew Hussey argues, that concept may have come from reading verses on Paris by the nineteenth-century poet Charles Baudelaire, and may also have come from a recent popular novel by Jean-Paul Clébert, *Paris Insolite* (*Strange Paris*), which was based on accounts of wanderings in the city. Who suggested these readings, or further shaped these ideas, is unknown. But Ralph Rumney claimed that he was the one who introduced Debord to *Homo Ludens*. The classic 1938 book by the Dutch social scientist Johan Huizinga explores the importance of play in civilization.[32] The idea of play was already shaping discussions of architecture among members of the Independent Group, a diverse circle that gathered around the Institute of Contemporary Art in London, and for Debord, they would profoundly color his attitudes to art and work and the wider purpose of activities like *dérive*.

The Situationists defined psychogeography as "the study of the precise effects of the geographical milieu, whether consciously arranged or not, and its direct influences on the affective behavior of individuals."[33] While they believed that the modern city was a force that deadened life, they also hoped that there were cracks in its defenses, that there were marginal points where its rule was weak. Here, Debord felt, you could begin to actually feel things, unpredictable things, passions. If you wound your way through the city, ignoring its major arteries and moving against its structures, you could taste these changing atmospheres. But could you? One of the Situationists produced a psychogeographical report on Les Halles, the old Paris market that was a favorite of the group, but it ended up richer in data than it was in passion, and it struggled to identify what it was that attracted them to it.[34] Perhaps the feeling was too ineffable to capture.

But there were a few inspirations that pointed the way, and for a long time, the most potent and compelling of those were provided by Constant. He had first emerged as a Surrealist-influenced painter but, like Debord, he came to believe that images were a falsification of experience, and that the world required a new form of cultural experience. He became interested in architecture, and this brought him into contact with the Dutch architect Aldo van Eyck, whose work demonstrated ways in which art and play could be introduced to the modern city. From the late 1940s onward, Van Eyck was responsible for building a staggering seven hundred playgrounds in Amsterdam.[35] Some were shaped in part by modern art, in particular a relief sculpture by Sophie Taeuber-Arp, *Rectangular Relief* (1936), whose cubic and cylindrical patterns, holes, and projections gave him ideas for play equipment. He wrote, "If we create a playground well, we create a world in which man rediscovers what is essential, in which the city rediscovers the child."[36] After Constant started moving in circles of modernist architects in Holland, he had taught himself about reinforced concrete, titanium, aluminum, and steel. Van Eyck helped him obtain commissions to build his own playgrounds, and the artist produced designs for swings and seating as well.

By the early 1950s, Constant was living in Paris and began to hang about Moineau's bar and became close to Debord. It was around this time that he began to dream of a city he called New Babylon. It would be a place in which work had ended because technology had automated all the most laborious activities, leaving humanity at ease. Factories, buried underground, would run by themselves; trains connecting them would be sunk out of view. The old "terrestrial" cities on the ground would be abandoned as obsolescent technology, or their ruins would be repurposed. And raised above the ground, on mighty columns fifteen to twenty meters high, would be the world's "new skin," a sprawling complex almost entirely enclosed, with great expanses of freely structured space linked together in a network.

Everything would be housed in lightweight enclosures, twelve to twenty-five acres in size, in which every aspect of the artificial environment could be modified at will. Lighting could be raised or lowered, so, too, the temperature, the sound, and the air quality. Inhabitants could move floors, ramps, bridges, partitions, and stairs, and as they did so, new environments would be produced. The shape and feel of the world wouldn't be planned, it would simply come into being, like some spontaneous expression of the popular will. The critic and historian Mark Wigley calls Constant's New Babylon "a huge atmosphere jukebox that can only be played by a completely zed society."[37] New Babylon was a phrase popular in the late nineteenth century to point to the commercial phantasmagoria that had lately come into being in Paris—an irony, given that the Situationists were opposed to this very transformation of their cities. Debord believed it should be named Dériville, since here humans could endlessly and pleasurably wander through labyrinths of their own design. Constant described the city as "a camp for nomads on a planetary scale."[38] The liberated people who wandered its terrain would rise in the morning and immediately lose themselves, encountering new things and new people. To service these nomads, a string of transit hotels would be created. The family home would no longer be needed, so the nuclear family would wither way, along with all the other social institutions that structured traditional society.

Constant worked on the idea of New Babylon for several years, constantly enlarging it, producing new models and plans. Yet while its extent, and possibility, seemed to grow in his imagination, its detail remained vague and tended to be supplemented by the ideas of Debord and others who also entertained dreams of a renovated city. Chtcheglov, who had plotted the destruction of the Eiffel Tower, had raised the prospect of "states-of-mind" districts, in which different quarters of the city would encourage different moods. There would be a Bizarre Quarter, a Sinister Quarter, a Historical Quarter, and a Useful Quarter. A Happy Quarter would be reserved for residences, a Noble and Tragic Quarter would, for some reason, be reserved "for good children."[39] Debord imagined streets furnished with trash cans made of ivory; streetlamps that had switches so they could be turned on and off at will; public sculpture would be replaced by scaffolding and carefully arranged cranes; he wanted the Paris Métro kept open after the trains had stopped running so that people could wander the tunnels; and the city's roofs would be open for strolling. The parks, too, would be accessible at night, and while Debord would have preferred them to be kept dark, he allowed that "in some cases, a weak illumination may be justified by psychogeographic considerations."[40] While the notion of New Babylon certainly came, in part, from Constant's work on playgrounds and the new ideas that Aldo van Eyck brought to that work, Debord's ideas of city life also emerged from his wanderings, and from his experience of the ordinary, interstitial, mixed-use quarters of the city. From these he built notions of the city that would supersede the functionalism of a previous generation and be given over instead to luxury. Instead of efficiency, there would be extravagance.

The notion of New Babylon is charming, but it is, of course, resolutely fantastical. Mark Wigley describes it as a collection of "unusable, uninhabitable, unthinkable dream spaces."[41] That troubled some people, Constant included. He felt that it was all very well to dream of a better world, but one should also take some concrete steps to bring it about, in whatever compromised form was possible. Debord, however, remained opposed to any concessions to a reality he perceived as fallen. For him, small-scale efforts were akin to reformism, an approach that made concessions to whatever it opposed. Utopias that remained utopias retained their power to criticize and inspire. This is certainly one of the reasons why Debord increasingly maintained a distance from those around him who would make art and culture in the name of the Situationists.

Many critics split the life of the Situationist International into two phases, with the first phase, given over to art, coming to an end in 1962, after which Debord adopted what amounted to a culture boycott, in which he perceived the production of art as a kind of reformist gesture. He would say that the SI was camped at the gates of culture and wouldn't go inside; to do so would be to become just another avant-garde to entertain the enemy. It's likely that Debord's policy of abstention would have led the Situationists into obscurity by the late 1960s. But instead, events intervened that Debord might have encouraged in print, might even have daydreamed into being, but which he would never, ever have imagined would occur. Paris erupted in protests.

The trouble started in April 1968 at the university in Nanterre, a suburb of northern Paris not far from where the Duchamps had once lived in Puteaux. A handful of activist students were held up on disciplinary charges. The mood was ugly enough for the university to be temporarily closed and infectious enough to light a fury among the students' allies at the Sorbonne, and spark demonstrations in Paris. By 4:00 p.m. on May 3, the Sorbonne was surrounded by police, who were reinforced by riot squads. They arrested protesters, who were bundled into a column of vans. As the vans drove away, students pelted them with a hail of bottles, ashtrays, and mustard pots taken from cafés. Fighting continued, and the Sorbonne was closed. Three days later, military police were outside the Sorbonne as students began marching. In the ensuing hours, protesters ripped paving stones out of the ground, tore up the railings around trees on the streets, and burned cars. The police answered with volleys of tear gas and counted five hundred injuries among their own ranks. The protesters no doubt suffered many more.

It's certainly true that the events of May 1968 would have never occurred had the authorities not made a series of missteps, but no one imagined that the protests could escalate so far and so fast. By the middle of the month, a general strike paralyzed France, closing factories, offices, oil refineries, shipyards, banks, department stores, and schools. It became the largest urban insurrection that France had seen since the Paris Commune of 1871. It was very, very real, yet the rhetoric that caught the students' imagination spoke of dreams and imagination, and they often borrowed from the Situationists' slogans. "Imagination Is Seizing Power" read a poster that was pinned on the doors of the Sorbonne on May 13. Observers at the time responded in similar terms. Tom Nairn, who was involved in student protests in London, repeatedly invoked dreams to describe the Paris events, likening them to "a vivid, troubled dream experienced just before waking," or "a secret, haunting dream of release turned into reality." "The apocalypse prefigured in the dream is already here," he wrote.[42] Certainly, the events seemed to exceed reality, and in the fog of the situation, imaginations took over. Paris began to reverberate with rumors that there were tanks surrounding the city, that the police had thrown bodies into the Seine, that the wounded had been beaten on their stretchers. The Canadian-born writer Mavis Gallant was in her late forties when she reported on the protests for *The New Yorker*, and her fear and confusion are palpable in her writing. She described the city thronged with marching crowds which charged police; by night, the noise continued, and she would hear the feet of people running past her building. Tear gas was everywhere, creeping up into apartments, descending into the subways where the passengers rubbed smarting eyes. The artist and writer Jean-Jacques Lebel kept a diary, and noted that at 6:00 a.m. on May 11, "Still fighting outside . . . The police are searching house by house, room by room. Anybody with black hands and gas spots on clothes . . . or wounds is beaten and arrested. . . . Many people in cars and taxis volunteer to take us out of the police zone. Everywhere we see enormous buses full of our people, tired, beaten, bloody prisoners."[43]

The Situationists would later claim that they held the Sorbonne for three days at the height of the troubles, and in subsequent years, Debord's sense of his own role in the events only deepened. He noted that some felt he had a "grave responsibility" for them, that he was even in command.⁴⁴ In fact, the SI's role was fairly insignificant, and it warrants only a few lines in most histories. Yet in hindsight, Debord's writing seems prescient in its description of the dulling power of spectacle; he knew it in forms like television and advertising; we have come to experience much the same thing through social media, and the whole spectacularized world that the internet puts before us. Certainly, Debord's renown, and that of his avant-garde, were greatly enhanced in the aftermath as people struggled to understand what had happened. The fact was that the tinder was there for the fire, but most simply hadn't noticed. Technology was changing the French economy, elevating some, impoverishing others. President de Gaulle presided over all this disquiet with grim authority, oblivious to change and wanting only to stop any and all protests.

/

IN THE EARLY EVENING of November 30, 1994, Guy Debord shot himself through the heart and died. It isn't clear if this came as a surprise to his friends. He did it, most likely, out of a mixture of pride and despair. He was sixty-two, and even by the time he was fifty he had been suffering from gout and walking with a cane. He no longer lived in Paris, and instead spent several months of the year hiding out in remote reaches of the mountainous Auvergne, a full six hours from the capital. Debord's avant-garde had retreated.

Although a leader who drew people to him, Debord was progressively casting off those same people from the very beginning. No sooner had he and Gil Wolman ousted Isou back in 1952, than Debord ousted Wolman from the Letterist International for living "a ridiculous lifestyle." The group's journal, *Potlach*, reported Wolman dead ("He was twenty-seven years old").⁴⁵ There was some confusion over why so faithful and early an adherent as Wolman should have been so rudely denounced, but Rumney suspected it was because he had recently married and had a child. Shortly thereafter, Rumney was ejected for a similar offense when he married Pegeen Guggenheim, the daughter of the art collector, Peggy.[46] Other victims, expelled for a variety of other crimes, included Piero Simondo, who had helped birth the Situationists by organizing the meeting in Cosio. Accused—along with his friend Walter Olmo—of being "enemies of reality" and "anti-experimental," both were dismissed in January 1958.[47] And Raoul Vaneigm was exiled for being on holiday in the south of France during the events of May '68.[48] What exactly prompted these expulsions or who implemented them is sometimes difficult to say. In Andrew Hussey's account, Constant resigned after he became the target of abuse and accusations that he was "technocratic"; in other accounts it's said that he was expelled after it was discovered that one of the architects he worked with had built a church.[49] Even Constant seemed to have been unclear what happened: "You couldn't understand everything in the Situationist International," he said. And so it continued, the names of the denounced listed in the SI's journal. By 1965, seventy people has passed through the group, and only Debord and Bernstein remained from the eight who had gathered at Cosio di Arroscia.[50] By April 1972, when the SI was formally dissolved, it consisted merely of Debord and a young Communist, Gianfranco Sanguinetti. The philosopher and sociologist Henri Lefebvre saw the pattern early on and determined not to join the group precisely because it could only end in his expulsion. Lefebvre believed that the purpose of all these removals was to keep Debord "in a pure state, like a crystal," though it's probably nearer to the truth to say that he did it because he enjoyed the exercise of power and ruthlessness, even when it was quite arbitrary.[51] The critic and historian Peter Wollen once remarked that the group's "habit of vitriolic denunciation" left him feeling "relieved that these writers never enjoyed real public power or influence." Wollen was later vitriolically denounced.[52]

DEBORD LEFT PARIS IN 1972. Partly, he did so out of disgust. The city had been "ravaged," he complained. "Whoever sees the banks of the Seine sees our grief: nothing is found there now save the bustling columns of an anthill of motorized slaves."[53] But it was also true that success had opened new avenues to Debord, and he found he had a taste for them. Whatever the minor role the Situationists played in the events of May '68, Debord found considerable fame in its wake. This was only helped along by his publisher's determination to market *The Society of the Spectacle* as a guide to the students' views, however misleading that might have been, and the success of the book brought Debord a prosperity he had never known. So even while the Situationists' activity in Paris seemed to be winding down in the late 1960s, they were attracting their widest acclaim. Today, the Situationists continue to remain in the shadows of Debord's great book, partly because it is the most substantial, accessible, and engaging text to come out of their work, but also because they left little art behind, so there are fewer opportunities to revive them for audiences. This leaves the Situationists as a kind of tragic cult, a philosophical avant-garde that self-destructed—and did so rather than compromise.

That posture would always suit Debord more than success, and as acclaim grew for his circle, he withdrew. He first made for the hills of Chianti in Central Italy. Then he moved into a fourteenth-century palazzo in Florence, where he drank in bars with the city's petty criminals. He had always enjoyed wine, and he drank as freely as ever, but now he dipped into cognac and grappa. He continued to write, though less often than before, and fancied himself a modern Machiavelli, an intellectual who had wielded power and could advise on its use. As he puts it in *Panegyric*, one of his brief, atmospheric, and lordly memoirs, he is "a person who has led an action," and he "[knows] what sovereignty is, how many kinds there are, how one acquires it, how one keeps it, how one loses it."[54] When he did return to Paris he often resided at a spacious apartment on the rue du Bac, furnished with antiques and paintings. He spent time in Spain, summers in Arles, and other periods in the Auvergne. Visitors from Paris might arrive in the summer, but in the winter the snow would fall for days on end and pile up in drifts. Violent winds pounded the region, bending trees on the moors and assaulting the woodland on the hillsides. Storms could move in from all directions. The wind would pick up gently, flashes of light would illuminate the horizon, and then rain would arrive with such force as to give Debord the unhappy feeling that he was in a fortress under siege. He recalled one night when lightning had struck nearby. "The whole landscape was equally illuminated for one startling instant." He reflected that, for all his hopes, art had never really given him anything of such "irrevocable brilliance."

Having lost this sovereignty, Debord was in no fit state to regain it. He was in increasingly poor shape, and he lacked the energy for new maneuvers. The closest he came to his earlier commanding heights was in the evenings, when he played a board game he had devised called "Game of War." His energy had dissipated in feelings of stagnation and failure. He had no regrets: he explained himself in *Panegyric* by citing the nineteenth-century writer Chateaubriand, who claimed that "'of the modern French authors of my time, I am almost the only one whose life resembles his works.'" Debord added that, "In any case, I have most certainly lived as I have said one should."[55] And he was happy to escape. As he put it, now that the Situationists could take pride in "having achieved the most revolting fame among this rabble, we fully intend to become even more inaccessible, even more clandestine. The more famous our theses become, the more shadowy our own presence will."[56]

EPILOGUE

The Future of an Illusion

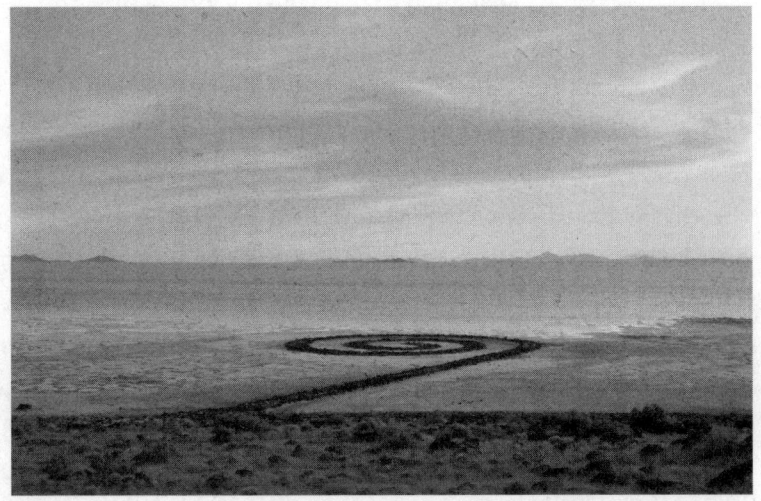

Robert Smithson, Spiral Jetty, *1970*

IN 1970, THE AMERICAN ARTIST ROBERT SMITHSON built a huge, coiling earthwork on the remote northern shoreline of the Great Salt Lake in Utah. He constructed it with 6,650 tons of black basalt rock and earth, using bulldozers to heave the material into the spiraling shape, which is roughly fifteen hundred feet in length and fifteen feet wide. The salinity of the lake is such that white salt crystals quickly formed on the rocks that lay in the water, and the algae that gathers in that part of the lake lends the water a blood-red discoloration.

The coil motif refers to an old myth that an ancient vortex originally formed the lake, yet *Spiral Jetty*, as the work is titled, creates the impression of a terrifying, postapocalyptic future, as much as it does of some lost past. Time was a central theme for Smithson, and he was fascinated with how crystals grow in a spiral formation, slowly marking time as they do. Ideas like this came to Smithson in the late 1960s, when the technological optimism of the early part of the decade had disappeared, pounded first by an economic slump and then by the public's horror at the destruction being wrought by advanced arms in Vietnam. For Smithson, as for many other American artists of the period, modernity seemed to be winding down, its energy exhausted; now time could only bring decay and collapse. In fact, Smithson knew there was a risk that *Spiral Jetty* could be entirely submerged if the waters in the lake rose, and indeed they did shortly after it was built, making the earthwork disappear entirely from view. The waters receded for a time in the 1990s, briefly restoring the jetty to view before it was submerged again. It reemerged in 2002 and remains visible on the shore of the lake to this day. At least, photographs and reports in the press attest to this; I've never seen *Spiral Jetty*. There are plenty of famous artworks that I haven't seen in person, and this wouldn't be noteworthy were it not for the fact that Smithson thought a great deal about how his audience might get to "see" his artworks. He knew that there would be many like me who might never see his large earthworks—only hear about them. This means that for most who take an interest, Smithson's *Spiral Jetty* isn't any kind of object you can buy, or any kind of thrilling and authentic experience you can readily partake in. It's a kind of myth, which itself is about a myth.

For me, as for so many others, *Spiral Jetty* is one of the greatest artworks of the 1960s. It's romantic, sci-fi, conceptual, and in its time it defied all the conventional modes of contemporary art, exceeding them in its sheer scale and remoteness. The achievement also has a patina of tragedy about it, given that Smithson was killed in a helicopter accident only three years after making it, while surveying a site for another earthwork. The jetty's site is cared for today by the Dia Foundation, a strange and wonderful institution developed in the 1970s to fund the kind of ambitious, large-scale work that was popular in the period. But you could never domesticate the jetty, never bring it indoors in some marble edifice of a museum and stick a label on it. It's wild and cannot be tamed.

But is it avant-garde? Yes and no. Yes, because it breaks with the conventional mediums of art, and because it aspired to break out of the framework of the museum. No, because Smithson himself didn't behave like the avant-gardists of the past. He had no grand diagnosis of contemporary society, no charged manifesto, no plan for how his work was going to transform the world. He was too conscious of the centrality of art to our society and culture to imagine that his work could somehow escape it, let alone bring it to an end. And, like many of his peers, he was far too much of an individualist, too suspicious of collective activity of any kind to bind together under some movement, with some new Breton or Marinetti at the helm. Indeed, to him avant-gardism seemed like a thing of the past, all its tricks worn thin. He once bemoaned the idea that artists should form themselves into "an avant-garde of dissipated scandals," who would devote themselves to grabbing the patrons' attention with more and more outrageous stunts.[1]

One of the inspirations for this book was a slim volume titled *Theory of the Avant-Garde*, which was published by the German academic Peter Bürger in 1974.[2] He argued that the whole project of the European avant-garde could be understood as an attack on the status of art in bourgeois society. Their aim wasn't simply to displace earlier forms of art, he believed, but art itself, understood as an institution separate from life. For the avant-garde, art needed to "become practical once again." That didn't mean that modern painters should paint realistic images of the social world or great moments in history as their predecessors had done; it meant instead that they should strive to change how art functions in society, the job it does. Bürger was the first to put forward the argument that there was a generational effort, around the 1910s and '20s, to integrate art and life, and in so doing to end art and improve life. He argued that that effort had failed, and that it could not be revived.

Bürger wrote in the knowledge that that there were plenty of artists working in the 1960s and '70s whose work seemed ambitious and unconventional enough to warrant comparison with the old avant-gardes. There were innovators like Andy Warhol, who created sculptural copies of Brillo soap pad boxes; or the German artist Joseph Beuys, with his sculptures made of felt and fat, and his mission to educate; or the wildly energetic Japanese Gutai Group and their performance painting; or the Italian prankster Piero Manzoni, who canned his own shit. For some critics, these artists deserved to be called the "Neo-avant-garde," but for Bürger their efforts are null and void, and to the extent that they revived some old avant-garde tactics, they only served to institutionalize them, dulling them of the power they once had and turning them into museum pieces.

Bürger's book has been enormously influential because it puts forth reasoned arguments about a highly consequential series of art movements. And his ideas bear on a wide range of questions, only a few of which I've been able to raise here. But the book is a flawed one, as many critics have argued over the years, and some of the complaints center on his dismissal of a new generation.[3] One way to confront these is to first reflect on the supposed failure of the historical avant-garde. In a certain sense they would seem to have failed, since so many called for the end of art and for some great accompanying transformation, and yet art today is no utopia, and old-fashioned art would seem to be in rude health. But how seriously are we to take these calls to end a central occupation in human civilization? Is it not better to think of these calls as cries for change, as rhetorical outbursts of the kind Marinetti and Breton so loved?

Viewed in this way, the avant-garde's "failure" to end art isn't such a failure after all, since in so many ways their work was influential, provoking successive generations of artists to think ambitiously, to think radically about the place and purpose of their art in the world. If that is the case, then perhaps we should look differently upon the Neo-avant-garde and not see their efforts, as Bürger does, as a pale rerun of the authentic avant-garde. For Smithson's attempts to challenge the museum were also powerfully effective and influential, and similar efforts by artists across his generation were often equally so, and they remain important even if museums today are still—just like art—in rude health. The critic Hal Foster argues that rather than seeing the original avant-garde as a heroic failure and the Neo-avant-garde as a farcical one, we should attend to their different aims. He argues that the earlier artists were principally mounting an attack on the conventions of art, its modes and genres. That explains why they introduced so many new forms to the visual arts, like the manifesto, the use of performance, collage, the ready-made, and the constructed sculpture. The Neo-avant-garde, by contrast, aimed to challenge the institutions of art, the way art is mediated through commercial galleries and museums. So even if the new generation dumped the habits and postures of the old avant-garde, it's fair to say that their outlook is still in some measure avant-garde; it still seeks art's realignment in the world.

Smithson was particularly alert to the problem of museums. He complained in one essay about how contemporary art was caught in a "culture of containment," one that determined that every artwork must find a home in a domesticating institution. Works like *Spiral Jetty* demonstrated an alternative, one that sets up challenges for any institution that might seek to contain it; it is simply too large and too remote for them. It's this aspect of *Spiral Jetty* that most attracts me to it: it presents itself as a nameless and forgotten monument, an edifice created perhaps even before the idea of art as we recognize it today. It feels almost *un*mediated, *un*processed, raw and outside the system, though Smithson wasn't too naïve on that score, as he knew that there would always be some institutional vantage point, some perspective conditioning the way his sculptures were seen.

It's hardly surprising that art world institutions like museums were a focus of concern in the 1960s. The art world had developed some significantly layered complexity by that time. Its museums were powerful, influential edifices—none more so than the Museum of Modern Art in New York, that richly endowed temple that critics once referred to as the "Vatican" of modern art. A boom in the postwar economy in the West had also lifted the fortunes of the commercial art world, creating many more small galleries to answer to the growing interests of a prosperous middle class. And then there were critics who wielded the power to crown new stars or depose old ones (and those critics had vastly more power to do so than critics today). In sum, the art world was a place of powerful and interlocking institutions, and in the 1960s artists were much more alert to the power of those things. They were also much less sanguine about the possibilities of escaping the system entirely. I suspect that vanishingly few among that later generation thought that an art world without institutions was ever likely, but that didn't dampen the determination of their efforts.

So what about today? Are there still artists seeking to challenge our understanding of art's place in the world? Yes, there are. There are countless examples I could offer, but I'll cite one exemplary project that seeks to return our thoughts to the First World War, that horrific and catalytic event that brought so many avant-gardes into being. Its creator was the British artist Jeremy Deller, who in 2016 was commissioned to devise an artwork to commemorate the hundredth anniversary of the first day of the Battle of the Somme. That day, July 1, 1916, was the nadir in the fortune of Allied troops. A dayslong artillery barrage had been meant to soften German defenses, leaving the way clear for thousands of troops to easily cross no-man's-land in the early morning. Instead, they were met by heavy machine-gun fire. By the end of the first day, an estimated 19,240 lay dead on the British side. By the time the Battle of the Somme concluded, four and a half months later, it had claimed the lives of 420,000 British troops, 200,000 French, and 500,000 German.

Deller's project was aimed at public remembrance, a difficult

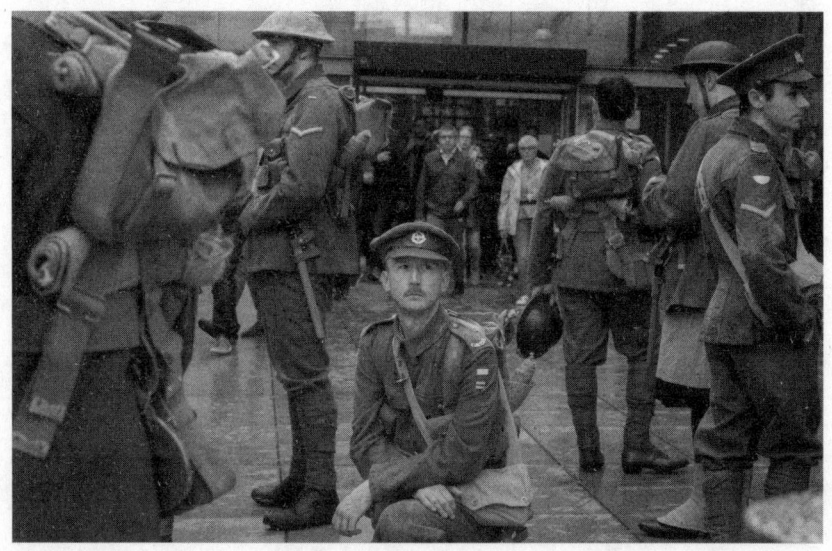
Jeremy Deller, "We're Here Because We're Here," 2016

task when the events have receded far out of living memory, and when our culture struggles to remember what happened last week, never mind a century ago. To effect it, he enlisted the help of a team of fifteen hundred volunteers, all nonprofessional performers from ordinary walks of life, who dressed up in the uniforms of British soldiers of the period. And on the morning of the anniversary, they were sent out into British towns and cities, sometimes marching down streets, sometimes sitting around and smoking and waiting, but otherwise silent. Occasionally, they would break out in song, singing, "We're here because we're here," a refrain that troops of the period used to sing in the trenches to the tune of "Auld Lang Syne"; it was these words that lent Deller's project its title. If members of the public approached them, they would silently hand them little cards with the names of the dead soldier that they were commemorating. One typical card read: "Private John Hayes. 2nd Battalion Gordon Highlanders. Died at the Somme on 1st July 1916. Aged 18 years." The sight of all these soldiers, apparently walking out of the past and into the everyday present, was jarring and arresting. It brought history to life in the present, and in a manner that was sobering rather than celebratory. Yet with soldiers who wouldn't speak, and could only be observed, it suggested that history could not be so easily recovered and redeemed; what was done was done.

Deller's project wasn't concerned with the end of art or museums, but it was avant-garde in its determination to evade the clutches of both. It didn't present itself as art that might be difficult and that might reward us with some erudition if we paid it attention. It occurred completely outside the walls of museums, its galleries being the high streets of ordinary places. What it did challenge was the idea that there can be no broad public for art, and certainly not for one with serious, commemorative, historical concerns. Earlier in the book, I argued that the culture of art at the new fairs has a decadent, trivial air, as if it is happy to celebrate the end of any serious and demanding culture. But Deller's project was instead hopeful. It sought a broad, new, democratic audience for art, and did so while rallying a country in an act of remembrance.

I began this book moaning about art fairs, and I must end it that way. My first complaint about the experience at Miami Art Basel was that it was incoherent. There was so much art, and it was all so different—superficially, at least—that it was difficult to make any sense of it. That's a typical problem at art fairs. The organizers of these fancy malls have various means of bringing order to the chaos, by separating galleries into sections, by encouraging some to show fewer artists, and so forth, but it's difficult to contain the clamor of all those objects crying out, like puppies in the pound, to find a home. A better place to see art is in a museum or gallery, where a curator has made careful selections and arranged artworks in an order that puts forth a kind of argument, almost in the way I'm trying to do here. So perhaps I should conclude that fairs are not for me, and that art itself should not have to come to an end simply because I dislike them, just as food should not come to an end because I dislike brussels sprouts. Yet the problem with art fairs is that they are a symptom of a changing art world.

I first began to look at a lot of contemporary art in London in the 1990s. The city's gallery scene was significant, but it was not large. The public galleries had a presence, though funding cuts had long ensured that they were neither rich nor powerful. The commercial galleries were far fewer than today, and I don't recall any having the international outposts that so many do today. There were a lot of galleries, but with some diligent work you could see most of what was worth seeing, most of the time. Back then, I used to write about the exhibitions for art magazines. Not many people read the magazines, but enough did to make it feel like the debate that took place in them mattered. This was an art scene with a balanced diet: some public culture, some private culture, and some discussion between the two. But since then, much has changed. London has become, like New York, a hub for galleries with an international reach, some of which have taken on the scale of mini-conglomerates with multiple divisions and offshoots.

And fairs have become a key driver of sales. Not so many years ago, exhibitions were the gallery's shop window. Collectors who wanted to purchase work had to go to exhibitions and see all the work displayed; some went to artists' studios to see more work and discuss the artists' ideas. But now those same collectors skip all the exhibitions and the studios and the conversations, and they just go to the fair. The fair organizers will tell you that they have opened up art to the crowds and that they bring exhibitors from far-flung parts, which otherwise might rarely have an opportunity to show their artists internationally. There's much truth in that, but it's also true that the fairs have turned the culture of art into a spectacle of selling. It only takes a glance at the press coverage of fairs to see that part of the attraction is the excitement of high-dollar transactions and the prospect of rubbing shoulders with money and celebrity.

What is most sad, though, is how the fairs elevate and celebrate the most conservative modes of art and do so with little or no interest in bringing change to art. Over a hundred years ago, a generation of artists were serious and ambitious enough to question art's purpose in the world and to ask whether it might be put to new ends. Could we use it for protest? Could we wrap it around ourselves in total environments? Could we use art's inventions to create new and vivid products for sale in a revolutionary society? Could we abandon art objects in favor of walks in the city? For sure, there are great, ambitious artists working today who still want to confront questions like these, but the aim of the fairs isn't to highlight them, it's to promote the most salable object to decorate a room. Walk the halls of the fairs today and you'll find the collectors chilled and informal, in hoodies and sneakers, liberal in opinion and very much in touch with themselves, but in a sense they are the same as the top-hatted bourgeoisie of the nineteenth century, who wanted no more from art than an oil painting to hang over the hearth. It's almost as if art never ended.

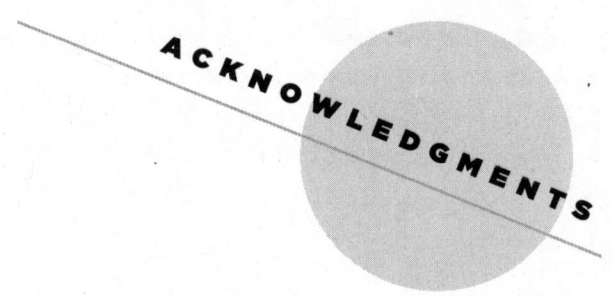

ACKNOWLEDGMENTS

COUNTLESS PEOPLE HAVE HELPED ME IN THE PROCESS OF writing this book, but I would particularly like to thank Amy Cherry, Huneeya Siddiqui, Michael Signorelli, Amy Whitaker, Andrew Hemingway, and Carol Duncan. I would like to thank my colleagues, particularly Ann-Marie Richard, for giving me the time to write, and Eric Wolf for his good cheer. I could not have written anything without the staff of the Art and Architecture Collection at the New York Public Library. And I would not have sustained the will to continue without the support of my family, Mariska, Anton, and Elliot.

Introduction: On the Coast

1. On Marinetti's early years, see Giovanni Lista, "Une enfance égyptienne," in *Marinetti* (Paris: Seghers, 1976). See also R. W. Flint, ed., *Marinetti: Selected Writings* (New York: Farrar, Straus and Giroux, 1972).
2. Eric Hobsbawm, *The Age of Empire, 1875–1914* (London: Abacus, 1994), 1–2.
3. F. T. Marinetti, "An Italian Egypt in Lombardy," in *Let's Murder the Moonshine: Selected Writings*, ed. R. W. Flint (Los Angeles, CA: Sun and Moon Press, 1991), 183.
4. Daniel Heller-Roazen, "On Tradition's Destruction: On the Library of Alexandria," *October* 100 (Spring 2002): 135.
5. Michael Haag, *Alexandria: A City of Memory* (New Haven, CT: Yale University Press, 2004), 19.
6. Marinetti, "An Italian Sensibility Born in Egypt," in *Marinetti: Selected Writings*, 225.
7. Flint, ed., *Marinetti: Selected Writings*, 9.
8. Marinetti, "An Italian Sensibility Born in Egypt," 305–10.
9. Flint, ed., *Marinetti: Selected Writings*, 9.
10. F. T. Marinetti, *Selected Poems and Related Prose*, ed. Luce Marinetti, trans. Elizabeth Napier and Barbara Studholme (New Haven, CT: Yale University Press, 2002), 7.
11. On Milan's modernization, see Christine Poggi, *Inventing Futurism: The Art and Politics of Artificial Optimism* (Princeton, NJ: Princeton University Press, 2008), 70–72.
12. Marinetti, "An Italian Egypt in Lombardy," 176, 174.
13. Marinetti, "The Founding and Manifesto of Futurism," in *Let's Murder the Moonshine*, 47–52.
14. Clare McAndrew, *The Survey of Global Collecting 2023*, Art Basel and UBS, 2023, 20.
15. Marinetti, "The Founding and Manifesto of Futurism," 47–52.

16. Marinetti, "Against Past-Loving Venice," in *Marinetti: Selected Writings*, 55–58.
17. John Milner, *Vladimir Tatlin and the Russian Avant-Garde*, 137.
18. Theo van Doesburg, "The End of Art," Paris, 1925, published in *De Stijl*, series XII, 9, 1924–25, 135–36, available at Bibliotheek Voor de Nederlandse Letteren, https://www.dbnl.org/tekst/_sti001stij03_01/_sti001stij03_01_0175.php.
19. T. J. Clar, *Image of the People: Gustave Courbet and the 1848 Revolution* (Berkeley, CA: University of California Press, 1973), 20.
20. Günter Berghaus, "Futurist *Serate* and Gallery Performances," in Vivien Greene, ed., *Italian Futurism 1901–1944: Reconstructing the Universe* (New York: Guggenheim Museum, 2014), 90.
21. Flint, ed., *Marinetti: Selected Writings*, 9.
22. Ernest Ialongo, *Filippo Tommaso Marinetti: The Artist and His Politics* (Teaneck, NJ: Fairleigh Dickinson University Press, 2015), 49.

1: Leaving Montmartre

1. Pierre-Marcel Adéma, *Apollinaire*, trans. Denise Folliot (New York: Grove Press, 1955), 120, 130.
2. T. J. Clark, quoted in David Cottington, *Radical Art: The Formation of the Avant-Garde* (New Haven, CT: Yale University Press, 2022), 77.
3. Gautier, quoted in Cottington, *Radical Art*, 76.
4. Murger, quoted in Jerrold Seigel, *Bohemian Paris: Culture, Politics, and the Boundaries of Bourgeois Life, 1830–1930* (New York: Viking Penguin, 1986), 3.
5. Seigel, *Bohemian Paris*, 31.
6. On Murger, see Seigel, *Bohemian Paris*, chap. 2.
7. Seigel, *Bohemian Paris*, 4.
8. Seigel, *Bohemian Paris*, 25.
9. Martin Sorrell, introduction, *Selected Poems*, by Guillaume Apollinaire, trans. M. Sorrell (Oxford: Oxford University Press, 2015), ix.
10. Roger Shattuck, *The Banquet Years: The Arts in France, 1885–1918* (New York: Harcourt Brace Jovanovich, 1958), 256.
11. Shattuck, *The Banquet Years*, 256.
12. John Richardson, *A Life of Picasso: Volume I, 1881–1906* (New York: Knopf, 1991), 327.
13. Adéma, *Apollinaire*, 24.
14. Richardson, *A Life of Picasso: Volume I*, 159–60.
15. Richardson, *A Life of Picasso: Volume I*, 162.
16. Richardson, *A Life of Picasso: Volume I*, 385.
17. Calvin Tomkins, *Duchamp: A Biography* (London: Pimlico, 1998), 10.
18. Shattuck, *The Banquet Years*, 274.
19. Richardson, *A Life of Picasso: Volume II, 1907–1916* (New York: Knopf, 1996), 21.

20. For *l'affaire des statuettes*, see Richardson, *Picasso, Volume II*, chap.13.
21. Seigel, *Bohemian Paris*, 350.
22. Seigel, *Bohemian Paris*, 352.
23. The subtitle of Shattuck's book reads "The Origins of the Avant-Garde in France, 1885 to World War I," but he uses the term "avant-garde" in the loose, broader sense to designate advanced art, not in the narrower sense used in this book.
24. Gertrude Stein, *The Autobiography of Alice B. Toklas* (New York: Harcourt Brace Jovanovich, 1933), 126.
25. Seigel, *Bohemian Paris*, 221.
26. Adema, *Apollinaire*, 224.
27. Guillaume Apollinaire, "Zone," in *Alcools: Poèms, 1898–1913* (Paris: Gallimard, 1920), 7–15. Translated by the author.
28. As Mark Ford notes in his review of Sorrell's translation, that final image has had many different translations: "Decapitated Sun" (William Meredith); "Sun slit throat" (Anne Hyde Greet); "The sun a severed neck" (Roger Shattuck); "Sun neck cut" (Beverley Bie Brahic); "Let the sun beheaded be" (David Lehman). See Mark Ford, "Dancing and Flirting," *London Review of Books*, May 24, 2018, 35.
29. As Martin Sorrell points out, although Eliot was reading French poetry around 1920, there is no direct evidence that "Zone" was an inspiration for "The Waste Land." See Sorrell, introduction, *Selected Poems*, xviii.
30. My definition of modernism comes from Charles Harrison, "Modernism," in Robert S. Nelson and Richard Shiff, *Critical Terms for Art History*, 2nd ed. (Chicago: University of Chicago Press, 2003), 188–201.
31. Sorrell, introduction, *Selected Poems*, xix.
32. David Cottington, *The Avant-Garde: A Very Short Introduction* (Oxford: Oxford University Press, 2013), 5.
33. On Saint-Simon see Matei Calinescu, *Five Faces of Modernity* (Durham, NC: University of North Carolina Press, 1987), 100ff.
34. Cottington, *Radical Art*, 14.
35. Starr Figura, Isabelle Cahn, and Philippe Peltier, *Félix Fénéon: The Anarchist and the Avant-garde* (New York: Museum of Modern Art, 2020), 21–22. See also Mitchell Abidor, "Letter to the Editor," *New York Review of Books*, May 14, 2020.
36. David Cottington, *Cubism and Its Histories* (Manchester, UK: Manchester University Press, 2004), 23–26.
37. See Hal Foster, Rosalind Krauss, Yve-Alain Bois, and Benjamin A. E. Buchloh, *Art Since 1900: Modernism, Antimodernism, Postmodernism* (London: Thames & Hudson, 2016), 90.
38. William Rubin, "Picasso," in *"Primitivism" in 20th Century Art*, ed. Rubin (New York: Museum of Modern Art, 1984), 262. Rubin notes that scholars have traditionally associated four types of tribal mask with the *Demoiselles*, yet he notes that there is no clear and certain evidence that any of them provided a model for Picasso.

39. Shattuck, *The Banquet Years*, 253.
40. Christopher Green, *Art in France, 1900–1940* (New Haven, CT: Yale University Press, 2000),19.
41. Leah Dickerman, *Dada: Zurich, Berlin, Hannover, Cologne, New York, Paris* (Washington D.C.: National Gallery of Art, 2005), 2.
42. James Joll, *Intellectuals in Politics* (London: Weidenfeld & Nicolson, 1960), 137.
43. Christine Poggi, *Inventing Futurism: The Art and Politics of Artificial Optimism* (Princeton, NJ: Princeton University Press, 2008), 30.
44. Joll, *Intellectuals in Politics*, 138.
45. Selena Daly, *Italian Futurism and the First World War* (Toronto: University of Toronto Press, 2016), 3.
46. Walter Adamson in *Italian Futurism 1901–1944: Reconstructing the Universe*, ed. Vivien Greene (New York: Guggenheim Museum, 2014), 175.
47. Joll, *Intellectuals in Politics*, 150.
48. Joll, *Intellectuals in Politics*, 151.
49. Caroline Tisdall and Angelo Bozzolla, *Futurism* (London: Thames & Hudson, 1985), 177.
50. Berghaus, *Theater, Performance, and the Historical Avant-Garde* (London: Palgrave Macmillan), 101.
51. Berghaus, *Theater, Performance, and the Historical Avant-Garde*, 105.
52. On the Futurists engagement with Cubism, see Neil Cox, *Cubism* (London: Phaidon, 2000), 196–99.
53. Marjorie Perloff, *The Futurist Moment: Avant-Garde, Avant-Guerre, and the Language of Rupture* (Chicago: University of Chicago Press, 1986), xvi.
54. Perloff, *The Futurist Moment*, xvi.
55. Marianne Martin, "Futurism, Unanism, and Apollinaire," *Art Journal* 28 (Spring 1969), 258.
56. James Joll, *Three Intellectuals in Politics* (New York: Pantheon Books, 1961), 138.
57. Joll, *Three Intellectuals in Politics*, 138.

2: Can You Make Works Which Are Not Works of Art?

1. For more on Duchamp's childhood and family, see "Blainville," in Calvin Tomkins, *Duchamp: A Biography* (London: Pimlico, 1998),15–30.
2. Tomkins, *Duchamp: A Biography*, 34.
3. Tomkins, *Duchamp: A Biography*, 34.
4. Details of the afternoons spent in Puteaux come from Tomkins, *Duchamp: A Biography*, 60.
5. On Duchamp's early days in Paris, see "Swimming Lessons" in Tomkins, *Duchamp: A Biography*.
6. On Picabia's childhood and education, see William A. Camfield, *Francis Picabia: His Life and Times* (Princeton, NJ: Princeton University Press, 1979).

7. Mark Polizzotti, *Revolution of the Mind: The Life of André Breton* (Boston: Black Widow Press, 2009), 105.
8. On the Salon Cubists' interests in science, see Neil Cox, *Cubism* (London: Phaidon, 2000), 180–94.
9. On Kupka's pictures, see Leah Dickerman, *Inventing Abstraction, 1910–1925: How a Radical Idea Changed Modern Art* (New York: Museum of Modern Art, 2012), 16–17, 64–66.
10. Arturo Schwarz, *Marcel Duchamp* (New York: Harry N. Abrams, 1975).
11. Tomkins, *Duchamp: A Biography*, 83.
12. Tomkins, *Duchamp: A Biography*, 133.
13. Hal Foster, Rosalind Krauss, Yve-Alain Bois, and Benjamin A. E. Buchloh, *Art Since 1900: Modernism, Antimodernism, Postmodernism* (London: Thames & Hudson, 2016), 155.
14. Tomkins, *Duchamp: A Biography*, 143.
15. Tomkins, *Duchamp: A Biography*, 162.
16. For the events surrounding Duchamp's attempt to exhibit *Fountain*, see Tomkins, *Duchamp: A Biography*, 181ff. Also see William Camfield, *Marcel Duchamp: Fountain* (Houston, TX: Houston Museum of Fine Arts, 1987).
17. Thierry De Duve, "Given the Richard Mutt Case," in *The Definitively Unfinished Marcel Duchamp*, ed. De Duve (Cambridge., MA: MIT Press, 1991), 226, n.9.
18. De Duve, "Given the Richard Mutt Case," 194.
19. See Christopher Green, *Art in France, 1900–1940* (New Haven, CT: Yale University Press, 2000), 77-79.
20. Tomkins, *Duchamp: A Biography*, 245.
21. Green, *Art in France*, 78.
22. Green, *Art in France*, 78
23. Tomkins, *Duchamp: A Biography*, 302.
24. Tomkins, *Duchamp: A Biography*, 302.
25. Tomkins, *Duchamp: A Biography*, 246.
26. Tomkins, *Duchamp: A Biography*, 246.
27. Tomkins, *Duchamp: A Biography*, 32.
28. Schwarz, *Marcel Duchamp*.
29. Dawn Ades, Neil Cox, and David Hopkins, *Marcel Duchamp* (London: Thames & Hudson, 1999), 139.
30. Jason Farago, "A (Grudging) Defense of the $120,000 Banana," *New York Times*, December 8, 2019.

3: The Wandering Prophets

1. Nicholas Fox Weber, *The Bauhaus Group* (New Haven, CT: Yale University Press, 2009), 207.
2. Fox Weber, *The Bauhaus Group*, 210.
3. Fox Weber, *The Bauhaus Group*, 210.

4. Fox Weber, *The Bauhaus Group*, 204.
5. Fox Weber, *The Bauhaus Group*, 209.
6. Kandinsky seen as aristocratic: Will Grohmann, *Wassily Kandinsky: Life and Work*, trans. Norbert Guterman (New York: Harry N. Abrams, 1958), 9.
7. Fox Weber, *The Bauhaus Group*, 206.
8. Betsy F. Moeller-Sally, "Inner Simmering," *Russian Review* 61, no.1 (January 2002): 52.
9. These are the famous opening words of Mann's short story "Gladius Dei" (1902). See Thomas Mann, *Stories of the Three Decades*, trans. H. T. Lowe-Porter (New York: Knopf, 1979).
10. Peg Weiss, *Kandinsky in Munich: The Formative Jugendstil Years* (Princeton, NJ: Princeton University Press, 1979), 3.
11. Ulrich Herbert, *A History of Twentieth Century Germany*, trans. B. Fowkes (New York: Oxford University Press, 2019), 17.
12. Robert Eben Sackett, *Popular Entertainment, Class and Politics in Munich 1900–1923* (Cambridge, MA: Harvard University Press, 1982), 65.
13. Wassily Kandinsky, "On the Spiritual in Art," in *Kandinsky: Complete Writings on Art*, vol. 1, eds., Kenneth C. Lindsay and Peter Vergo (Boston, MA: G. K. Hall & Co., 1982), 128.
14. Peg Weiss, "Kandinsky and the 'Jugendstil' Arts and Crafts Movement," *Burlington Magazine* 117, no. 866 (May 1975): 270–77, 279.
15. Weiss, *Kandinsky in Munich*, 36.
16. On Ball's ideas, see Philip Mann, *Hugo Ball: An Intellectual Biography* (London: Institute for Germanic Studies, University of London, 1987), passim.
17. On Ball's interest in Nietzsche, see Mann, *Hugo Ball*, 15–18.
18. Weiss, *Kandinsky in Munich*, 96.
19. John Richardson, *A Life of Picasso: Volume II, 1907–1916* (New York: Knopf, 1996), 348.
20. Selena Daly, *Italian Futurism and the First World War* (Toronto: University of Toronto Press, 2016), 50.
21. Daly, *Italian Futurism and the First World War*, 52.
22. Daly, *Italian Futurism and the First World War*, 53.
23. Daly, *Italian Futurism and the First World War*, 53.
24. Daly, *Italian Futurism and the First World War*, 60.
25. Daly, *Italian Futurism and the First World War*, 71.
26. Daly, *Italian Futurism and the First World War*, 170, n.52.
27. See Eric Hobsbawm, *The Age of Empire, 1875–1914* (London: Abacus, 1994), chap. 13, "From Peace to War."
28. Hobsbawm, *The Age of Empire*, 311.
29. Hobsbawm, *The Age of Empire*, 303.
30. Hobsbawm, *The Age of Empire*, 325–26.
31. Vivien Greene, ed., *Italian Futurism 1901–1944: Reconstructing the Universe* (New York: Guggenheim Museum, 2014), 176.
32. Ernest Ialongo, *Filippo Tommaso Marinetti: The Artist and His Politics* (Teaneck, NJ: Fairleigh Dickinson University Press, 2015), 1, 63.

33. Hans Richter, *Dada, Art and Anti-Art* (New York: Oxford University Press, 1978), 9.
34. Hugo Ball, *Flight Out of Time*, ed. J. Elderfield, trans. Ann Raimes (New York: Viking Press, 1974), lii.
35. Gerhardt Steinke, *The Life and Work of Hugo Ball* (The Hague, Netherlands: Mouton & Co., 1967), 111.
36. Ball, *Flight Out of Time*, 10.
37. Richard Huelsenbeck, *Memoirs of a Dada Drummer*, ed. Hans J. Kleinschmidt, trans. J. Neugroschel (Berkeley, CA: University of California Press, 1969), 6.
38. On Ball's early years, see John Elderfield, introduction, in Ball, *Flight Out of Time*, passim.
39. Quotes from Huelsenbeck, *Memoirs of a Dada Drummer*, 2–3.
40. Ball, *Flight Out of Time*, xlix.
41. Thomas F. Rugh, "Emmy Hennings and the Emergence of Zurich Dada," *Woman's Art Journal* 2, no. 1 (Spring-Summer 1981): 1.
42. Hubert Van Den Berg, "The Star of the Cabaret Voltaire: The Other Life of Emmy Hennings," in B. Pichon and K. Riha, eds., *Dada Zurich: A Clown's Game from Nothing*, vol. 2 of *Crisis and the Arts: The History of Dada*, ed. Stephen C. Foster (New York: G. K. Hall & Co., 1996), 69.
43. Huelsenbeck, *Memoirs of Dada Drummer*, 4.
44. Leah Dickerman, *Dada: Zurich, Berlin, Hannover, Cologne, New York, Paris* (Washington D.C.: National Gallery of Art, 2005), 19.
45. Ball, *Flight Out of Time*, 18.
46. Ball, *Flight Out of Time*, 4.
47. Ball, *Flight Out of Time*, 16.
48. On the *Chat Noir*, see Seigel, *Bohemian Paris*, 216-41.
49. Denis Calandra, "Karl Valentin and Bertolt Brecht," *Drama Review* 18, no. 1 (March 1974): 90.
50. Debbie Lewer, "Hugo Ball, Iconoclasm and the Origins of Dada in Zurich," *Oxford Art Journal* 32, no. 1 (2009): 28.
51. Huelsenbeck, *Memoirs of a Dada Drummer*, 14.
52. Dickerman, *Dada*, 20.
53. Huelsenbeck, *Memoirs of a Dada Drummer*, 9.
54. Huelsenbeck, *Memoirs of a Dada Drummer*, 12.
55. Dickerman, *Dada*, 27.
56. Dickerman, *Dada*, 28.
57. Dickerman, *Dada*, 36–38.
58. Dickerman, *Dada*, 20.
59. Van Den Berg, "The Star of the Cabaret Voltaire," 79.
60. Van Den Berg, "The Star of the Cabaret Voltaire," 74.

4: The Pope

1. On Tzara's arrival in Zurich, see Marius Hentea, *Da Da Ta Ta: The Real Life and Celestial Adventures of Tristan Tzara* (Cambridge, MA: MIT Press, 2014), 59ff.

2. Hentea, *Da Da Ta Ta*, 1.
3. Leah Dickerman, *Dada: Zurich, Berlin, Hannover, Cologne, New York, Paris* (Washington D.C.: National Gallery of Art, 2005), 35.
4. In most cases, biographical details for Breton come from Mark Polizzotti's excellent and exhaustive biography, *Revolution of the Mind: The Life of André Breton* (Boston, MA: Black Widow Press, 2009).
5. Polizzotti, *Revolution of the Mind*, 15.
6. Polizzotti, *Revolution of the Mind*, 197.
7. Polizzotti, *Revolution of the Mind*, 170.
8. Polizzotti, *Revolution of the Mind*, 145.
9. On *La Révolution Surréaliste*, see Polizzotti, *Revolution of the Mind*, 201–3.
10. Polizzotti, *Revolution of the Mind*, 93–94.
11. As Polizzotti notes, Breton was not the inventor of automatic writing, and the ideas has roots at least as far back as the eighteenth century, but his way of thinking about it, not purely as therapy or purely as artistic technique, but as a means to bridge art and the unconscious, was novel. See *Revolution of the Mind*, 94–95.
12. André Breton and Philippe Soupault, *Magnetic Fields*, trans. David Gascoyne (London: Atlas Press, 1985), 39.
13. My treatment of this narrative comes from André Breton, *Nadja* (New York: Grove Press, 1984).
14. Louis Aragon, *Paris Peasant*, trans. Simon Watson Taylor (London: Cape, 1971), 13.
15. Breton, *Nadja*, 55–56.
16. Polizzotti, *Revolution of the Mind*, 146.
17. Hal Foster, Rosalind Krauss, Yve-Alain Bois, and Benjamin A. E. Buchloh, *Art Since 1900: Modernism, Antimodernism, Postmodernism* (London: Thames & Hudson, 2016), 214.
18. Polizzotti, *Revolution of the Mind*, 245.
19. Polizzotti, *Revolution of the Mind*, 253.

5: The Monument without a Beard

1. John Richardson, *A Life of Picasso: Volume II, 1907–1916* (New York: Knopf, 1996), 254.
2. On Tatlin's youth, see John Milner, *Vladimir Tatlin and the Russian Avant-Garde* (New Haven, CT: Yale University Press, 1983), 3–9.
3. They studied at an atelier called La Palette, at which Henri Le Fauconnier also taught. See Milner, *Vladimir Tatlin and the Russian Avant-Garde*, 71.
4. Christina Lodder, *Russian Constructivism* (New Haven, CT: Yale University Press, 1983), 11.
5. Brik's words as reported by Lila. Bengt Jangfeldt, *Mayakovsky: A Biography*, trans. H. D. Watson (Chicago: University of Chicago Press, 2014), 121.
6. Jangfeldt, *Mayakovsky*, 12, 21.

7. Herbert Marshall, *Mayakovsky and His Poetry* (London: Pilot Press, 1945), 29.
8. Jangfeldt, *Mayakovsky*, 98
9. John Reed, *Ten Days That Shook the World* (London: Penguin Classics, 1977).
10. Sheila Fitzpatrick, *The Commissariat of Enlightenment: Soviet Organization of the Arts and Education Under Lunacharsky* (Cambridge: Cambridge University Press, 1970), 9.
11. Fitzpatrick, *The Commissariat of Enlightenment*, xii.
12. Fitzpatrick, *The Commissariat of Enlightenment*, 2.
13. Lodder, *Russian Constructivism*, 8.
14. Milner, *Vladimir Tatlin and the Russian Avant-Garde*, 3.
15. Quote from Igor Grabar's account. See Christina Lodder, "Lenin's Plan for Monumental Propaganda," in M. C. Bown and B. Taylor, *Art of the Soviets* (Manchester, UK: Manchester University Press, 1993), 18.
16. Maria Gough, quoted in Leah Dickerman, "Monumental Propaganda," *October* 165 (Summer 2018): 181.
17. Norbert Lynton, *Tatlin's Tower: Monument to Revolution* (New Haven, Conn.: Yale University Press, 2009), 65.
18. Lodder, *Russian Constructivism*, 61.
19. Lodder, *Russian Constructivism*, 88.
20. Hubertus Gassner, "The Constructivists: Modernism in the Way to Modernization," in *The Great Utopia: The Russian and Soviet Avant-Garde, 1915-1932* (New York: Guggenheim Museum, 1992), 299.
21. Gassner, "The Constructivists," 299.
22. Kiaer, *Imagine No Possessions: The Socialist Objects of Russian Constructivism* (Cambridge, MA: MIT Press, 2005), 71, 74, 76, 83, 86.
23. Quoted in Kiaer, *Imagine No Possessions*, 7.
24. Will Grohmann, *Wassily Kandinsky: Life and Work*, trans. Norbert Guterman (New York: Harry N. Abrams, 1957), 161.
25. Kiaer, *Imagine No Possessions*, 201.
26. On the expulsion of intellectuals, see Lesley Chamberlain, *The Philosophy Steamer: Lenin and the Exile of the Intelligentsia* (London: Atlantic Books, 2006).
27. Chamberlain, *The Philosophy Steamer*, 1, 331 n.1.
28. S. A. Smith, *Russia in Revolution: An Empire in Crisis 1890–1928* (Oxford: Oxford University Press, 2017), 334.
29. Fitzpatrick, *The Commissariat of Enlightenment*, 120.
30. Jangfeldt, *Mayakovsky*, 162.
31. Jangfeldt, *Mayakovsky*, 225. Among the other poets left in Russia were Mandelstam, Pasternak, Anna Akhmatova, Klyuyev, and Yesenin.
32. On "Fifth International," see Jangfeldt, *Mayakovsky*, 164–69.
33. "The Suicide Note," from *Vladimir Mayakovsky: Selected Poems*, trans. James H. MacGavran III (Evanston, IL: Northwestern University Press, 2013), 155.
34. Milner, *Vladimir Tatlin and the Russian Avant-Garde*, 224.
35. Milner, *Vladimir Tatlin and the Russian Avant-Garde*, 220.
36. Jangfeldt, *Mayakovsky*, 555.

37. Rodchenko quote from David Elliott, ed., *Rodchenko and the Arts of Revolutionary Russia* (New York: Pantheon Books, 1979), 104.

6: Saint-Peter of the Straight Line

1. Hans Janssen, *Piet Mondrian: A Life* (London: Ridinghouse, 2022), 160.
2. Janssen, *Piet Mondrian: A Life*, 306.
3. Piet Mondriaan shortened his name to Mondrian when he came to France and found the French could not pronounce it. See Janssen, *Piet Mondrian: A Life*, 297.
4. Michel Seuphor, *Piet Mondrian: Life and Work* (New York: Harry N. Abrams, 1956), 44.
5. Alister E. McGrath, "Shapers of Protestantism: John Calvin," in A. E. McGrath and Darren C. Marks, *Blackwell Companion to Protestantism* (Oxford: Blackwell, 2004), 53–65.
6. Janssen, *Piet Mondrian: A Life*, 153–56.
7. Janssen, *Piet Mondrian: A Life*, 153.
8. Piet Mondrian, "Toward the True Vision of Reality," in *The New Art, The New Life: The Collected Writings*, ed. and trans. Harry Holtzman and Martin S. James (Boston, MA: G. K. Hall, 1986), 338–41.
9. Mildred Friedman, ed., *De Stijl 1917–31: Visions of Utopia* (Oxford: Phaidon, 1982), 33.
10. Janssen, *Piet Mondrian: A Life*, 89, 165.
11. On Theosophy, see Edward L. Queen II, Stephen R Prothero, and Gardiner H. Shattuck, Jr., *The Encyclopedia of American Religious History* (New York: Facts on File, 1996), 663–65.
12. Robert P. Welsh, *Piet Mondrian Centennial Exhibition* (New York: Guggenheim Museum, 1971), 40.
13. Michael White, *De Stijl and Dutch Modernism* (Manchester, UK: Manchester University Press, 1983), 24.
14. White, *De Stijl and Dutch Modernism*, 25.
15. Michael White, "Theo van Doesburg: A Counter-Life," in *Van Doesburg & the International Avant-Garde: Constructing a New World*, Gladys Fabre and Doris Wintgens Hötte, eds. (London: Tate, 2009), 68.
16. White, "Theo van Doesburg," 70.
17. Carel Blotkamp, *De Stijl: The Formative Years 1917–22*, trans. C. L. Loeb and A.L. Loeb (Cambridge, MA: MIT Press, 1982), 4.
18. Seuphor, *Piet Mondrian: Life and Work*, 149.
19. White, "Theo van Doesburg," 68.
20. Blotkamp, *De Stijl: The Formative Years*, 6.
21. White, *De Stijl and Dutch Modernism*, 40.
22. Joost Baljeu, *Theo van Doesburg* (New York: Macmillan, 1974), 20.
23. Reyner Banham, *Theory and Design in the First Machine Age* (New York: Praeger, 1967), 151.
24. Blotkamp, *De Stijl: The Formative Years*, 8.

25. Fabre and Hötte, *Van Doesburg & the International Avant-Garde*, 77.
26. White, *De Stijl and Dutch Modernism*, 1.
27. Fabre and Hötte, *Van Doesburg & the International Avant-Garde*, chap. 1, Doris Wintgens Hötte, "Van Doesburg Tackles the Continent," 11.
28. White, *De Stijl and Dutch Modernism*, 3; Blotkamp, *De Stijl: The Formative Years*; Doris Wintgens Hötte, "Van Doesburg Tackles the Continent," 19.
29. William J. R. Curtis, *Modern Architecture Since 1900* (London: Phaidon, 1996), 154.
30. Baljeu, *Theo van Doesburg*, 20.
31. Van Doesburg quoted in April 1920, Fabre and Hötte, *Van Doesburg and the International Avant-Garde*, 10.
32. On Mondrian's return to Paris, see Janssen, *Mondrian: A Life*, 49–51.
33. Yve-Alain Bois, *Piet Mondrian 1872–1944* (Boston, MA: Bullfinch Press, 1994), 193.
34. Mark Cheetham, *The Rhetoric of Purity: Essentialist Theory and the Advent of Abstract Painting* (Cambridge: Cambridge University Press, 1991), 104.
35. On the shifts in Mondrian's work, see Bois, *Piet Mondrian 1872–1944*, 315–16 and passim.
36. On stained glass, see Gladys Fabre, "A Universal Language of the Arts," in Fabre and Hötte, *Van Doesburg & the International Avant-Garde*, 47. For remarks about writing paper, see Evert van Straaten, *Theo van Doesburg: Constructor of the New Life* (Otterlo, The Netherlands: Kröller-Müller Museum, 1994), 11.
37. Yve-Alain Bois, "Mondrian and the Theory of Architecture," *Assemblage*, no. 4 (October 1987), 116.
38. Robert P. Welsh, "De Stijl: A Reintroduction," in *De Stijl 1917–31: Visions of Utopia*, ed. Mildred Friedman, ed. (Oxford: Phaidon, 1982), 33.
39. Janssen, *Piet Mondrian: A Life*, 68.
40. Theo van Doesburg, "The End of Art," Paris, 1925, published in *De Stijl*, series XII, 9, 1924–25, 135–36, available at Bibliotheek Voor de Nederlandse Letteren, https://www.dbnl.org/tekst/_sti001stij03_01/_sti001stij03_01_0175.php.
41. Seuphor, *Piet Mondrian: Life and Work*.
42. On Mondrian's interiors, see Nancy Troy, *The De Stijl Environment* (Cambridge, MA: MIT Press, 1983).
43. Bois, "Mondrian and the Theory of Architecture."
44. Reyner Banham, *Theory and Design in the First Machine Age* (Cambridge, MA: MIT Press, 1980), 155.
45. Curtis, *Modern Architecture*, 159.
46. Kenneth Frampton, "Neoplasticism and Architecture," in Friedman, *De Stijl 1917–31: Visions of Utopia*, 105.
47. Banham, *Theory and Design in the First Machine Age*, 160.
48. Seuphor, *Piet Mondrian: Life and Work*, 171.
49. Cheetham, *The Rhetoric of Purity*, 113.
50. Cheetham, *The Rhetoric of Purity*, 105.
51. Banham, *Theory and Design in the First Machine Age*, 149.
52. White, *and Dutch Modernism*, 173.
53. Bois, "Mondrian and the Theory of Architecture," 123.

54. Craig Eliason, "All the Serious Men Are Sick: Van Doesburg, Mondrian and Dada," *Simiolus* 34, no.1 (2009–10), 53.
55. Bois, *Piet Mondrian 1872–1944*, 106.
56. Blotkamp, "Mondrian," *De Stijl: The Formative Years*, 71.

7: The School, the Cathedral, and the Whitewashed Die

1. On Gropius's experiences during the First World War, see Fiona MacCarthy, *Gropius: The Man Who Built the Bauhaus* (Cambridge, MA: Belknap Press, 2019), 72–101.
2. Frank Whitford, ed., *The Bauhaus: Masters and Students by Themselves* (Woodstock, NY: Overlook Press, 1993), 21.
3. MacCarthy, *Gropius*, 67.
4. On Muthesius and ideas in German design, see William J. R. Curtis, *Modern Architecture Since 1900* (London: Phaidon, 1996), 99–111.
5. Gropius quoted in Marco De Michelis, "Walter Determann: Bauhaus Settlement Weimar, 1920," in *Bauhaus: Workshops for Modernity*, eds. Barry Bergdoll and Leah Dickerman (New York: Museum of Modern Art, 2009), 86–89.
6. Gropius quoted in Charles W. Haxthausen, "Walter Gropius and Lyonel Feininger. Bauhaus Manifesto. 1919" in Bergdoll and Dickerman, *Bauhaus*, 64–67.
7. MacCarthy, *Gropius*, 108.
8. Gillian Naylor, *The Bauhaus Reassessed: Sources and Design Theory* (New York: Dutton, 1985), 81.
9. Naylor, *The Bauhaus Reassessed*, 78.
10. Frank Whitford, *Bauhaus* (London: Thames & Hudson, 1984), 54.
11. Whitford, *Bauhaus*, 55.
12. Naylor, *The Bauhaus Reassessed*, 77.
13. Leah Dickerman, "Bauhaus Fundaments," in Bergdoll and Dickerman, *Bauhaus*, 17.
14. On Expressionism and Itten, see Curtis, *Modern Architecture*, 185.
15. Christopher Wilk, "Marcel Breuer and Gunta Stölzl, 'African Chair,' 1921" in Bergdoll and Dickerman, *Bauhaus*, 100–103.
16. MacCarthy, *Gropius*, 109; On food shortages, see Justus H.Ulbricht, "Un-German Activities: Attacks from the Right, 1919–1933," in Philipp Oswalt, ed., *Bauhaus Conflicts* (Ostfildern: Hatje Cantz, 2009), 18.
17. Whitford, *Bauhaus*, 52.
18. MacCarthy, *Gropius*, 4, 137.
19. On Bauhaus parties, see MacCarthy, *Gropius*, 118–19.
20. Whitford, *Bauhaus*, 117.
21. Whitford, *Bauhaus*, 118.
22. MacCarthy, *Gropius*, 141.
23. MacCarthy, *Gropius*, 140.
24. MacCarthy, *Gropius*, 141.
25. Quote and other details of Moholy-Nagy's biography come from Sibyl

Moholy-Nagy, *Moholy-Nagy: Experiment in Totality* (New York: Harper and Brothers, 1950), 6.
26. Moholy-Nagy, *Moholy-Nagy*, 30.
27. The words of his wife, Sibyl Moholy-Nagy. See *Moholy-Nagy*, 44.
28. Whitford, *Bauhaus*, 127.
29. Whitford, *Bauhaus*, 128.
30. Frederic Schwartz, *Wilhelm Wagenfeld and Carl Jakob Jucker. Table Lamp. 1923–24*, n Bergdoll and Dickerman, *Bauhaus*, 138–41.
31. De Michelis, "Walter Determann," in Bergdoll and Dickerman, *Bauhaus*, 89.
32. Bergdoll, "Bauhaus Multiplied: Paradoxes of Architecture and Design in and After the Bauhaus" in Bergdoll and Dickerman, *Bauhaus*, 47.
33. Magdalena Droste, *Bauhaus 1919–1933* (Cologne: Taschen, 1990), 105.
34. Droste, *Bauhaus 1919–1933*, 105.
35. Marcel Franciscono, *Walter Gropius and the Founding of the Bauhaus in Weimar* (Urbana, IL: University of Illinois Press, 1971), 166.
36. Naylor, *The Bauhaus Reassessed*, 60.
37. Naylor, *The Bauhaus Reassessed*, 60.
38. Hal Foster, Rosalind Krauss, Yve-Alain Bois, and Benjamin A. E. Buchloh, *Art Since 1900: Modernism, Antimodernism, Postmodernism* (London: Thames & Hudson, 2016), 212.
39. Foster, Krauss, Bois, and Buchloh, *Art Since 1900*, 212.
40. MacCarthy, *Gropius*, 161.
41. On Gropius's Dessau building, see Curtis, *Modern Architecture*, 196.
42. Criticism quoted in Curtis, *Modern Architecture*, 195.
43. Whitford, *Bauhaus*, 185.
44. Curtis, *Modern Architecture*, 199.
45. Whitford, *Bauhaus*, 187–89.
46. For more on the Bauhaus in the United States, see Achim Borchardt-Hume, *Albers and Moholy-Nagy: From the Bauhaus to the New World* (London: Tate, 2006).
47. Borchardt-Hume's essay, *Albers and Moholy-Nagy*, 76.

8: Situations

1. Andrew Hussey, *The Game of War: The Life and Death of Guy Debord* (London: Jonathan Cape, 2001), 92.
2. Hussey, *The Game of War*, 126.
3. Andrew Hussey, *Speaking East: The Strange and Enchanted Life of Isidore Isou* (London: Reaktion Books, 2021), 7.
4. Ivan Chtcheglov believed a drift should be months long. See Simon Sadler, *The Situationist City*, 93.
5. Hussey, *The Game of War*, 93.
6. Hussey, *The Game of War*, 50.
7. Guy Debord, *Panegyric* (New York: Verso, 2004), 29.
8. Details of Breton's departure and life in the United States come from *Revo-*

lution of the Mind: The Life of André Breton (Boston, MA: Black Widow Press, 2009), 445, 450–51.
9. Pollizoti, *Revolution of the Mind*, 450.
10. On the surrealists in New York, see Charles Darwent, *Surrealists in New York: Atelier 17 and the Birth of Abstract Expressionism* (London: Thames & Hudson, 2022).
11. Ernest Ialongo, *Filippo Tommaso Marinetti: The Artist and His Politics* (Teaneck, NJ: Fairleigh Dickinson University Press, 2015), 298.
12. Hussey, *The Game of War*, 112. On the "Report on the Construction of Situations," see 113–16.
13. Hussey, *The Game of War*, 112.
14. Hussey, *The Game of War*, 13, 15.
15. Hussey, *The Game of War*, 22.
16. Debord, *Panegyric*, 12.
17. Hussey, *Speaking East*, 206ff.
18. On Isou's Letterism see Hussey, *Game of War*, 33–45, and Anselm Jappe, *Guy Debord* (Oakland, CA: PM Press, 2018), 45–62.
19. Hussey, *The Game of War*, 38.
20. Hussey, *The Game of War*, 48.
21. Adrian Dannatt, "Obituary: Gil J. Wolman," *The Independent*, August 2, 1995.
22. Hussey, *The Game of War*, 51.
23. Hussey, *The Game of War*, 318.
24. Hussey, *The Game of War*, 329.
25. Hussey, *The Game of War*, 214.
26. Hussey, *The Game of War*, 67–68.
27. Sadler, *The Situationist City*, 105.
28. Guy Debord, "Report on the Construction of Situations," in Tom McDonough, ed., *Guy Debord and the Situationist International: Texts and Documents* (Cambridge, MA: MIT Press, 2002), 38.
29. On Debord's attitudes to art, see Jappe, *Guy Debord*, 63–72.
30. Guy Debord, "Editorial Notes: The Sense of Decay in Art," *October* 97 (Winter 1997): 106. Debord stated that situations were the opposite of works of art on the basis that artworks "are attempts at the absolute valorization and preservation of the present moment."
31. Jappe, *Guy Debord*, 67.
32. Hussey, *The Game of War*, 73.
33. Hussey, *The Game of War*, 126.
34. Sadler, *The Situationist City*, 70.
35. Robert McCarter, *Aldo Van Eyck* (New Haven, CT: Yale University Press, 2015), 39.
36. McCarter, *Aldo Van Eyck*, 51.
37. Mark Wigley, *Constant's New Babylon: The Hyper-Architecture of Desire* (Rotterdam: 010 Publishers, 1998), 13.
38. Wigley, *Constant's New Babylon*, 12.
39. Sadler, *The Situationist City*, 120.

40. On Debord's reimagined Paris, see Sadler, *The Situationist City*, 104–9.
41. Wigley, *Constant's New Babylon*, 33.
42. Tom Nairn and Angelo Quattrocchi, *The Beginning of the End: France, May 1968* (London: Verso, 1998), 104–5.
43. David Caute, *'68: The Years of the Barricades* (London: Paladin, 1988), 189.
44. Kristen Ross, *May '68 and Its Afterlives* (Chicago: University of Chicago Press, 2002), 193–94.
45. Hussey, *The Game of War*, 111, 117.
46. Hussey, *The Game of War*, 117.
47. Hussey, *The Game of War*, 116.
48. Hussey, *The Game of War*, 273.
49. Hussey, *The Game of War*, 170.
50. Hussey, *The Game of War*, 196.
51. Kristin Ross, "Lefebvre on the Situationists: An Interview," in McDonough, *Guy Debord and the Situationist International*, 275.
52. Peter Wollen, "Bitter Victory: The Art and Politics of the Situationist International," 2001, in Elisabeth Sussman, ed., *On the Passage of a Few People Through a Rather Brief Moment in Time: The Situationist International, 1957–1972* (Cambridge, MA: MIT Pres, 1989), 59, n.30. For the attack on Wollen, see T. J. Clark and Donald Nicholson-Smith, "Why Art Can't Kill the Situationist International," *October* 79 (Winter 1997).
53. Debord, *Panegyric*, 39.
54. Debord, *Panegyric*, 44, 37.
55. Debord, *Panegyric*, 40.
56. Hussey, *The Game of War*, 274.

Epilogue: The Future of an Illusion

1. Robert Smithson, *The Writings of Robert Smithson*, ed. Nancy Holt (New York: New York University Press, 1979), 216.
2. Peter Bürger, *The Theory of the Avant-Garde*, trans. Michael Shaw (Minneapolis, MN: University of Minnesota Press, 1984).
3. Among the most notable critiques include Hal Foster, "Who's Afraid of the Neo-Avant-Garde" in *The Return of the Real* (Cambridge, MA: MIT Press, 1996), and Benjamin Buchloh, "Theorizing the Avant-Garde," *Art in America*, November 1984.

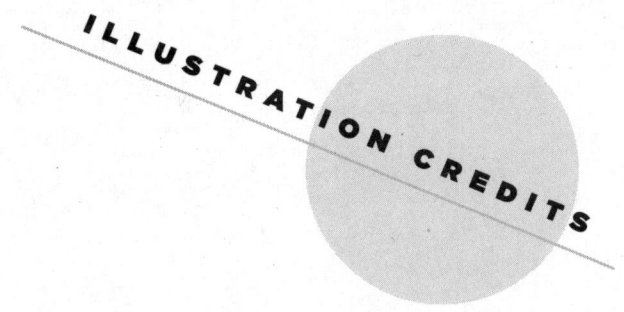

ILLUSTRATION CREDITS

1	Photo by Emilia Sommariva. Archivio GBB / Alamy Stock Photo.
15	Hi-Story / Alamy Stock Photo.
41	Bygone Collection / Alamy Stock Photo.
65	DLA Marbach.
93	Photo by Henri Manuel, 1927. Archivio GBB / Alamy Stock Photo.
117	Heritage Image Partnership Limited / Alamy Stock Photo.
122	GL Archive / Alamy Stock Photo.
143	Photo by Rogi André. Album / Alamy Stock Photo.
171	Heritage Image Partnership Ltd. / Alamy Stock Photo.
189	Zuma Press, Inc. / Alamy Stock Photo.
197	Mondadori Portfolio / Electa / Giorgio Maffei / Bridgeman Images.
223	Nathan Allred / Alamy Stock Photo.
229	Chris Bull / Alamy Stock Photo.

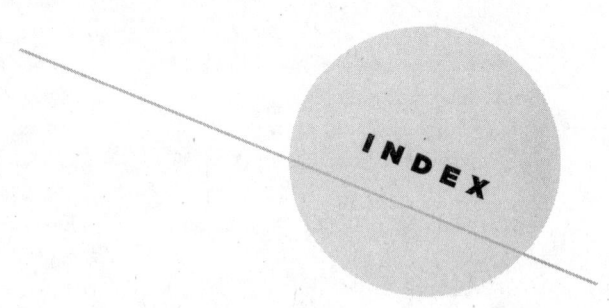

INDEX

Page numbers in *italics* indicate a figure on the corresponding page.

abstraction, 10, 166
    abstract art, 70, 88, 128, 166, 180
    abstract photography, 40
    Cubism and, 49–50, 154
    extreme abstraction of the avant-garde, 10, 166
    high Modernist abstraction, 88
    Mondrian and, 147–50
    in Russian art, 88, 122, 129, 132, 140
    among the Situationists, 210–11
    the spiritual, abstract art behind geometric ornament, 70, 128
    in theater and caberet performance, 73, 83, 85–86, 88–89
    Van Doesburg and, 152–54, 159
    See also geometry
Academy of Fine Arts, Amsterdam, 146
Adrianople, 35
Advertisement Constructors Mayakovsky-Rodchenko, 134
advertising, 105–6, 120, 133–34, 194, 196, 203, 218
    as "commercial, industrial agitation," 135
    sexuality in, 115
    the treason of working in, 120, 133–35, 194, 196, 207

"Advice to the Romans" (Marinetti), 37
Africa, 6, 85, 109, 210
    African and Oceanic masks, 31, 87, 114
    Etoumbi region of the Congo, 31
    tribal art, 26, 87, 207, 237n38
    See also North Africa
African Chair, the, 181
Agero, Auguste, 24
agitation, 130, 135, 208–9
"air-bicycle," 139
Ai Wei Wei, 140
Akhmatova, Anna, 243n31
"A la Villette" (At La Villette), 84
Albers, Anni, 175
Albers, Joseph, 175, 186, 195
Alexandria, Egypt, 1–2, 11, 35
Algiers, 204–5, 206
alienation, 113, 210
"All Meetinged Out" (Mayakovsky), 138
Alpine Architecture watercolor series, 176
Alps, 73
Alsace, France, 171
Altstadt, Switzerland, 94
American spiritualism, 148

Amorpha, Fugue in Two Colors (Kupka), 49
Amorpha, Warm Chromatic (Kupka), 49
"amplitude" (amplification), 205
Amsterdam, 146, 152, 157, 213
Amsterdam Academy of Fine Arts, 146
Amsterdam School of architecture, 156
anarchism, 28–29, 81, 120
anarcho-syndicalism, 19
Anglophilia, 99
anomie, 48
anti-Semitism, 95, 101
anxiety, 48, 113
apocalyptic and postapocalyptic future, 71, 223
Apollinaire, Guillaume, *15*, 15–40, 47–48
    arrest of, 23
    on the Cubists, 31–32, 51
    in Deauville, 72
    early life of, 19–20
    influence on Breton, 97, 100, 105
    influence on Debord, 204
    meeting Picasso, 21–23
    at war and death of, 72–73
    "Zone," 25–27
applied arts, 46, 88, 178
Aragon, Louis, 100–101, 103–4, 108, 111
architects, 83, 153–54, 156
architecture
    Amsterdam School, 156
    Beaux Arts architecture, 164
    concept of a *Stadtkrone* (City Crown), 177
    De Stijl and, 156, 159, 161, 163–67
    Debord's thoughts on, 209–10, 212–13
    experimental, 40
    Expressionism and, 69
    Futurists in, 156
    Gropius's views on, 177–78
    Independent Group, 212
    International Style, 193
    Mondrian's thoughts on, 162–63
    Schröder House, Utrecht, 163
    social housing, 194
    technology and, 176–77
    See also Bauhaus; Gropius, Walter
"architecture-as-environment," 163
Arensberg, Walter, 54–58, 61
Aristotle, 2
Arles, France, 221
Armory Show, New York, 52–53, 54
Arnhem, Netherlands, 144
Arp, Hans, 84, 87–88, 97
art
    applied arts, 46, 88, 178
    art-as-construction, 131
    authenticity in, 50, 98, 181, 206, 212, 224, 226–27
    as commodity, 131, 211
    the end of, 8–9, 32, 160, 226, 230
    equilibrium and, 158–60, 166
    fine art, 10, 88, 95–96, 175, 178, 196, 211
    looking at art through a scientific lens, 49–50
    manifestos on various elements of the arts, 37, 39–40
    the more, the better, 7
    motifs of, 26, 112, 115, 148, 186
    a new religion of art, 12, 31
    ornament and objects, 155
    role in society, 30–31, 190, 203–4, 210
    as a "safety valve" for society, 12, 81
    in search of a spiritual abstract art, 70, 128
    as spectacle, 77, 115, 130, 203, 210–11, 218, 220, 231
    tribal art, 26, 87, 207, 237n38
    unconventional art, 31, 206, 226
    understanding art and life through a walk in the city, 109–14
    See also avant-garde; modern art

"Art and Technology—A New Unity" (Gropius), 187
Art Basel Miami Beach, 5–14, 62–63, 230–32
art fairs
    Art Basel Miami Beach, 5–14, 62–63, 230–32
    attendants, 63
    the attraction of destroying the modern art fair, 8–9
    See also art, why kill it
art galleries. See galleries; museums
artists
    the author takes up painting, 42–45
    branding, 33, 170
    in collaboration, 28, 87–88, 153, 156, 166, 177, 211
    as "essential art workers," 46–47, 60
    "fine artists," 47, 60
    handicraft among, 184, 191
    as "men of imagination," 27
    as *respirateurs* ("breathers"), 60
    sexuality of female artists, 91
    special role in society, 27, 69, 211
    suicides of, 89–90, 138, 140, 218
    thinking in relationships, 144, 150
    turning into engineers, 131, 134, 139
    See also group identity
Artist's Shit (Manzoni), 226
art movements and styles
    Art Nouveau, 69, 146–48
    Arts and Crafts movement, 154, 155, 156, 174, 175–78, 189, 192
    Barbizon School of painting, 146
    Blaue Reiter group, 70
    Divisionism, 38, 148
    Elementarism, 168
    Expressionism, 69–71, 89, 180–81, 192
    Fauvism, 31, 42, 48, 50
    folk arts, 82, 118, 122, 181
    Hague School, 146
    Impressionism, 28, 48, 122
    "Neo-Impressionism," 28
    Neo-Plasticism, 150, 153, 158, 160–61, 169
    Post-Impressionism, 50
    Rayonism, 122
    realism in, 146–47, 225
    World of Art group, 122
    See also abstraction; avant-garde; group identity; manifestos
Art Nouveau, 69, 146–48
Arts and Crafts movement, 154, 155, 156, 174, 175–78, 189, 192
art schools, 45, 67
    Amsterdam Academy of Fine Arts, 146
    École des Beaux Arts, 46–47, 164
    Harvard Graduate School of Design, 195
    Illinois Institute of Technology, 196
    Imperial Academy of the Arts, 127
    Kunstgewerbeschule (Grand Ducal School of the Arts and Crafts), 174
    Weimar Academy of Art, 174
    Zurich School of Applied Arts, 87
    See also Bauhaus
art, why kill it
    "Art ends with us," 131
    "Art has poisoned our life," 9, 160
    "Art is dead," 9
    the end of art, 8–9, 32, 160, 226, 230
    the self-destruction of art, 205
    See also art fairs
"art workers," 46–47, 60
art world
    collectors of, 54, 58–59, 118, 196, 211, 219, 231–32
    commercialization of, 170

art world (*continued*)
    conventions of, 10, 26, 32, 39, 49–50, 63, 202, 227
    magazines, 28, 54, 100–101, 104, 151, 154, 161, 208, 231
    museums, 6–8, 12–13, 67, 130, 227–28, 230
    in New York, 44
    in Paris, 38, 44, 51, 62
    today, 202, 227–32
    See also art fairs; art schools
Aseyev, Nikolay, 125
assemblage, 39–40
Athenian Mouseion, 2
Austria, Vienna, 35, 112–13, 179
Austro-Hungarian Empire, 34–35, 74, 86, 184–85
Auteuil, France, 16, 26, 46
authenticity, 50, 98, 181, 206, 212, 224, 226–27
automatic writing, 105, 242n11
automobiles, 5, 25–26, 48, 69, 115, 130, 160
Auvergne, France, 218, 221
avant-garde, 1–14, 223–32
    ambition to bring art *into* life, 18–19
    authenticity and the, 50, 98, 181, 206, 212, 224, 226–27
    "banquet years" of, 23
    the Bauhaus, 75, 171–96
    the Bohemians, 15–20, 33, 81–82, 206
    a bowl of "avant-garde" noodles, 11
    the city of the, 33
    the Constructivists, 117–41
    contesting the value of bourgeois culture, 63, 120, 203, 225
    the Cubists, 30–32, 39, 48–54
    Dada, 9, 77–78, 83, 87–89
    De Stijl, 9, 151–57, 165–68
    as a distinctly Western phenomenon, 30–31
    the extreme abstraction of the, 10, 166
    female artists of the, 88–92
    forms, 39–40
    the Futurists, 15–40, 73–77
    institutionalization of the, 175
    later avant-gardes, 223–32
    the Lettrists, 197, 204–5, 208–9, 211, 218
    "neo-avant-garde," 226–27
    outrage in the DNA of the, 25–32, 38, 63
    as perpetual agitation, 208–9
    relentless logic of, 208–9
    the Situationists, 36, *197*, 197–3, 204, 209–11, 217, 220
    the Surrealists, 9, 31, 36, 102, 105–13, 114–15, 198, 204
    the Symbolists, 4, 70, 98, 101, 122, 125, 146, 148
    the term, 11, 27–28, 43, 237n23
    See also group identity; manifestos; *specific artists and artforms*

Bakunin, Mikhail, 88
Balkans, 11, 35
Ball, Hugo, 9, 10, 65, 70, 78, 79–90, 95–97, 114
Banham, Reyner, 165–66
"banquet years," 23
Barbizon School of painting, 146
Barcelona, Spain, 30, 77, 165
Baron, Jacques, 103
Barrès, Maurice, 101
Bateau Lavoir studio, 16, 21, 23, 24
Baudelaire, Charles, 3, 212
Bauhaus, 75, 171–96
    the African Chair, 181
    geometry in, 181, 183–90, 192
    Haus am Horn, 187–88, 191
    manifestos of, 175–77, 187–88
    move to Dessau, 175, 191, 192–93
    Movement for an Imaginist Bauhaus, 209–10
    the New Bauhaus, 195, 210
    as not avant-garde in the conventional sense, 175

place of art in, 189–91
Preliminary Course, 178–79, 186, 188, 190
under state scrutiny, 191–95
in the United States, 195–96
See also Gropius, Walter
Bauhaus Stairway (Schlemmer), 191
Bayer, Herbert, 175
beautiful, the
of the city, 68, 80
confined to art, 9
Dada's disgust of the beautiful, rational, and thoughtful, 87
Mondrian's views on, 159, 163
war as beautiful, 35
Beaux Arts architecture, 164
Becker-Ho, Alice, 207
Behrens, Peter, 173
Belgium, 72, 78, 98, 144, 152
Belle Epoque, 28–29
Bellows, George, 55
Belyi, Andrei, 133
Berlage, Hendrik Petrus, 156
Berlin, 77, 192
bourgeoisie in, 173, 174
Dada in, 97
Emmy Hennings in, 90
"The Exhibition of Futurist Painters," 36
Hugo Ball in, 79–80, 84
Kapp putsch, 192
Kunstgewerbeschule (Grand Ducal School of the Arts and Crafts), 174
Mark Twain in, 68
Moholy-Nagy in, 185–86
Tatlin in, 118
See also Bauhaus
Bernstein, Michèle, 198–99, 207, 219
Beuys, Joseph, 226
bicycles, 3, 52, 53–54, 73, 139, 160
Bicycle Wheel (Duchamp), 52, 53–54
Bill, Max, 210
Billy, André, 72
Blainville, France, 45

Blaue Reiter group, 70
Blavatsky, Madame, 149
Blind Man, The (magazine), 54–55
Bloc des gauches, 29
Blue Nude (Matisse), 53
Boccioni, Umberto, 35–39, 73–74
Bohemians, 15–20, 33, 81–82, 206
as distinct from the avant-garde, 17
and a life of "perpetual dispersion," 23
on the margins of the bourgeoisie, 16–19, 23
in Munich, 68, 70
Bolshevik Revolution (October Revolution), 60, 119, 125–28, 131, 137–38
Bolz, Fritz, 91
bombardment, during the First World War, 75, 96, 152
bombing, domestic, 29
Bonset, I. K., 151, 167
Bottle, The (Tatlin), 128
Bourbon restoration, 27
Bourgeois Galleries, New York, 54
bourgeoisie
appealing to the, 82–85
the avant-garde contesting the value of culture, 63, 120, 203, 225
in Berlin, 173, 174
Bohemians on the margins of the, 16–19, 23
confusing the, 12
war as antidote to the bourgeois torpor, 76
Brancusi, Constantin, 53
branding, 33, 170
Brandt, Marianne, 175
Braque, Georges, 24, 30, 38–39, 48–49, 148
Brecht, Bertolt, 82
Breton, André, 9, 10, 93, 97–106, 114–16, 225, 226
apartment in New York City, 199–200

Breton, André (*continued*)
    Apollinaire's influence on, 97, 100, 105
    arrest of, 200
    art and life through a walk in the city, 109–14
    on Duchamp, 46, 59
    early life of, 97–98
    during the First World War, 75, 97–99, 101
    Freud and, 112–13
    influence on Debord, 200–201, 203–4, 207–8
    Jacques Vaché and, 99–100, 105
    l'amour fou (mad love) of, 109
    Nadja, 107–9, 111–16
    among the Surrealists, 103–6, 114–16
    Tristan Tzara and, 96–97, 100–101
    on writing, 101–2, 105–6, 242n11
Breuer, Marcel, 175, 181, 194
Brevoort Hotel, 201
Bride Stripped Bare by Her Bachelors, The (Duchamp), 61
Brik, Lili, 124–25, 134–35, 136, 137, 138
Brik, Osip, 123–26, 134–35, 136, 137, 138
Brillo soap pad boxes, 226
Bruant, Aristide, 84
Brussels, Belgium, 36
Bucharest, Romania, 94–95, 205
Buenos Aires, Argentina, 57
Buffet-Picabia, Gabrielle, 100
Bulgaria, 35, 121
Buñuel, Luis, 114
bureaucracy, 76, 113, 120, 137–38
Bureau of Surrealist Research, 104
Bürger, Peter, 225–27
Burliuk, David, 123, 124
Burliuk, Marusya, 124
Buscher, Alma, 188

cabaret
    abstraction in theater and cabaret performance, 73, 83, 85–86, 88–89
    Cabaret Pantagruel, Zurich, 83
    Cabaret Voltaire, Zurich, 78, 83–92, 94–97
    chant nègre, 85
    Elf Scharfrichter (Eleven Executioners) cabaret, Munich, 82–83
    Emmy Hennings's career in, 79–80, 82–83
    as political performance, 10, 88
Café de Flore, Paris, 22
Calvinism, 145
Camfield, William, 48
Camini, Aldo, 151
cannabis, 206
canned shit (Manzoni), 226
Cannes film festival, 204
Capture of Rome (1870), 73
Carrà, Carlo, 36, 38–39
Caruso, Enrico, 37
Casagemas, 20–21
Catholicism, 3, 19, 90, 150, 155, 164
Cattelan, Maurizio, 62–63
Cavern of Anti-Matter (Pinot-Gallizio), 211
Cendrars, Blaise, 118
censorship
    art as uncensored thought, 104
    Cheka, 136
    in Germany, 82–83
    obscenity trials, 38, 90
    pornography, 22, 201
    in Russia, 136, 138
Cézanne, Paul, 50, 148
Chagall, Marc, 118
chance, importance of, 40, 87, 107, 109, 111
chant nègre, 85
chaos, 38, 70, 75
Chaplin, Charlie, 82, 101
Charcot, Jean-Martin, 102–3

Chateaubriand, 221
Chat Noir (Black Cat) club, Paris, 82
Cheka, 136
Chekhov, Anton, 84
Chérif, Ali Pacha, 2
chess, 57–58
Chez Moineau, Paris, 198
Chicago, 68, 195–96
Chirico, Giorgio de, 114
Chopin, Frédéric, 129
Christian Reformist School, Amersfoort, 145
"Christosophists," 150
Chtcheglov, Ivan, 206–7, 214, 247n4
cinema. *See* film
"ciselant" (chiseling, paring away), 205
city life
    the atomization of, 69
    automobiles, 5, 25–26, 48, 69, 115, 130, 160
    chance, importance of, 40, 87, 107, 109, 111
    Debord's Dériville, 214
    dérive ("drift"), 197–99, 211, 212, 247n4
    electric lights, 43, 164, 194, 214
    menacing squirrels of, 201
    New Babylon (utopian city), 213–215
    urban planning, 176
    See also bourgeoise; modernity; *specific cities*
City Rises, The (Boccioni), 38
Civil War in Russia, 134–35, 137
Clark, T. J., 16, 207–8
classes dangereuses, 16
Clébert, Jean-Paul, 212
collaboration, 28, 87–88, 153, 156, 166, 177, 211
collage, 6, 39–40, 61, 87, 105, 180, 227
collectors, 54, 58–59, 118, 196, 211, 219, 231–32
Collège Saint-François Xavier, Alexandria, 3

Comedian (Cattelan), 63
commercial galleries, 7, 62, 227, 231
commercialization of art, 170
Communism, 120, 128, 134, 138, 165. *See also* Soviet Union
Communist Manifesto, The (Marx and Engels), 33
Communist Third International, 10, 120, 138
"community-art" (*gemeenschapkunst*), 156
Composition C (Mondrian), 162–65
Concerning the Spiritual in Art (Kandinsky), 70–71
Congo, 31
"Conquest of the Stars, The" (Marinetti), 4
conscription, 46, 76, 98, 206
Constant (Nieuwenhuys), 209–15, 219
Constructivism, 117–41
    "composition" vs. "construction," 131
    geometry in, 132, 140
    legacy of, 139–40
    support of the Bolsheviks, 60, 119–20
    when "constructive" rather than "constructivist," 140
consumer society, 59, 198, 210–11
contemporary art, 8, 63, 84, 224, 227, 231
conventions of art, 10, 26, 32, 39, 49–50, 63, 202, 227
convergence, in De Stijl, 156–57
Corinth, Lovis, 68
Corner Counter-Relief (Tatlin), 129
Corpse, A (pamphlet), 102
Cosio di Arroscia, Italy, 209, 219
Cottington, David, 29–30
Crevel, René, 103–4, 106
Cubist Painters, The (Apollinaire), 31
Cubists, 30–32, 39, 48–54
    abstraction among the, 49–50, 154

Cubists (*continued*)
    Apollinaire on the, 31–32, 51
    French Cubism, 148–49
    the Futurist war against, 38–39, 48–49
    influence of, 122, 148, 154, 156, 185
    the Salon Cubists, 48–54, 121
Cult of the Self, The (Barrès), 101
culture
    clashes of culture, 201
    "culture of containment," 227
    high culture, 60, 63, 84, 89
    "isms," the invention of, 31–32
    utopian thinking, 27, 43–44, 139–40, 155, 165, 170, 193, 213–15
curation, 230
Curtis, William, 164–65

Dada, 9, 77–78, 83, 87–89
    in Berlin, 97
    the diversity of, 165
    finally ceding to Surrealism, 103
    Futurist influence on, 96
    in New York, 77
    nihilism of, 120
    in Paris, 77
    Première Exposition Dada (Tzara), 95
    in Zurich, 77–81, 87–89, 92, 93, 96–97
Dalí, Salvador, 114–15
Dances at the Spring (II) (Picabia), 53
Danton, Georges, 129
Deauville, France, 72
Debord, Guy, *197*, 197–99, 201–19, 248n30
    Apollinaire's influence on, 204
    on architecture, 209–10, 212–13
    Breton's influence on, 200–201, 203–4, 207–8
    city, 198
    Dériville, 214
    early life of, 201–3
    leaving Paris, 220–21
    "Report on the Construction of Situations," 203–4
    Society of the Spectacle, 203, 220
    on sovereignty of the person, 220–21
    suicide of, 218
Debord, Martial, 204
de Gaulle, Charles, 218
Delaunay, Robert, 31, 49
Deller, Jeremy, 228–30, *229*
Derain, André, 108
dérive ("drift"), 197–99, 211, 212, 247n4
Dériville (Debord), 214
"Der Stijl" (the Style), 10, 153. *See also* De Stijl movement
design
    Bauhaus and modern industrial design, 175–76, 184–86, 188–89, 193–96
    commodification of, 170
    contemporary, 196
    as a field, 133
    notion of "good design," 155–56
    repulsive idea of design for industry, 184
Desnos, Robert, 106
Dessau, Germany, 175, 191, 192–93
De Stijl (journal), 151, 154, 166
De Stijl movement, 9, 151–57, 165–68
    architecture of, 156, 159, 161, 163–67
    convergence in, 156–57
    "Der Stijl" (the Style), the search for, 10, 153
    the diversity of tje, 153–54, 156
    Futurist influence on, 154, 156, 185
    geometry in, 152, 154, 156, 163
    manifestos of, 153–55
    Schröder House, Utrecht, 163
    technological utopianism of, 165
Dia Foundation, 224
diagonals, use of, 167
Dickerman, Leah, 191

Dieuze, France, 78, 80
disillusionment, 34, 76, 78, 81
disorder, 23, 206
Divisionism, 38, 148
d'Oettingen, Baroness, 118
Dolet, Etienne, 111
Domburg, 143–45, 148
"Donnerwetterleid" (Thunder Song), 84
Dorpskerk (Mondrian), 146, 148
Dosso Casina, 74
Dostoyevsky, Fyodor, 129
Doucet, Jacques, 103
Drabbe, Mies-Elout, 144
dream interpretation. *See* unconscious, the
Dreyfus affair, 101
Duchamp, Eugène, 45
Duchamp, Gaston, 45, 48, 51, 52
Duchamp, Marcel, 20, 41, 44–51, 54, 77, 106, 114
    biographers, 59
    birth of the Readymade, 51–57
    and the contemporary art market, 61–63
    Fountain, 44, 55–63
    later work and life of, 57–61
    Nude Descending a Staircase No. 2, 51, 52–53
    optical "playtoy," 59
    relationship with patrons, 58
    retreat into chess, 57–58
    Rotoreliefs, 59, 61
    Sonata, 50
    studio in Neuilly, 45, 51
    the "swimming lessons" of, 50, 59–60
    variable motivations of, 45, 51–53, 56
Duchamp, Raymond, 45, 48, 51, 52
Duchamp, Suzanne, 45, 50, 54, 57
Dutch Calvinism, 145
"dynamic equilibrium," 159
Dynamism of a Speeding Horse and Houses (Boccioni), 39

École des Beaux Arts, 46–47, 164
Eenheid (weekly journal), 151
Egypt, 2–5, 11, 35
Eiffel Tower, 25, 26, 130, 207, 214
electric lights, 43, 164, 194, 214
"Elefantenkarawane" (Elephant Caravan; Ball), 86
Elementarism, 168
Elf Scharfrichter (Eleven Executioners) cabaret, 82–83
Eliot, T. S., 26, 237n22
El Lissitzky, 165
Eluard, Paul, 100
embellishment, 170
"end of art," 8–9, 32, 160, 226, 230
Ephraim, Jan, 83, 85–86
Erffa, Helmut von, 183
Ernst, Max, 114, 201
Etoumbi region of the Congo, 31
Europe
    facing a apocalyptic and postapocalyptic future, 71, 223
    militarization of the late nineteenth century, 76
    moving away from ancient Greece and Rome, 25
    political crises around 1905, 29–30
    during the Second World War, 11, 166, 193, 199–200, 202
    See also First World War; *specific countries*
Everling, Germaine, 100
Evolution (Mondrian), 149–50
"excentroconcentroconcepticorationaloorphism," 31
"Exhibition of Futurist Painters, The," 36
Expressionism, 69–71, 89, 180–81, 192
Exquisite Corpse (game), 106

fairs. *See* art fairs
Farben, I. G., 194
fascism, 76–77, 202

Fauvism, 31, 42, 48, 50
Feininger, Lyonel, 177–78, 181
Fénéon, Félix, 28–29, 36
Ferdinand, Franz, 76
Feuillette, Pierre, 206
"Fifth International" (Mayakovsky), 138
film
    at the Bauhaus, 190
    Cannes film festival, 204
    found footage, 204–5
    Gaumont film company, 49
    On the Passage of a Few Persons Through a Rather Brief Period of Time (Debord), 211
    Prix de l'Avant-Garde, 205
    Treatise on Slime and Eternity, 204
    Un Chien Andalou, 114
fine art, 10, 88, 95–96, 175, 178, 196, 211
"fine artists," 47, 60
First Balkan War, 35
First State Cotton-Printing Factory, Moscow, 132
First World War, 9, 11–12, 29–30, 33–34, 74–78, 202, 228
    armistice, 73
    in Belgium, 72, 78, 98, 144, 152
    bombardment, 75, 96, 152
    Dosso Casina, 74
    exile in Zurich during, 80
    France under German occupation, 198–201
    impact of, 117–19
    neutrality, 75, 80, 152
    a visit to battlefield sites of northern France, 86–87
    "We're Here Because We're Here" (Deller), 228–30, *229*
Fitzpatrick, Sheila, 126–27
Flavin, Dan, 140
Flight Out of Time (Ball), 90
Florence, Italy, 37, 40, 220
folk arts, 82, 118, 122, 181
Fontana, Lucio, 210

formmeister (form master), 178
Foster, Hal, 227
found footage, 204–5
Fountain (Duchamp), 44, 55–63
Fountain of Light (Ai), 140
"fourth dimension," 50
Fraenkel, Théodore, 104
France
    Alsace, 171
    Arles, 221
    Auteuil, 16, 26, 46
    Auvergne, 218, 221
    Barbizon School of painting, 146
    Blainville, 45
    Bloc des gauches, 29
    Bourbon restoration, 27
    Cannes film festival, 204
    Deauville, 72
    Dieuze, 78, 80
    Dreyfus affair, 101
    French Cubism, 148–49
    French Revolution, 129
    German occupation of, 198–201
    government support of artists, 27–28
    humanism in the French lycée, 3
    Lille, 107, 116
    Nanterre, 216
    Nantes, 99
    Neuilly, 45, 51
    Nice, 72, 204
    Paris Commune of 1871, 29, 217
    Puteaux, 45
    the Resistance, 205
    Rouen, 46–47
    St. Tropez, 42
    student protests of 1968, 203, 216–18, 220
    See also Bohemians; Paris
France, Anatole, 102
free association, 103
freedom, 60
    in anarchism, 28–29, 81
    artistic, 29, 56, 59–62

the Bohemians' radical version
of, 23, 81
felt through purposeless walking,
110
individualism and, 18, 29, 34, 70,
101, 153–54, 192, 210
the limits of, 56
nihilism and, 99
promised by the Bolshevik Revolution, 120, 125, 127, 138
unequal freedoms for women, 91
utopian thinking and, 43–44,
158
"free genius," 107
French Revolution, 129
Freud, Sigmund, 102, 103, 112–13
Fry, Roger, 152
fumisterie, 23–24, 82
Futurist Manifesto, 32–33, 91
Futurist Political Party of Italy, 11, 77
Futurists, 15–40, 73–77
in architecture, 156
collaboration and group identity,
153
"Futurism" around the provinces,
123, 124
"The Exhibition of Futurist
Painters" in Berlin, 36
influence in Russia, 122–26, 137
influence on Dada, 96
influence on De Stijl, 154, 156,
185
legacy of performance, shock,
and confusion, 85–86
serate evenings, 10, 13, 37, 102
their mountain, Dosso Casina, 74
their views on pasta, 33–34
their war against the Cubists,
38–39, 48–49

Gabo, Naum, 140
Gagosian, Larry, 62
Galerie Bernheim-Jeune, Paris, 36,
38–39
Gallant, Mavis, 217

galleries
Bourgeois Galleries, New York, 54
commercial galleries, 7, 62, 227,
231
curation at, 230
Futurist war against, 8
Galerie Bernheim-Jeune, 38, 39
small galleries, 7, 202
Gaumont film company, 49
Gautier, Théophile, 16
gemeenschapkunst ("community-art"),
156
geometry, 50–51
in Bauhaus design, 181, 183–90,
192
in Constructivism, 132, 140
in De Stijl, 152, 154, 156, 163
diagonals, use of, 167
interest in "the fourth dimension," 50
in Latin American art, 166
non-Euclidean geometry, 50
the spiritual, abstract art behind
geometric ornament, 70, 128
turning into engineers, 131, 134,
139
See also abstraction; Cubism
Georgia, 123
Germany
authoritarianism of the German
Empire, 68–70
censorship in, 82–83
Dessau, 175, 191, 192–93
election of 1932, 194–95
German Expressionism, 71, 181
Kapp putsch, 192
martial law in Thuringia, 192
rise of the Nazis, 192–95
Wandervogel movement, 182
Weimar, 172–73, 174, 177, 182,
192
See also Berlin; Munich
Gesamtkunstwerk, 70. *See also* "total
work of art"
Gide, André, 99

Glackens, William, 55, 56
glass, 10, 129–30, 140, 152, 155, 176–77, 187, 193
Gleizes, Albert, 29, 49, 51, 121
globalization, 7, 96, 193, 210
Goldstein, Jean-Isidore, 205
Goudeau, Émile, 23
Gough, Maria, 130
Graber, Igor, 67
Great Salt Lake, Utah, 223
Great War, the. *See* First World War
Green, Christopher, 58
Gris, Juan, 21
Gropius, Manon, 174
Gropius, Martin, 173
Gropius, Walter, 75, *171*, 171–82
    affair with Alma Mahler, 174
    "Art and Technology—A New Unity" lecture, 187
    on Bolshevism, 192
    early life of, 173
    during the First World War, 171–72
    resignation of, 194
    Siedlung, a planned settlement, 177, 187
Gross, Hans, 191–92
group identity
    collaboration among artists, 28, 87–88, 153, 156, 166, 177, 211
    how group dynamics encourage extremism, 34
    marginalization of women and, 91
    membership structures and, 36–37, 153–54
    youthful energy and, 206
Guggenheim, Pegeen, 219
Guggenheim, Peggy, 67, 219
GUM state department store, Moscow, 135
Gutai Group of Japan, 226

Haag, Michael, 2
Hague School, 146

Hamsun, Knut, 102
handicraft, 184, 191
handwerksmeister (master craftsman), 178
Ha'nish, O. Z. A., 179
Harvard Graduate School of Design, 195
Haus am Horn, 187–88, 191
Häuser, Rudolf, 182
Hausmann, Raoul, 96
Haussmann, Baron, 16
Hayter, William Stanley, 200–201
Hegel, G. W. F., 208
Hennings, Emmy, 9, 10, 65, 78–92, 96–97
Hilbersheimer, Ludwig, 195
Hildebrandt, Lily, 188
Hitler, Adolf, 68, 115, 195
"Hive, The," 118
Hobsbawm, Eric, 75–76
Hochschule für Bildende Kunst (Weimar Academy of Art), 174
Holländische Meierei Café (Dutch Dairy Café), Zurich, 83
Homo Ludens (Huizinga), 212
Höxter, John. *See* Ball, Hugo
Huelsenbeck, Richard, 77, 78, 79, 84–85, 88–89, 95, 97
Hugnet, Georges, 200
Huizinga, Johan, 212
"human aquariums," 111–12
humanism in the French lycée, 3
Hundred Towers of Rouen, The (Duchamp), 46–47
Hungarian folk art, 181
Hungarian Soviet Republic, 185
Hungary, 184–85
Hussey, Andrew, 204, 209, 212, 219
Huszár, Vilmos, 153
hypnotic trances, 103, 105
hysteria, 103

"I am the soul in limbo," 108
icons, Russian, 118, 121–22
IKEA, 170

Illinois Institute of Technology, Chicago, 196
"Imagination Is Seizing Power" (slogan), 217
Imperial Academy of the Arts, St. Petersburg, 127
Impressionism, 28, 48, 122
    Divisionism, 38, 148
    "Neo-Impressionism," 28
    Pointillism, 42
    Post-Impressionism, 50
In Advance of the Broken Arm (Duchamp), 53
Independent Group, 212
individualism, 18, 29, 34, 70, 101, 153–54, 192, 210
industrial design, 175–76
industrialization, 68
"industrial painting," 211
Inkhuk (Institut Khudozhestvennoi Kul'tury), 128, 131
Institute of Contemporary Art, London, 212
Internationale Lettriste (journal), 208
Internationale Situationiste (journal), 210
International Style of modern architecture, 193
irrational forces of the modern world, 10, 70, 77, 81
"isms," the invention of, 31–32
Isou, Isidore, 197, 198, 204–6, 208–12, 218
Italy
    Alba, 210
    Cosio di Arroscia, 209, 219
    Dosso Casina, 74
    earthquake in Messina, 32
    fascism in, 76–77, 202
    first Italo-Ethiopian War, 34
    Florence, 37, 40, 220
    Futurist Political Party of, 11, 77
    invasion of Libya, 11, 35
    Milan, 4, 32, 37, 39, 60, 73, 202
    national love of pasta, 33–34
    Rome, 11, 37, 73
    the Stella d'Italia, 2
    Trieste, 34–35, 37
    unification of, 4, 34, 73
Itten, Johannes, 179–81, 183–84, 186, 189, 190

Jacob, Max, 84
Janco, George, 84
Janco, Marcel, 83–85, 87, 93–95, 97
Janssen, Hans, 145
Japan, 226
Jarry, Alfred, 204
Jastrebzoff, Serge, 118
Jesuits, 3
Jewish people and communities, 68, 94, 192
J. L. Mott Iron Works, 54
Jorn, Dane Asger, 209–211
Joyce, James, 80
Jucker, Carl Jakob, 186–87

Kahn, Gustave, 49
Kahnweiler, Daniel-Henry, 48, 61–62
Kaier, Christina, 132
Kamensky, Vasily, 123
Kandinsky, Wassily, 65–71, 83, 88, 127–28
    as aristocratic, 250n6
    at the Bauhaus, 175, 183, 189, 195
    Concerning the Spiritual in Art, 70–71
    on spirituality in the arts, 70–71, 152
    synesthesia of, 65–66, 70, 181
    time back in Russia, 128, 133
    time in Munich, 67, 71, 181
    "total work of art," 70, 71, 83, 165
    The Yellow Sound, 71–72
Kapp putsch, 192
Kapp, Wolfgang, 192
Kiev, Ukraine, 123
kitsch, 169–70

Klee, Lily, 66
Klee, Paul, 68, 175, 183
Klimt, Gustav, 174
Klyuyev, Nikolai, 243n31
Kok, Antony, 154, 166
Kokoschka, Oskar, 174
Kostrowitzky, Guillaume Albert Wladimir Alexandre Apollinaire de. *See* Apollinaire, Guillaume
Kun, Béla, 185
Kunstgewerbeschule (Grand Ducal School of the Arts and Crafts), 174
Kupka, František, 45, 49
Küpper, Christian Emil Marie, 151
Kutaisi, Georgia, 123

La Bohème (Puccini), 17
"L'amiral cherche une maison à louer" (The Admiral Is Looking for a House to Rent), a "simultaneous poem," 85
l'amour fou (mad love), 109
landscape with vagina (Masson), 201
Lapré, Marcelle, 24
Laren, Netherlands, 150, 153, 154
La Révolution Surréaliste (journal), 104
Large Glass, The (Duchamp), 61
Latin American art, 166
Laurencin, Marie, 16, 24–25
Lautréamont, Comte de, 204
la vie de bohème, 20–21. *See also* Bohemians
"Le Douanier." *See* Rousseau, Henri
Le Fauconnier, Henri, 49
Lefebvre, Henri, 219
Le Figaro (newspaper), 33, 123
League of Nations, 149
Lebel, Jean-Jacques, 217
Left Bank, 16, 206, 207
Léger, Fernand, 49, 118
Lenin, Vladimir, 80, 126–27, 129, 133, 137–38
Leopardi, Giacomo, 3
Leroy, Raoul, 102

Les Demoiselles d'Avignon (Picasso), 30, 31, 103, 237n38
Les Lettres Moderne (review), 23
Letatlin (Tatlin), 120, 139–40
Letterist International, 208, 211, 218
Letterists, 197, 204–5, 208–9, 211, 218
Levin, "John," 140
Lex Heinze, 82–83
liberty. *See* freedom
Libya, 11, 35
lighting, 164, 194, 214
Lille, France, 107, 116
Limbour, George, 103
Lipchitz, Jacques, 118–19
literature
 call for the end of, 9, 102
 illegal, 124
 the prestige of, 98
 as "safety valve" for society, 81
 search for alternatives to, 105
 See also poetry; theater
Littérature (magazine), 100–101, 102
Lombard Battalion of Volunteer Cyclists and Motorists, 73
London, 11, 36, 189, 217, 212, 231
London Psychogeographical Committee, 209
Loos, Adolf, 179
Lossky, Nikolai, 136
Louis Vuitton, 170
Louis XVIII of France, 27
Louis XVI of France, 27
Ludwig I of Bavaria, 67
Ludwig II of Bavaria, 67
Lunacharsky, Anatoly, 126–27, 129, 137–38
Luxe, Calme et Volupté (Luxury, Calm and Voluptuousness; Matisse), 42–44

MacCarthy, Fiona, 174
Macke, August, 84
Mademoiselle Pogany I (Brancusi), 53
Mafarka the Futurist (Marietti), 38

magazines. *See* art magazines
Magnetic Fields (Breton and Soupault), 105, 113
Mahler, Alma, 174, 179
Mallarmé, Stéphane, 98
Mandelstam, Osip, 243n31
manifestos, 32–33, 96, 101, 103, 227
    of the Bauhaus, 175–77, 187–88
    Cabaret Voltaire as manifesto, 89
    of De Stijl, 153–55
    of Elementarism, 168
    the Futurist Manifesto, 32–33, 91, 122–23
    misogyny in, 91
    refusing to sign, 163, 225
    of the Situationists, 203–4
    of the Surrealists, 103, 105–6, 115
    on various elements of the arts, 37, 39–40
Mann, Thomas, 68
Man Ray, 104
Manzoni, Piero, 226
Marbaix, Ghislain de, 206
Marinetti, Amalia, 2, 3
Marinetti, Enrico, 2
Marinetti, Filippo Tommaso, *1*, 1–5, 8–13, 32–40, 76–78
    "Advice to the Romans" speech, 37
    arrests of, 11, 35
    death of, 202
    and De Stijl, 154
    Futurist Political Party, 11, 77
    misogyny of, 91
    serate evenings, 10, 13, 37, 102
    visit to Russia, 122–23
    at war, 73–74
    Zang Tumb Tumb (Marinetti), 35
Marinetti, Leone, 4
Marx, Karl, 33, 129, 208
masks, African and Oceanic, 31, 87, 114
mass audience, 32
Masson, André, 201

mass production, 158, 168, 176, 181, 194
materialism, 69, 133
Matisse, Henri, 21, 42–44, 53
Maxim Ensemble vaudeville theater, 81
Maximilian II of Bavaria, 67
Mayakovsky, Vladimir, 9, 10, 120, *122*, 123–25, 137–41
    "All Meetinged Out," 138
    arrests of, 124
    "150,000,000," 137–39
    Vladimir Mayakovsky (play), 124–25
Mazdaznanism, 179, 185
McCullagh, Francis, 36
"metagraphics," 205–6
Metzinger, Jean, 49, 51, 121
Meyer, Hannes, 194
Miami Beach Art Basel, 5–14, 62–63, 230–32
middle class, the, 23, 27, 33, 68, 76, 136, 228. *See also* bourgeoisie, the
Mies van der Rohe, Ludwig, 175, 194–96
Milan, Italy, 4, 32, 37, 39, 60, 73, 202
militarization of the late nineteenth century, 76
Milner, John, 129
Minimalists, 140
Miró, Joan, 201
modern art
    character of the modern art world, 202
    Debord on, 211–12
    marginal position in Western society, 30–31
    Museum of Modern Art, New York, 228
    as technical drawing for progress, 49–50
    trying on different styles, 50
    in the United States, 54–56, 196
modernism, 26–27, 31, 67, 237n30
    dissonant modernism, 137–38
    enthuiasm for abstraction and fantasy, 85–86

modernism (*continued*)
    high Modernist abstraction, 88
    and the invention of "isms,"
    31–32
    in Russia, 119–21, 128
    after the Second World War, 202
modernity
    bureaucracy, 76, 113, 120, 137–38
    champions of modernity, 3
    chance, importance of, 40, 87, 107, 109, 111
    chaos, 38, 70, 75
    consumer society, 59, 198, 210–11
    dérive ("drift"), 197–99, 211, 212, 247n4
    globalization, 7, 96, 193, 210
    individualism, 18, 29, 34, 70, 101, 153–54, 192, 210
    industrialization, 68
    irrational forces of the modern world, 10, 70, 77, 81
    mass audience, 32
    mass production, 158, 168, 176, 181, 194
    social change and, 70–71, 203
    sovereignty, of the person, 220–21
    starker difference between public and private selves, 113
    See also city life; freedom; warfare
Modifications series (Jorn), 211
Modigliani, Amedeo, 21, 84
Moholy-Nagy, László, 175, 184–87, *189*, 190, 191, 194, *195*, 196
Mollet, Jean, 21
Mondriaan, Johanna Christina, 145
Mondriaan, Louis, 146
Mondriaan, Pieter Cornelius, 145
Mondriaan, Willem Frederik, 146
Mondrian, Carel, 146
Mondrian, Frits, 146
Mondrian, Piet, 9, 10, 41, *143*, 244n3
    abstraction and, 147–50
    on architecture, 162–63

    Composition C, 162–65
    discovering I. K. Bonset's true identity, 151
    in Domburg, 143–45, 148
    Dorpskerk, 146, 148
    early life and work of, 145–47
    Evolution, 149–50
    influence on Van Doesburg and De Stijl, 152–54, 165–70
    kitsch, 170
    painting in "noncolor," 158
    in Paris, 147–50, 157–61
    studio of, 160–61
    thoughts on architecture, 162–63
    views of the beautiful, 159, 163
Monte Carlo Bonds (Duchamp), 61
Montmartre, Paris, 15–29, 45, 48
Montparnasse, Paris, 20, 48, 118, 157
Monument to the Third International (Tatlin), 10, 120, 130–31, 140–41
More, Thomas, 155
Morise, Max, 103
Morris, William, 155, 176, 177
Moscow, Russia, 66–67, 118, 121, 124, 132–35, 139
Mossel'prom "Red Star" caramels, 134–35
motifs, 26, 112, 115, 148, 186
Movement for an Imaginist Bauhaus, 209–10
Muche, Georg, 188
Mühsam, Erich, 84, 90, 91
Munch, Edvard, 146
Munich, 51–52, 66–72, 79–82, 128
    Blaue Reiter group, 70
    Elf Scharfrichter (Eleven Executioners) cabaret, 82–83
    Hennings in, 88–90
    middle class of, 68
    Schwabing district of, 68, 70
    Simplicissimus club, 79–80, 91
    Third Congress of the Situationist International, *197*
Murger, Henry, 17–18

Museum of Modern Art (MoMA), New York, 228
museums, 6–8, 12–13, 67, 130, 227–28, 230
Mussolini, Benito, 11, 76, 202
Mussorgsky, Modest, 129
mustard gas, 98
Muthesius, Hermann, 176
Mutt, R., 44–57, 60

Nadelman, Elie, 84
Nadja (Breton), 107–9, 111–16
nagel, gustav, 182
Nairn, Tom, 217
Nanterre, France, 216
Nantes, France, 99
Narkompros (People's Commissariat of Enlightenment), 126
Navaille, Pierre, 115
Nazis, rise of the, 192–95
"neo-avant-garde," 226–27
"Neo-Impressionism," 28
Neo-Plasticism, 150, 153, 158, 160–61, 169
Netherlands
    Amersfoort, 145
    Arnhem, 144
    Domburg, 143–45, 148
    Laren, 150, 153, 154
    River Gein, 146
    Tilburg, 152–54
    Utrecht, 150, 151, 154, 163
Neuilly, France, 45, 51
neutrality, 75, 80, 152
New Babylon (utopian city), 213–215
New Bauhaus, 195, 210
New Economic Policy, 134
New York, 52, 53, 149, 179
    Bourgeois Galleries, 54
    Breton's apartment in, 199–200
    Brevoort Hotel, 201
    Museum of Modern Art (MoMA), 228
    Seagram Building, 196

69th Regiment Armory Show, 52–53, 54
New Yorker, The (magazine), 217
Nice, France, 72, 204
Nicolle, Emile, 44–45
Nietzsche, Friedrich, 47, 70–71, 76, 173
Nieuwenhuys, Constant, 209–15, 219
"noncolor," 158
nonlinear typography, 40
noodles, a bowl of "avant-garde," 11
North Africa, 109, 210
    Alexandria, Egypt, 1–2, 11, 35
    Algiers, 204–5, 206
novelty, 39, 185, 188
Novodevicky Monastery, Moscow, 139
Nude Descending a Staircase No. 2 (Duchamp), 51, 52–53

Oberdan, Guglielmo, 35
obscenity trials, 38, 90
October Revolution (Bolshevik Revolution), 60, 119, 125–28, 131, 137–38
Odessa, Ukraine, 121, 123
O'Keeffe, Georgia, 57
Oktoberfest, 67
Olcott, Henry Steel, 149
Olivier, Fernande, 21, 24
Olmo, Walter, 219
"150,000,000" (Mayakovsky), 137–39
On the Passage of a Few Persons Through a Rather Brief Period of Time (Debord), 211
opium, 22, 47–48, 72
ornament, 155
"ornithopter, an," 139
"Orphism," 31
Osorgin, Mikhail, 136
Ottoman Empire, 2
Oud, J. J., 154, 156, 162, 163, 166

Pace Gallery, 62
painting
    the author takes up painting, 42–45

painting (*continued*)
    Barbizon School of painting, 146
    Gropius's views on, 177–78
    "industrial painting," 211
    Mondrian painting in "noncolor," 158
    "pure painting," 31
    "telephone paintings," 190–91
Panegyric (Debord), 220–21
Pan (Hamsun), 102
Papini, Giovanni, 40
Paris
    during the Belle Epoque, 28–29
    Café de Flore, 22
    Chat Noir (Black Cat) club, 82
    Chez Moineau, 198
    Cuban embassy in Paris, 47
    Eiffel Tower, 25, 26, 130, 207, 214
    first abstract pictures exhibited in, 49
    Galerie Bernheim-Jeune, 38, 39
    Gare d'Orsay, 20
    Grand Palais, 49
    Haussmann's rationalization of, 16
    Île de la Cité, 198
    La Pitié hospital, 99
    Left Bank, 16, 206, 207
    Les Halles, 212
    Louvre, 22
    May '68 protests, 203, 216–18, 220
    Montmartre, 15–29, 45, 48
    Montparnasse, 20, 48, 118, 157
    Notre-Dame, 206
    Opéra, 107
    Picasso's Bateau Lavoir studio, 16, 21, 23, 24
    rail strike in, 197
    Restaurant Foyot, 29
    Rive Gauche culture of, 198, 205, 207
    Sorbonne, 49, 205, 216–17
    Vert-Galant, 198
    See also Bohemians
Paris Commune of 1871, 29, 217
Paris Insolite (*Strange Paris*; Clébert), 212
pasta, 33–34
Pasternak, Boris, 243n31
People's Commissariat of Enlightenment (Narkompros), 126
Peret, Roger Vitrac, 103
performance
    abstraction in theater and cabaret performance, 73, 83, 85–86, 88–89
    cabaret as political performance, 10, 88
    Futurist legacy of performance, shock, and confusion, 85–86
    puppetry, 82, 88
    "rigolo" (comic amusements), 23
    See also cabaret; theater
Perloff, Marjorie, 39
Pétain, Philippe, 200
Pevsner, Antoine, 140
Philadelphia Museum of Art, 58
Piatti, Ugo, 73
Picabia, Francis, 47–50, 53, 100, 114
Picasso, Pablo, 20–24
    Bateau Lavoir studio, 16, 21, 23, 24
    Les Demoiselles d'Avignon, 30, 31, 103, 237n38
    relationship with patrons, 58
    Tatlin and, 118–19, 128
    and traditional genres of still life and portrait, 39
Pichot, Ramon, 24–25
Pieret, Géry, 22–23
Pinot-Gallizio, Giuseppe, 210–11
"Pipifox." *See* Van Doesburg, Theo
Pissarro, Camille and Lucien, 28
Plasticism. *See* Neo-Plasticism
"plastic mathematics," 150
play
    chess, 57–58
    Duchamp's optical "playtoy," 59
    Exquisite Corpse game, 106

importance to civilization, 212
playgrounds in Amsterdam, 213, 215
Poesies (Lautréamont), 208
poetry
    contemporary, 84, 105
    motifs of classical pastoral poetry, 26
    without punctuation, 26
    reducing verse to its smallest component, the letter, 205
    rimes suivies, 26–27
    a "simultaneous poem," 85
    "utilitarian poetry," 133
Poincaré, Henri, 50
Pointillism, 42
Poland, 137
polenta, 66
Politburo, 137
political cabaret, 10, 88
Polizzotti, Mark, 48, 105, 242n11
Pollock, Jackson, 10, 169
Polonskaya, Veronika, 138
Pope's Aeroplane, The (Marinetti), 35
Popova, Liubov, 121, 132–33
pornography, 22, 201
Portrait of a Woman (Rousseau), 24
Post-Impressionism, 50
Potlach (journal), 208, 218
Pour une Architecture de Situation (Constant), 209
Preliminary Course at the Bauhaus, 178–79, 186, 188, 190
Première Exposition Dada (Tzara), 95
Princet, Maurice, 50
Princip, Gavrilo, 76
Prix de l'Avant-Garde, 205
Productivists, 131–33
"propaganda of the deed," 29
prostitution, 16, 30, 89
psychoanalysis, 102, 112–13. *See also* unconscious, the
psychogeography, 212, 215
Puccini, Giacomo, 17
Pugin, A. W. N., 155
puppetry, 82, 88
"pure painting," 31
Pushkin, Russia, 135, 136
Puteaux, France, 45

"R. Mutt," 44–57, 60
Rámirez, Julián Gómez, 119
Raynal, Maurice, 24
Rayonism, 122
ready-made sculpture, 39
Readymades (Duchamp), 51–57
realism, 146–47, 225
Rectangular Relief (Taeuber-Arp), 213
Red/Blue Chair (Oud), 163
Reed, John, 126
Rees, Jacob van, 146
Reich, Lilly, 175, 195
Reklam-Konstructor Mayakovsky-Rodchenko (Advertisement Constructors Mayakovsky-Rodchenko), 134
religion and spirituality
    American spiritualism, 148
    Calvinism, 145
    Catholicism, 3, 19, 90, 150, 155, 164
    Kandinsky on spirituality in the arts, 70–71, 152
    Mazdaznanism, 179, 185
    the spiritual, abstract art behind geometric ornament, 70, 128
    spiritualism, 148, 151, 200
    Theosophy, 148–50, 151, 158, 167–68, 179
    unconventional modes of spirituality, 152, 167–68, 177, 189
    See also beautiful, the
"Report on the Construction of Situations" (Debord), 203–4
respirateur, artist as, 60
Restaurant Foyot, Paris, 29
"Revoluzzerlied" (Revolution Song), 84
"Richard Mutt Case, The," 55, 60
Richardson, John, 22

Richter, Hans, 77, 96, 165
Rietveld, Gerrit, 154, 163–65
Rigaut, Jacques, 103
"rigolos" (comic amusements), 23
Rimbaud, Arthur, 99, 204
rimes suivies, 26–27
Risorgimento, 4, 34, 73
Robespierre, Maximilien, 129
Roché, Henri-Pierre, 54, 59
Rodchenko, Aleksandr, 131, 134, 135, 141
Romania, 94–95, 205
Rome (ancient), 26–27
Rome (modern), 11, 37, 73
Rosenstock, Samuel, 94
Rossi, Paulette, 204
ROSTA state telegram bureau, 134
Rothko, Mark, 10
Rotoreliefs (Duchamp), 59, 61
Rouen, France, 46–47
Rousseau, Henri, 3, 23–24, 206
Rubin, William, 237n38
Rumney, Ralph, 206, 209, 212, 218–19
Ruskin, John, 155
Russia, 10, 119, 125–33, 165, 202
    abstraction in Russian art, 88, 122, 129, 132, 140
    anarch, 88
    Futurists' influence in, 122–26, 137
    icons in Russian art, 118, 121–22
    Imperial Academy of the Arts, 127
    Moscow, 66–67, 118, 121, 124, 132–35, 139
    Pushkin, 135, 136
    Rayonism, 122
    St. Petersburg, 11, 122–24, 126, 127, 130, 137
    Union of Youth artists' society, 122
    World of Art group, 122
    See also Constructivism; Soviet Union
Russolo, Luigi, 36, 38, 74

Sachsen Hilburghausen, Therese von, 67
Sailor, The: A Self-Portrait (Tatlin), 121
St. Gerulfus church, Domburg, 144
"Saint-Peter of the Straight Line" ("I. K. Bonset"), 167
St. Petersburg, Russia, 11, 122–24, 126, 127, 130, 137
Saint-Simon, Henri de, 27, 43
St. Tropez, France, 42
Salmon, André, 15–16, 24–25, 84
Salon Cubists, 48–54, 121
Salon d'Automne, 39, 48–49
Salon des Indépendants, 48
Salon, the, 27, 62
Sanguinetti, Gianfranco, 219
Sant'Elia, Antonio, 73–74, 156
Scenes of Bohemian Life (Murger), 17
Schinkel, Karl Friedrich, 173
Schlemmer, Oskar, 186, 191
Schoenberg, Arnold, 174, 179
Schoenmaekers, Mathieu, 150, 157
Schröder House, Utrecht, 163
Schröder, Truus, 163–64
Schulz, Lucia, 185
Schwabing district of Munich, 68, 70
Schwartz, Frederic, 186
Schwarz, Arturo, 50
sculpture
    Constructivist clear plastic, 140
    in De Stijl, 153, 156
    Duchamp's Readymades, 51–57
    Gropius's views on, 177–78
    manifestos on, 33, 37, 227
    of the 1960s and '70s, 225–26
    Picasso's hybrid of sculpture and painting, 119
    public, 215
    ready-made sculpture, 39
    of Sophie Taeuber, 88, 213
    traditional, 39
Seagram Building, New York City, 196
Second World War, 11, 166, 193, 199–200, 202

Seigel, Jerrold, 17–18, 23
serate evenings, 10, 13, 37, 102
Serge, Victor, 200
Seuphor, Michel, 145, 152, 161
Seurat, Georges, 28, 48
Severini, Gino, 36, 38–39
sexism, 133, 207
sexuality
 of female artists, 91
 pornography, 22, 201
 prostitution, 16, 30, 89
 the unconscious and, 209
shadow plays, 82
Shattuck, Roger, 23, 237n23, 237n28
Shchukin, Sergei, 118, 121
shit, canned (Manzoni), 226
Shterenberg, David, 140
Siedlung (a planned settlement; Gropius), 177, 187
Signac, Paul, 28, 42
Simondo, Piero, 219
Simplicissimus club, Munich, 79–80, 91
"simultaneous poem," 85
Sironi, Mario, 73
Situationist International, 197, 208, 216, 218, 219
Situationists, 36, *197*, 197–203, 204, 209–11, 217, 220, 248n30
 abstraction among the, 210–11
 manifestos of, 203–4
 Third Congress of the Situationist International, *197*
69th Regiment Armory in New York, 52–53, 54
Slovenia, 184
Smithson, Robert, *223*, 223–25, 227
"socialism of vision," 187
Société des Artistes Indépwendants, 54, 56
Society of the Spectacle, The (Debord), 203, 220
Somme, Battle of the, 228–30, *229*
Sonata (Duchamp), 50
Sorbonne, Paris, 49, 205, 216–17

Sorel, George, 35
Sorrell, Martin, 26, 237n28, 237n29
Sottsass, Ettore, 210
Soupault, Philippe, 100, 103, 105, 113
South Africa, 146
Soutine, Chaim, 118
sovereignty, of the person, 220–21
Soviet Union
 Bolshevik Revolution (October Revolution), 60, 119, 125–28, 131, 137–38
 censorship in, 136, 138
 Cheka, 136
 Civil War, 134–35, 137
 Inkhuk (Institut Khudozhestvennoi Kul'tury), 128, 131
 Monument to the Third International, 10, 120, 130–31, 140–41
 Mossel'prom "Red Star" caramels, 134–35
 New Economic Policy, 134
 People's Commissariat of Enlightenment (Narkompros), 126
 Politburo, 137
 Red Army, 135
 See also Constructivism
Spain, 30, 72, 77, 96, 165
Spanish flu, 73, 185
spectacle, 77, 115, 130, 203, 210–11, 218, 220, 231
Spiral Jetty (Smithson), *223*, 223–25
spiritualism, 148, 151, 200
spirituality, unconventional modes of, 152, 167–68, 177, 189
Stadtkrone (City Crown), 177
stained glass, 152, 155, 187
Stalin, Joseph, 120, 202
Stark & Reise enamel sign factory, 190
steel, 10, 130, 213
Stein, Gertrude, 24
Stein, Leo, 24
Stella d'Italia, 2
Stella, Joseph, 54
Stepanova, Varvara, 131–33, 135

INDEX   273

Stettin, 137
Stieglitz, Alfred, 55–56, 57, 62
Stölzl, Gunta, 181
strip clubs, as Surrealist, 111
suicides, 89–90, 138, 140, 218
Suriname, 146
Surrealists, 9, 31, 36, 102, 105–13, 114–15, 198, 204
    Breton among the, 103–6, 114–16
    Bureau of Surrealist Research, 104
    the "Centrale" offices, 112
    A Corpse (pamphlet), 102
    Dada finally ceding to Surrealism, 77–78, 103
    Freud on the, 112–13
    manifestos of, 103, 105–6, 115
    strip clubs as Surrealist, 111
    in the United States, 201–2
"swimming lessons," 50, 59–60
Switzerland, 47, 128, 168, 210
    Altstadt, 94
    Art Basel, the original, 6
    neutrality of, 80, 95
    See also Zurich
Symbolists, 4, 70, 98, 101, 122, 125, 146, 148
synesthesia, 65–66, 70, 181
Szeged, Hungary, 184

Taeuber(-Arp), Sophie, 84, 87–88, 97, 213
Tanning, Dorothea, 200
Tatlin, Vladimir, 10, *117*, 117–19, 121, 122–28, 139–41
    in Berlin, 118
    early life of, 119–20
    Monument to the Third International, 10, 120, 130–31, 140–41
    return to Moscow, 125
    The Sailor: A Self-Portrait (Tatlin), 121
Taut, Bruno, 176, 177, 178, 186–87, 193

tear gas, 217
"telephone paintings," 190–91
theater, 10, 37, 70–71, 79–89
    abstraction in, 73, 83, 85–86, 88–89
    vaudeville, 81
    See also cabaret
Theory of the Avant-Garde (Bürger), 225
Theosophical Society, 149
Theosophy, 148–50, 151, 158, 167–68, 179
Thuringia, Germany, 192
Tilburg, Netherlands, 152–54
Tolstoy, Leo, 129
"total environment," 170, 188, 232
"total work of art," 70, 71, 83, 165
Toulouse-Lautrec, Henri de, 48
Treatise on Slime and Eternity (Isou), 204
tribal art, 26, 87, 207, 237n38
Trieste, Italy, 34–35, 37
Tsindel, Emil, 132
Tsindel Factory, 132
Turgenev, Ivan, 84
Twain, Mark, 68
"type forms," 176
Tzara, Tristan, 77, 83–85, 88, 93–97, 100–101, 114, 205

Udaltsova, Nadezhda, 121
Ugrimov, Alexander, 136
Ukraine, 119, 121, 123
"umour," 100
Un Chien Andalou (film), 114
unconscious, the, 112–15, 209, 242n11
unconventional art, 31, 206, 226
Union of Youth artists' society, 122
United Kingdom, 68
    Anglophilia, 99
    during the First World War, 98, 228–30, *229*
    London, 11, 36, 189, 217, 212, 231

United States
   American spiritualism, 148
   Chicago, 68, 195–96
   creation of, 179
   dominance of, 202
   Harvard Graduate School of Design, 195
   modern art in, 54–56, 196
   new beginnings in, 195
   Philadelphia Museum of Art, 58
   Surrealism in, 201–2
   See also New York City
urban life. *See* city life
utopian thinking, 27, 43–44, 139–40, 155, 165, 170, 193, 213–15
Utrecht, Netherlands, 150, 151, 154, 163

Vaché, Jacques, 99–100, 105
vagina, landscape with (Masson), 201
Valentin, Karl, 82
van der Leck, Bart, 154, 166
Van Doesburg, Nelly, 183
Van Doesburg, Theo, 9, 10, 151–57, 160, 165–68
   abstraction and, 152–54, 159
   at the Bauhaus, 183, 191
   De Stijl (journal), 151, 154, 166
   as "I. K. Bonset," 151, 167
   manifestos of, 155, 168
   in Tilburg, 152–54
   See also De Stijl movement
Vaneigm, Raoul, 219
van Eyck, Aldo, 213, 215
Van Gogh, Vincent, 48, 148, 169
van 't Hoff, Robert, 153–54, 156, 166
Vantongerloo, Georges, 153, 166
vaudeville, 81
Velde, Henry van der, 174
Vienna, 35, 112–13, 179
Vietnam, 204, 224
Villon, François, 48
Villon, Jacques, 20, 48
violence, 3, 11, 29, 35, 38, 71, 74–75, 81, 108, 154

visual arts, 27–28, 115, 166, 205–6, 227
   collage, 6, 39–40, 61, 87, 105, 180, 227
   "metagraphics," 205–6
   wallpaper, 119, 129, 155, 194
   See also Letterists
Vladimir Mayakovsky (play), 124–25
Vorkurs. *See* Preliminary Course *under* Bauhaus

Wagenfeld lamp, 186–87
Wagenfeld, Wilhelm, 186–87
Wagner, Richard, 70
walking, 109–14, 144, 205
wallpaper, 119, 129, 155, 194
Wandervogel movement, 182
warfare, 32, 201
   as beautiful, 35
   bombardment, 75, 96, 152
   destructive materiality of, 153
   as fiction, 75
   First Balkan War, 35
   irrational spectacle of, 77
   life as total war, 108
   militarization of the late nineteenth century, 76
   mustard gas, 98
   Second World War, 11, 166, 193, 199–200, 202
   as "the sole hygiene of the world," 35
   tear gas, 217
   See also First World War
Warhol, Andy, 226
Waste Land, The (Eliot), 26
Weber, Nicholas Fox, 67
Wedekind, Frank, 84
Weimar Academy of Art, 174
Weimar, Germany, 172–73, 174, 177, 182, 192
"We're Here Because We're Here" (Deller), 228–30, 229
"Weisswurst patriots," 82
Western culture. *See* Europe

"White Leprous Giant in the Countryside, The" (Tzara), 101
White Russians, 134
Wigley, Mark, 214, 215
Wilhelm I of Germany, 118
Wilhelm II of Germany, 173
Wils, Jan, 153
Wollen, Peter, 219
Wolman, Gil, 206, 208, 218
women
    female artists of the avant-garde, 88–92
    with a free mind, 107
    misogyny in men's manifestos, 91
    sexism, 133, 207
    sexuality of female artists, 91
    See also sexuality
Wood, Beatrice, 54, 55, 59
World of Art group, 122
World War I. *See* First World War
World War II. *See* Second World War
Wright, Frank Lloyd, 156
writing
    automatic writing, 105, 242n11
    Breton on, 101–2, 105–6, 242n11
    Exquisite Corpse game, 106
    industrialization of, 102
    nonlinear typography, 40
    See also manifestos; poetry

Yellow Sound, The (Kandinsky), 71–72
Yesinin, Sergei, 243n31
Ypres, Battle of, 98

Zang Tumb Tumb (Marinetti), 35
Zola, Emile, 4
"Zone" (Apollinaire), 25–27
Zurich, 9, 89–90, 93, 95
    Cabaret Pantagruel, 83
    Cabaret Voltaire, 78, 83–92, 94–97
    Dada in, 77–81, 87–89, 92, 93, 96–97
    Holländische Meierei Café (Dutch Dairy Café), 83
    Lenin's exile in Zurich, 126
    along the Limmatquai, 80
    School of Applied Arts, 87